POLLY EVANS is very cowardly and not at all fond of danger. She does, however, have an unfortunate tendency to seek out discomfort and sometimes even downright pain, the result of which are the travel adventures *It's Not About the Tapas,* a *Boston Globe* bestseller and *People* "Great Reads: Travel" pick; *Fried Eggs with Chopsticks,* about Polly's journey through China; and *Kiwis Might Fly,* all available from Delta. When she's not on the road, Polly, an award-winning journalist, lives in London, where she is at work on the tale of her adventures dogsledding in Canada's frozen Yukon, which Delta will publish in 2009. Visit her website at www.pollyevans.com.

On a Hoof
and a Prayer

Exploring Argentina
at a Gallop

POLLY EVANS

DELTA TRADE PAPERBACKS

ON A HOOF AND A PRAYER
A Delta Book

PUBLISHING HISTORY
Bantam UK edition published March 2007
Delta trade paperback edition / May 2008

Published by
Bantam Dell
A Division of Random House, Inc.
New York, New York

Map illustration by Neil Gower
Book design by Glen M. Edelstein

Library of Congress Cataloging-in-Publication Data
Evans, Polly.
On a hoof and a prayer : exploring Argentina at a gallop / Polly Evans.
p. cm.
ISBN 978-0-385-34110-3 (trade pbk.)
1. Argentina—Description and travel. 2. Horsemanship—Argentina.
3. Evans, Polly—Travel—Argentina. I. Title.
F2817.E93 2008
918.2'047—dc22
2007040624

Printed in the United States of America
Published simultaneously in Canada

www.bantamdell.com

BVG 10 9 8 7 6 5 4 3 2 1

For Inaara,

with love

Contents

Tilcara

Salta
Cachi
Cafayate
Tucumán

PARAGUAY

Puerto Iguazú

Posadas

BRAZIL

Río Ceballos

Córdoba

URUGUAY

Mendoza

Buenos
Aires
Luján

Dolores

CHILE

ARGENTINA

San Martín
de los Andes

Bariloche

Puerto Madryn
Gaiman

PENÍNSULA
VALDÉS

N

0   Miles   500

0   Kilometers   800

El
Calafate

Ushuaia

Gower

On a Hoof and a Prayer

1

The Starting Gate

As a child, I longed to ride a horse. My girlish dreams were peppered with fantasies of bright red horse-show rosettes and deliciously exciting grooming sessions in which I would brush my pet's sleek coat till it gleamed like polished ebony.

I devoured the adventures of *Black Beauty*. I was given an old hardcover copy of *Jill's Gymkhana* with a sand-colored binding that must have been bought at a tag sale somewhere, and I read and reread it with avid enthusiasm. After all, if Jill had managed to happen upon enough money to buy herself a pony, why shouldn't I? I gazed enraptured through *National Velvet*. But those Grand National fences seemed nothing to the hurdle I faced: convincing my parents of my need.

For years I pestered them. I wanted riding lessons. They thought the piano more suitable. I still wanted riding lessons. But ballet was so much more ladylike. I wanted a horse. Where would it live? I thought the backyard would do fine. Who would look after it? I would, of course. Who was going to pay for it? Well, they could—couldn't they?

But realistically they could not, and so the horse was never forthcoming. Christmases and birthdays came and went, and I never unwrapped so much as a My Little Pony. Not even my Barbie doll was given a horse. Barbie, instead, received a bathtub and a wedding dress—clean, wholesome, morally upright playthings.

The time went by and the obsession died. Through my teenage years, I don't suppose I'd have been seen dead around a horse. In my twenties, I developed an unhealthy preoccupation with swimming and biking and running. It wasn't until I was in my mid-thirties that the niggling little thought began to trot around inside my head once more: Wouldn't it be fun to learn to ride?

But where should I go for lessons? I didn't much like the idea of plodding around a London park for ninety dollars an hour. And why spend week after week joggling around a riding-school ring attempting to master the very British rising trot, when there was a world out there with wide-open spaces to gallop through, places where nobody cared if my heels were down or my head was high? Why squeeze into an unflattering pair of jodhpurs when I could deck myself out in leather chaps and jingling spurs, and gallop with the cowboys through the ranches of Wyoming? Why strap on a hard black hat when I could wear a fur-trimmed bonnet and ride wild with the nomads across the Mongolian steppe?

There were the Berber horsemen of Morocco. Surely they could do with a new companion with whom to charge across the desert; perhaps they needed a tea girl to serve their mint infusions as they rested beneath the stars. Or maybe I should grab a saber and head to the spice-scented

East to ride with the Rajputs through the ancient battle-grounds of princely Rajasthan.

But the Rajputs' horse days were gone, and the offspring of those famously wild warriors probably spent their days not in the saddle but selling secondhand Ambassador cars on the streets of Jaipur. In any case, I reflected, it might make sense to take lessons in a country where I at least spoke the language. Should I, then, join up with the Canadian Mounties? Or with the *gardiens* of the Camargue? Or, perhaps, I could head for the far-flung south, to Argentina, and take my first equine steps among the gauchos.

Horsemanship courses through Argentina's fiery Latin veins. The country as we know it owes its very existence to the horse, for without their steeds the Spanish could never have conquered the ferocious native tribes who had inhabited South America for many thousands of years. The natives had never set eyes on these four-legged creatures before the Spaniards arrived, and they viewed them at first with utter, debilitating terror. They believed horse and rider formed a single supernatural monstrosity and that the Spaniards' gunfire constituted the roar of an animal enraged.

It didn't take long for them to conquer their fear. In 1536, the Spaniard Pedro de Mendoza founded the settlement of Buenos Aires, but he was soon overwhelmed by the indigenous population. Mendoza fled back to Spain, abandoning a handful of horses to run wild on the pampas. It was the perfect environment for them: There were endless grass plains, plenty of water, a temperate climate, and very few predators. The horses bred. By 1580, when Juan de Garay returned to retake Buenos Aires, he found the province full of wild herds—and, gradually, the natives learned to ride them.

Today, horses still play a vital role in Argentine life. The cattle on the *estancias,* or ranches, are herded on horseback just as they were a century ago. Horses continue to provide the principal form of transport for many rural folk. In the plush Buenos Aires district of Palermo, the polo ground plays host to the finest players in the world.

I did a little research. I sent some e-mails. I received a reply from Robin Begg, an Anglo-Argentine whose family had owned their six-thousand-acre cattle farm in Córdoba province for generations. Now Robin's father handled the cattle-breeding operation while Robin used the estancia to run horse-riding holidays for visitors. He invited me to his farm for a week. He would, he proclaimed with disarming confidence, teach me to ride. After my week at Robin's, I'd take off to tour the country for eight further weeks, riding horses wherever I could find them. I'd canter across Argentina's flat open grasslands, into its spectacular Andean mountains, and through its southern Patagonian parks where mighty condors would soar before snowcapped peaks and pristine lakes.

Joyfully, I drew a line through my diary from mid-October to mid-December: While in England the days would be drawing short and gray, in Argentina it would be springtime. The trees would be sprouting fresh green shoots, the cattle would be suckling their knock-kneed calves—and I'd be sauntering among them all, high on my horse.

"Aren't you scared?" my friends asked me again and again. After the tenth time, I started to wonder if, perhaps, they knew something I didn't.

"What will happen if you get there and find that you really hate riding?" some forward-thinking souls asked with the chipper confidence of those who know they are going to spend the next few months safe and warm in a centrally heated office with nothing more frightening than a weekend break to France thrown in to ease the tedium.

"Whatever you do, don't ride in jeans," my friend Ruth advised me when I told her of my forthcoming adventure. She pulled up her trouser legs and showed me scars on her calves: Ruth used to ride daily as a teenager, and the sores caused by denim seams rubbing her skin had apparently marked her for life. "Oh yes, and also, remember that after you've been riding you will really stink."

"Pack painkillers," said some.

"Take arnica," declared others.

"*Always* wear gloves," instructed my friend Jenny.

"You must take Elliman's horse liniment to rub into your legs," Pam, a septuagenarian friend, pronounced imperiously.

"Horse liniment? But isn't that for horses?" I asked, trying hard to hide my horror.

"Oh yes, but I know plenty of humans who use it too. It's powerful stuff and you might be needing it," she said in a no-nonsense kind of way.

I went nervously to the pharmacist. They didn't stock Elliman's; I settled for arnica and ibuprofen. I packed sweatpants—and threw in a pair of jeans just in case. I blithely ignored the instruction regarding riding gloves. And then, I boarded the plane.

2

A Foot in the Stirrups

Robin's driver, Fabio, collected me from the Córdoba airport in a longhooded Ford pickup. Its leather-upholstered banquette stretched wide enough to accommodate a family. We drove out of the city and passed through flat fields and grassland—some green, some the color of pale straw. Cattle and horses grazed. We came into the town of Río Ceballos, where Ford Dodges and huge, antiquated American cars ornamented with rust weaved through the streets.

"Argentines can't drive," Fabio said, shrugging as he swung out of the way of a truck intent on collision.

Leaving the Chevrolets, we turned right onto an unpaved track, then climbed higher and higher into the Sierra Chica hills. The land undulated green and gold for as far as the eye could see. The buzz of the city was far below us now.

"That building there." Fabio pointed across the hillside to a tiny, one-story whitewashed construction. "That's the local school. It's very small—only about ten or twenty children go there."

The schoolhouse was right in the middle of nowhere. No roads seemed to lead to it. I asked Fabio how the children traveled there each day.

"Oh," he said, "they ride there on horseback."

He said it nonchalantly, as if to ride one's horse to school were the most natural thing in the world.

"How old are the children?" I asked, trying to hide my urbanite's surprise.

"Oh, the youngest ones are probably about six, I suppose."

"And they ride a horse to school, all alone?"

"Oh, the little ones ride with the older kids."

So here I was at last in Argentina, where six-year-olds traveled to school on horseback. I was a long, long way from home, where harassed, highlighted mothers ferried their offspring through city streets in outsized SUVs. Here in the Sierra Chica there was no school bus. And if the six-year-olds were so competent, why, after a couple of lessons, shouldn't I be? A small current of euphoria sparked within me. I hadn't even made it to the corral, yet already I felt a powerful sense of arrival.

We wound our way higher into the hills. A tinamou scuttled out of our path. As we drove through the gates of Estancia Los Potreros, a pair of bright green monk parakeets flitted between the trees.

"You can teach those birds to talk," Fabio told me. "You have to cover up their cage, then give them a piece of bread soaked in wine. It loosens their tongues."

We rattled along a track until we finally arrived in front of an L-shaped whitewashed house. The house sat slightly elevated from the lawn that spread before it: At intervals, staircases of five or six stone steps led up to a terrace, raised to the same level as the floor of the house. Along the outside of the terrace a series of square white pillars supported a low-pitched corrugated metal roof. Robin was standing in front of the house as we drew up. He was in his mid-forties, his brown hair just starting to thin. He was dressed in beige chinos and a blue cotton short-sleeved shirt, and wore large horn-rimmed glasses.

"Hello, welcome!" He shook my hand in a very English way. Robin was born in Argentina, but went to boarding school in England from the age of thirteen. He then worked a long stint in London and married his English wife, Teleri, before returning to Argentina seven years ago. Robin and Teleri now had four children; at the time of my visit the oldest, Elicia, was eight. Teleri lived with the children during the week in the nearby village of La Cumbre, where there was an English school; the two older girls went to the regular Argentine school in the morning and studied the British syllabus in the afternoon.

Robin showed me to my room, where a wooden four-poster bed took prominence, its dark, polished pillars spiraling dramatically skyward. In the corner of the room a wood-burning stove sat alongside a basket full of logs. The floor was constructed from parquet squares of gleaming *algarrobo*—carob tree—wood the color of bitter chocolate; a vase of fresh pink roses stood on the table. On the wall hung old sepia photographs of Robin's family.

"There's a key here if you want it," said Robin, "but we never bother to lock anything ourselves."

Robin's family moved to Argentina in 1825, he told me
a little later over a lunch of *milanesas*—breaded cutlets—
and salad, which we ate on the terrace before the emerald
green lawn and rolling golden hills. The day was sunny without being hot, the perfect temperature for sitting out in
shirtsleeves.

"That wasn't the Begg branch of the family, but another
lot. They moved from Scotland with an entire community.
They brought everyone—the doctor, carpenters, bricklay-
ers, an architect, a schoolteacher—on three ships."

The head of this part of the family was William Grierson:
He was Robin's great-great-great-grandfather. Grierson was
a farmer. He sailed to Argentina on the *Symmetry* with his
family—his wife, Catherine, and, at that time, three children—
to help found the Monte Grande settlement just south of
Buenos Aires.

The wave of British immigration to Argentina in the
1820s was encouraged by a liberal government eager to at-
tract educated people to its shores. Europeans had first col-
onized this land three hundred years previously, but the
descendants of those early settlers had only very rudimentary education. Argentina needed to instill learning into its
people—but the process would take time. The government
therefore came up with the expedient solution of importing
a population ready-schooled.

The government drew up an attractive package of land
grants and financial incentives for its citizens-to-be. Still,
those Scots' pioneer optimism must have been blended with
a heady dread of the unknown that Friday in May 1825
when they assembled at Leith and prepared for their long
voyage across a tempestuous ocean. They knew next to
nothing about the land that would be their home, yet there
would be little opportunity ever to return to Scotland, for

the journey was horribly long and prohibitively expensive. Grierson wrote a diary during his Atlantic voyage which has subsequently been reprinted in a book, *From Caledonia to the Pampas.*

"Found the greatest confusion in every part, the Steerage baffles all description, Beds, Blankets, Clothes, Bales, Packages. Items of every kind all in a huddle. Sailors, Passengers, Strangers, sick, healthy old and young, sober, tipsy, crying, praying, scolding . . . If things are to continue as they begin, the sooner our voyage is at an end, the better," wrote Grierson in his diary on May 20, 1825, of his first boarding of the *Symmetry.*

From his diaries, Grierson comes across as a stalwart Georgian gentleman. When in need of light entertainment, he partook of a round of whist. On Sundays, he joined the captain in reading sermons in his cabin. He was not given to namby-pamby ailments such as seasickness—yet there must have been times during the voyage when even the ever-upright William Grierson wondered whether it had really been such a great idea to throw in his familiar life in Scotland in order to pitch and roll across the Atlantic just so he could set up home on a patch of grass he'd never seen.

On July 15, the *Symmetry* passed through a storm so severe that even William Grierson's punctuation took a battering:

"The ship trembled, the Capt. called, the sailors roared; the sails clashed; the ropes cracked. the Ladies screamed; the crockery clattered; the children cried.—surprise seized me, and I cannot tell what I felt.—I ran to the cabin door and peeped out.—most awful!!"

When at last land was sighted at the end of July, Grierson—whose diary had in the previous fortnight descended into little more than dry comments on the wind and readings of longitude and latitude—appeared to be moved almost to emotion. His prose, which with the monotonous raising and downing of sails had become as gray as the endless slate blue sea, was now festooned with color and floridity:

"Winds of Columbia beat us not from your shore—," he wrote on July 30, 1825. One can almost imagine his tears of desperation spattering the page as he dipped his pen in ink: Land had been sighted the previous day, but overnight the winds had blown the *Symmetry* on a backward course. "We are the Sons of Liberty.—we come to you because you are free.—we come to hail your Emancipation.—we bring you not fetters, slavery, nor Inquisition.—our prowess lies in the muscles of our arms, our weapons are the Implements of Ceres; her Seeds are in our Hold; our weather-beaten hands shall adorn your plains; we will become your Sons; our blood shall mingle with yours, and Columbian, and Briton shall have no distinction.—for, indeed, we are all weary of cross winds, and flashing storms."

Finally, the Grierson clan landed safely in Buenos Aires. After all that trouble, first impressions frankly weren't that great. Grierson described the country as bleak, the city as gloomy; the inhabitants looked "rather foreboding."

Nonetheless, the Monte Grande colony flourished, as did the Grierson family. There were more children, and then grandchildren—and one of these granddaughters, years later, married Robert Begg, whose parents had emigrated to Argentina from Scotland in the late 1850s. It was Robert's son Robin, the current Robin's grandfather (clearly nobody thought to bring from Scotland a book of imaginative baby names), who started to build up the farm that today is Estancia Los Potreros.

Over the years, times had moved on a little—wind generators high on the hill now provided electricity, and Robin had rigged up a complex telephonic system from which he could sometimes receive calls if he stood very carefully at a specific spot at the back of the kitchen—but Los Potreros was a place that enjoyed the trappings of tradition rather than the latest gadgetry. Some of the staff came from families who had worked here for three generations. Both the grandmother and the mother of one of the kitchen girls had worked in one or other of the estancia's houses. The headman's son worked on the farm.

"And his son—well, he's too young at the moment, but I daresay he will too," said Robin.

He rang a little bronze bell in the shape of a Dutch woman in traditional dress. A girl similarly attired in an apron and cap appeared from the kitchen, cleared our plates, and served us coffee.

"I've got a few things to do," said Robin as we drained our cups, "so why don't we meet at about four-thirty at the gate over there and I'll give you a riding lesson."

I went back to my room and slept off my journey and lunchtime wine on the four-poster bed among small hillocks of soft, feathery pillows. A while later, I woke, blissfully refreshed, to the sound of squawking parakeets outside the window.

I had some sartorial concerns about my riding attire. Back in England, I had made some cursory attempts to buy gear, but had soon given up.

"In Argentina people just don't wear this kind of stuff,"

the girl in one shop had told me conspiratorially as she'd waved at the rows of tweed hacking jackets and tight cream jodhpurs.

I had sent Robin an e-mail asking what I needed to bring. A sun hat and some sunscreen, he had replied.

In the end, I turned up at the gate in sweatpants and a baseball cap. I asked if my headgear was suitable.

"Yes, it's all right for you to wear a cap like that," said Robin, "but no one else can. Sometimes the gauchos turn up with them on and I say, 'These people haven't traveled halfway across the world to see you in a stupid American cap. Go and put a proper hat on!' "

José, a diminutive gaucho with a broadly beaming smile, was saddling up the horses. He wore on his head a knitted black beret that slouched to one side like a lopsided tea cozy. According to Robin these were all the rage among the men at the moment—and what's more, approved of by the establishment. José was apparently given a healthy supply of woolly berets by his enthusiastically knitting sister and brother-in-law. I could just imagine the pair of them sitting around the fire of an evening, sipping maté and roasting a side of beef as their knitting needles clickety-clicked in happily wedded harmony.

Robin, I noticed, was wearing jeans. I wondered whether he, too, had scarred inner calves, or whether his skin was made of sterner stuff. I suspected the secret might lie in his half chaps, a pair of which he lent me. Made of brown suede, they wrapped around the lower leg and were fastened with Velcro, while a strap under the foot held them in position.

"Er, no," said Robin as I tried to put them on back to front. "Same foot, but the other way around."

The tack room was immaculate. Sepia photographs of

the family decorated the walls as they did in my bedroom. One photograph dated back to 1890 and showed Robin's great-grandfather sitting on a horse with a baby—Robin's grandfather—clutched in front of him.

Back outside, Robin introduced me to my horse.

"This is Ídolo," he said. "It means Idol."

"Idle?" Excellent, I thought.

"Idol as in god," said Robin, "not as in lazy."

Frankly, this didn't sound quite so hopeful. Slow and slothful I could cope with. On my first day on a horse, such characteristics were even desirable. But an object of idolatrous devotion? Wouldn't such a name give him ideas above his station?

It wouldn't be the first time a horse had been idolized in this part of the world. In 1701, a Spanish writer, Juan de Villagutierre Soto-Mayor, told the intriguing tale of the fate of one of Hernán Cortés's horses farther north, in what is now Guatemala. Villagutierre has been accused by more recent historians of bias and inaccuracy; still, the story is an interesting one.

According to Villagutierre, Hernán Cortés—the Spanish conquistador who overthrew the Aztecs—had a black horse named El Morzillo of whom he was very fond. Unfortunately the horse injured his hoof and in 1525 Cortés was forced to leave him in the care of an Indian chief near Lake Petén Itzá.

The Spaniards went on their way, killing, conquering, and colonizing. It wasn't until 1697, more than a hundred and seventy years later, that their descendants returned to Petén Itzá. During that time the local population had never laid eyes on another horse. According to Villagutierre's narrative, their reaction to the Spaniards' arrival was a surprising one.

When the Spaniards rode in on their mounts, he wrote, one of the local chiefs "almost ran mad with joy and with astonishment. Especially the jumps and bounds made by the animals moved him to admiration, and going down on all fours he skipped about and neighed."

The Spaniards then found on an island in the middle of a lake the image of a horse carved in stone. The locals appeared to worship it as a god.

"These barbarous infidels adored the abominable and monstrous beast under the name of Tziunchan, God of Thunder, and the Lightning, and paid reverence to him," the horrified Villagutierre wrote.

It transpired that, after Cortés had left his horse there all those years before, the indigenous people had stabled him in a temple and fed him rich foods but, missing his oats or whatever, the horse had soon died. The Indians were terrified that his passing would enrage Cortés should he happen to return, so they made a carving of the animal in the hope that the statue might appease him. But Cortés never did come back and, over the generations, the carved horse's importance had become inflated until it was considered to be an object of divinity.

Fortunately, nobody had explained anything of this to Ídolo and he turned out to be a delightfully placid creature. Ídolo was a skewbald criollo. Criollo translates as Creole, and is the word used to refer to both horses and cattle indigenous to South America. (The word also denotes the human descendants of the early Spanish settlers, people who were of Spanish blood but born in America.) The criollo horse was not created by assiduous breeding; rather, it came into being through rigorous natural selection among those first horses who ran wild on the pampas.

"The horses brought from Spain most probably were of

the same stamp as the horses Velásquez painted, ridden on by Philip IV. They were of course the finest specimens of their race to be obtained in Spain. Short-backed, and without too much daylight showing beneath their bellies, they must have been admirably suited for the hard work of a campaign," Robert Cunninghame Graham wrote in *Horses of the Conquest*. As generations of these horses' offspring bred on the wild pampas, they developed the tenacity and stamina for which criollos are now famous—though I was hoping neither Ídolo nor I would be required to show a great deal of those two qualities on our first outing together that afternoon.

"We use British military saddles," said Robin, showing me how they rise high front and back. "They're made this way because the army doesn't want the soldiers falling off."

That sounded good and safe to me, and when José tied a big, soft sheepskin over the top, I began to wonder whether the arnica and ibuprofen were going to be needed after all.

"The Argentines hold the reins in the left hand," Robin explained, demonstrating as he mounted a gray called Gaucho. "This leaves the right hand free for a lasso, or a polo stick, or whatever."

If I wanted Ídolo to turn left, I was to hold the reins high over his neck, and gently move them to the left so that they merely brushed his skin. To turn right, I should hold them to the right. To ask Ídolo to start, a little kick was required, and to stop, the gentlest of tugs on the reins. Frankly, it looked easy.

This style of riding owes as much to the Spanish conquistadors as does the presence in Argentina of horses themselves. The sixteenth-century Spaniards were brilliant horsemen. In fact, the Spanish word for gentleman— *caballero*—literally translates as "rider of a horse." When the

Spaniards first sailed to South America, the Christians had just routed the Moors from the Iberian Peninsula after nearly eight hundred years of war. The Catholic monarchs Ferdinand and Isabella had finally conquered the last stronghold, Granada, in 1492.

The raids and scourges of Spain had taken place on horseback—and, over the centuries, the Moorish style of riding had influenced the Christians. Cunninghame Graham explained in *Horses of the Conquest* that, unlike northern Europeans, the Moors held the reins in a single hand and used a bit that worked on the neck, not directly on the mouth. This meant both that the horse suffered less, and that the rider was able to turn his mount more quickly. When the Spanish came to conquer South America, they favored this type of riding, which was so well suited to warfare. Over the years, some adjustments have been developed— for example, the New World settlers quickly adopted a longer stirrup length than had been traditional, as this made it easier to mount a semiwild horse—but still today, influences from the first conquistadors can be seen in the riding style of South America.

I mounted, clasping the reins in my left hand as instructed, gave Ídolo a little kick, and off we walked through the green paddock in front of the house. *Horneros,* or ovenbirds, waddled with their awkward gait across the grass to our left. These are the national birds of Argentina, named after the ovenlike mud domes they build as nests; their rather drab plumage is compensated for by the strikingly harmonious duets they sing as couples. We continued along an inclined path that led out into the open land of the estancia. On both sides, plump sheaves of pale gold *paja brava,* a type of tussock, swayed in the wind like thousands of perfectly bouffant heads of expensively highlighted hair. The grasses seemed to undulate down the hillside, turning a silvery yellow as they caught the breeze.

"You should always have a bit of weight in your feet; that way all your weight isn't floating around on the top," said Robin. "The easiest way to do that is to put your heels down."

José rode in front. "Look at the way José's body relaxes into the horse's stride," Robin suggested. I studied José's posture. He seemed enviably careless about the whole business. His spine just slouched onto the horse, it seemed to me, while his legs splayed outward at an angle that looked horribly uncomfortable.

"I'm not sure my hips extend at quite the angle José's do," I commented tentatively.

"Ah! It's that dreadful saddle he's sitting on!" remarked Robin, throwing his eyes to the blue sky. "The gaucho saddles are awful things. They're flat, like a dining table."

Robin later revealed that a guest had once been so impressed by José's horsemanship that he'd offered him a job in England as a jockey, but José had chosen to stay here in his native hills.

The lesson continued. Going downhill, I was to lean backward. Going uphill, I was to lean forward. And if Ídolo became bored with this whole business and thought it would be an awful lot more fun to trot, I was gently but firmly to rein him in.

Around us, Aberdeen Angus and Hereford cattle grazed. Robin's black Labrador, Pippa, galloped and frolicked alongside through the tall, softly rolling grasses, chasing delicious smells. Every now and then she eagerly dived her nose down a hole in the ground and rooted around while her bottom and fiercely wagging tail pointed high to the sky.

Alongside Pippa galloped José's dog, a sandy-colored

mutt called Earless. There was good reason for his name:
Earless only had one ear. But Earless wasn't his full name,
Robin told me. In formal circles, he was introduced as
Earless the Fearless.

We ambled gently back toward the house in the late afternoon sun, and Robin told me Earless's intrepid tale.

Several years ago Pippa had been in heat, and a horde of
neighborhood dogs had come around to have their wicked
way with her. Earless (who presumably was called something different then) had valiantly defended her to the
last—but the fight had been fierce. By the end of the battle,
the knightly Earless had lost an ear as well as dangerous
quantities of blood from his many wounds.

"I didn't think he'd survive," said Robin. "I was sure we
were going to have to put him down."

But Robin had underestimated Earless's indomitable
spirit. The dog recovered—and obviously Pippa appreciated
his help, because Earless went on to father her first litter of
puppies. Maybe it was love.

But then, as in all good romantic yarns, disaster struck.
The mettlesome Earless, high perhaps on success, got carried away. He went on the rampage to a neighboring farm
and killed a sheep. This is an unforgivable crime in the
Argentine countryside, and the unwritten law of the *estancieros* dictates that the dog involved must be banished.

"So we sent him away," Robin said. "There was no way he
could stay here, so we sent him to another farm about forty
miles away. But somehow he found his way back."

Duly Robin and José sent Earless away once more.
Again, he returned.

"Obviously forty miles wasn't far enough," said Robin,
"so this time we sent him to a different place, a really, really
long way away—I'd say at least a hundred miles."

For a while, this third banishment seemed effective—
and then one day, to Robin and Teleri's total astonishment,
Earless turned up at their house in La Cumbre, an hour's
drive from the estancia.

"We have no idea how he got there. He'd never even
been to La Cumbre before. I can only think that he was
nearby and smelled Poppy, our other Labrador, who we keep
down there. She comes up to the farm with us sometimes,
so he knew her."

However he found his way, this time Earless the Fearless
saw his tenacity rewarded. Robin brought him back to the
estancia and allowed him to stay.

The two dogs, happily reunited, gamboled along beside
us. The land here was immense, wide and open. The sky was
blue, the tussock was golden. I was entirely happy sitting
astride Ídolo and watching the incredible scenery slowly roll
by. None of the dire outcomes I had been warned about
seemed to be bearing fruit: My legs weren't sore, my skin
wasn't chafed, and Ídolo smelled really quite pleasant.

We rode for an hour or two, then returned to the house,
where tea and scones fresh from the oven appeared magically on the terrace alongside a pot of *dulce de leche,* the
sweet caramel that the Argentines so adore. I sat there, chatting with Robin, eating and drinking and thinking that yes,
this idea to come and learn to ride in Argentina had really
been rather a good one.

3

Meanwhile, Back at the Ranch . . .

"The important thing with horses is never to be afraid," said José cheerfully the next morning as we made circuits of the paddock. I was concentrating fiercely on trying to sit naturally. It was all very well to try to imitate José, but he must have started riding before he could walk. His limbs appeared to have formed around the flanks of a horse. It was no wonder the indigenous Americans had thought that the Spaniards and their steeds were one if those men had looked anything like this. Perhaps, I considered, José was directly descended from those warriors of old and his seat was congenital. He seemed a lot friendlier than those bloodthirsty, swashbuckling saber-rattlers, though. In fact, José wore a perpetual smile between his blousy blue cotton shirt and his woolly beret. Maybe perpetual happiness is what comes of knowing that you have a sister and brother-in-law who love you so much that they spend their evenings knitting your headgear.

I had woken fully refreshed after a luxurious night in the four-poster bed. During the night a storm had broken. Heavy raindrops had reverberated on the metal roof of my bedroom, rattling noisily as they struck the surface like the bursting of thousands of tiny water-filled balloons. Sporadic strobes of lightning had lit the room a bright bluish white. But I have always enjoyed storms, those violently expressive explosions of nature, and it had seemed wonderful to lie warm and dry among a heap of pillows, and from there to listen to the fierce detonations of the wild world outside.

By morning, though, the storm had cleared and the Córdoban skies shimmered cerulean. I'd ambled over to the dining room where I diligently fueled my horse-riding muscles with a breakfast of muesli and fruit in yogurt, fresh eggs and bacon, and toast with homemade marmalade. Where in this remote land had the cook managed to procure Seville oranges? I'd wondered. I later found out that a strain of bitter citrus grows conveniently nearby.

Other accoutrements of the breakfast table had come from farther afield. The delicate bone-handled butter knife had a blade engraved in an elaborate cursive script: "Thomas Ward & Sons, Sheffield." A silver toast rack looked as though it had been in the family for generations. The table mats featured Constable prints. And then, alongside this very English theme, there were touches of the pioneer New World: Above the large wooden table hung an old bellpull whose plaited leather was oiled smooth and pliant by generations of supplicatory hands. The cord disappeared through a hole in the wall and when it was pulled, *ding-ding,* a bell jingled in the kitchen next door. The latch would rise and a white-aproned girl would waltz through, as had her mother and grandmother before her, to clear the plates of one course and to bring in the next. I reflected on the dinners that bellpull must have presided over, and the stories it could tell if it talked.

The bookcases that lined the walls curved concave beneath the weight of age-speckled tomes: *Lady Chatterley's Lover,* Winston Churchill's *The Second World War,* and *The Complete Works of Shakespeare* in a tattered brown leather binding. I later discovered that these books hadn't been in the family for generations as the staff had but that, on hearing that Robin and Teleri were renovating a part of the estancia for paying guests, Anglo-Argentine residents of La Cumbre had cleared out unwanted reading matter and donated many volumes to them. Likewise, the *algarrobo* parquet floors were not rich with a patina imparted by the kitchen maid's grandmother's elbow grease. Despite their aged and uneven appearance, they were in fact brilliantly crafted circa 1990-something. These buildings in which I now ate and slept had been a part of the estancia for decades—Robin's father could remember studying for his private-school entrance exams on the very terrace where I had eaten lunch and tea yesterday—but they had fallen into disuse and only recently been renovated. Los Potreros was a vast establishment. There were countless houses: Robin's brother Kevin had his place a short distance down the track. His parents' home—which they used when they came here from Buenos Aires—was a good half hour's ride away. There were scattered buildings where the men lived, some with their wives, some alone. Other structures lay empty and crumbling, awaiting, perhaps, the day of their own redemption.

By the time José and I had finished our morning outing, two more guests had arrived at the estancia. Luciana and Marcelo were from Buenos Aires. Luciana worked in the Sheraton Hotel while Marcelo owned and managed a microbrewery. Despite their Argentine blood, these two weren't riders either. Luciana confessed to me that she had been taken by her father to learn to ride at the age of six. She had lost control of the horse, which had thrown her, bolted, and subsequently couldn't be found. Luciana's father had been so annoyed at the disappearance of the animal that he had refused ever to take his disgraced daughter riding again.

And so, later that morning, Luciana went on the second ride of her life, and I went on my third. Marcelo was marginally more experienced. For an hour or two, we sauntered gently through the estancia's grounds, returning just in time for an aperitif before lunch.

We relaxed into the plump cushions of the sitting room, glasses in hand, and were happily reliving our morning's experiences when a fourth guest arrived.

"Hello, I'm Charlotte Stoney," this tall, slender woman pronounced, striding into the room with imposing presence, tumbling reddish hair, and striking green eyes.

Charlotte lived in Dublin but she'd grown up in the west of Ireland in a castle complete with stables, horses, and a Norman keep. Her childhood, it seemed, had been dedicated more or less entirely to galloping hell-for-leather across the windswept beaches and lush green meadows of County Mayo. I was sad to hear that her family had eventually run out of cash and had been forced to sell the castle, because I quite fancied inviting myself over for a weekend.

"I like a horse that's forward-going," Charlotte instructed Robin. Robin stuttered slightly. He was beginning to look distinctly anxious.

We calmed our nerves with another glass of wine and settled together at the long table on the terrace for lunch—fabulously tender chicken that had been stewed with peppers and onions in a colossal circular metal pan over a barbecue. The cooking pot had, in a former life, been the wheel of a plough. Dessert came in the form of a slice of mild local cheese with sweet, ruby red quince jelly. We retired for a siesta in order to work up the energy for an afternoon ride—before which we managed to squeeze in a quick pick-me-up of tea and freshly baked apple cake. Really, it was easy to get used to the rigors of this particular riding school.

At about five o'clock we heaved our burgeoning bellies onto our long-suffering mounts and walked out once more through the *paja brava*. It was spring and, helped by last night's rains, there were faint wisps of green among the golden grasses. The hillsides burst with new life and springtime vibrancy. Wobbly-legged calves stood close to their mothers and stared startled and wide-eyed as we rode past. One cow tried to hide her offspring behind a tussock spray and gave bullish chase when Pippa the Labrador showed too close an interest.

I was riding Ídolo again; José was riding a spirited gray mare called Paloma, upon whom Charlotte had firmly fixed her eye for tomorrow.

"Er, yes, well, you can ride her if you like," said Robin, still looking worried.

A military starling with a bright scarlet breastplate flitted by; a black-chested buzzard eagle swooped and soared before us. We rode upward, past mares and their nervous newborn foals, until we arrived at "The Top of the World"— or the top of this small, rather perfect world, anyway. From the peak of the highest hill on the estancia's land, we could see Córdoba city and the flat, featureless plains that stretched beyond it toward Buenos Aires and the sea.

It was in these hills to the west of Córdoba that Argentina's most famous revolutionary grew up. Ernesto

Guevara, who was later nicknamed "Che" by his Cuban revolutionary comrades, moved to the town of Alta Gracia, just
to the south of where I was now, with his family in the 1930s
when he was four years old. His parents hoped that the dry
climate would cure his debilitating asthma, and, though
they'd planned to come only for a few months, they ended
up staying here for eleven years. It was curious to think that
Che Guevara would have been galloping about the hills a
short distance to the south at the same time as Robin's father would have been sitting on the terrace at Los Potreros
studying his Latin.

Che Guevara is best known as Fidel Castro's comrade-
in-arms: He sailed with Castro to Cuba and helped him to
overthrow the dictator Fulgencio Batista in 1959. He subsequently dreamed of leading the rest of Latin America to rise
up against their corrupt and damaging governments and to
unite—but in 1967 the CIA hunted him down in Bolivia and
shot him dead.

But Guevara's roots lay a long way from his subsequent
revolutionary activity. He was born into a middle-class
Argentine family: Both parents came from wealthy landowning stock. By the time they met, however, Ernesto's father's fortunes were dwindling, and when the shipyard in
which he had invested caught fire and burned to the ground,
what little remained of his inheritance quite literally went
up in smoke. The family still had assets—most important, a
yerba mate (maté leaf) plantation in the northeastern province
of Misiones bought with Ernesto's mother's inheritance—
but the Guevara family would always struggle financially,
and during their years here in the Sierra Chica their finances
became increasingly precarious.

The Guevara parents must have been pleased, therefore,
when their eldest son trained to be a doctor. By the time

Ernesto was in his early twenties, the family had moved to Buenos Aires and Ernesto was making excellent progress toward a respectable profession and a good income. He was even courting the daughter of one of the wealthiest families in Córdoba. In fact, he demonstrated no radical tendencies whatsoever until, in 1952, he set out with his friend Alberto Granado on a worn-out Norton 500 motorbike to travel through Latin America. His journal from that trip was later published as *The Motorcycle Diaries*. For the first time he smelled the stench of poverty and witnessed the gross inequalities between rich and poor—and his heart never returned to the comfortable enclave of middle-class Argentina.

Ernesto completed his medical training, but as soon as he had qualified he took off once more on his travels. His first port of call was Bolivia, whose new revolutionary government interested him: It had created a "Ministry of Peasant Affairs"—but Ernesto was enraged to see that, when the peasants themselves visited its offices, they were dusted at the door with DDT powder so that their lice didn't take up residence in the Ministry's carpets.

Back in Buenos Aires, his respectable family fretted. Biographer Jon Lee Anderson relates that Ernesto's father was so bothered by the fact that his son, having pawned his suit, would not be properly dressed that he sent him a parcel of newly tailored garments.

"When Ernesto received the new suit, blazer, and ties, he sent a letter to his father that said, 'What little value Argentine clothes have—for the whole lot I got only one hundred dollars!'"

Guevara then traveled north, through Peru, Ecuador, and Central America, barely surviving on the money he earned from sporadic odd jobs but nourishing his intellect with the writings of philosophers and revolutionaries, and with the conversation of the political exiles with whom he made friends. It was through his Cuban exile friends that Ernesto first met Fidel Castro in Mexico in 1955—and from that point, he embarked on his career as a revolutionary fighter in earnest.

Coincidentally, it was in the town of La Cumbre—where Robin and Teleri lived when they weren't at the farm—that Guevara enjoyed his first political escapade. Though he showed scant interest in politics in his youth, in 1944 Ernesto, aged about sixteen, and a friend embarked on an adventure with a political tone: They decided to carry out an undercover mission to a hotel in La Cumbre that was said to be a headquarters for Nazi operations in Argentina. Presumably they hoped to gather vital information and reveal the Fascist group's secret activities to the authorities. They crept up to the hotel, peered discreetly through a window, saw some men at a table—and then somebody spotted them. Shots were fired and Ernesto and his friend ran away. So began the political career of Ernesto "Che" Guevara.

Just a few miles away from the site of Che Guevara's adolescent retreat, we stood for a while and gazed at the view from our hilltop idyll. Pippa sat on the highest rock, her nose raised to the heavens, and looked out across the plains. The wind caught her ears so that they flew out sideways, flapping on the breeze like black velvet wings. Then we turned around and rode for home. As we approached the house, we could see smoke coiling up from the chimneys where fires and stoves had been lit in a delightful, warm welcome.

And so the days went rather blissfully by. I was starting to wonder if, perhaps, I could find a way of skipping the rest of Argentina. Would Robin mind very much if I abandoned the remainder of my trip and instead just shacked up here to spend the next couple of months cosseted in a whirl of panoramic rides and recuperative gin and tonics on the veranda? It was odd, really. Everyone at Los Potreros seemed so ridiculously happy. The horses whinnied, the dogs wagged their tails, José continued to beam. Even the kitchen girls couldn't stop grinning.

"What do you do to make them smile so constantly?" I asked Robin. Secretly I suspected he was slipping something in their maté.

"I pay them on time," he said. "Not everyone does that in Argentina."

We rode out over increasing distances across the estancia's land. Charlotte rode Paloma and proved that Robin had nothing to be nervous about. During those fairy-tale years in County Mayo she'd certainly learned a thing or two about horses. Ídolo was granted a reprieve and I progressed to Flopi, a black purebred *peruana* with a mouth so soft that she responded to the merest stroke of the reins.

"As one of our guests once said, Flopi is anything but floppy," Robin told me as he introduced us.

I thought Flopi was wonderful. She had a gloriously smooth gait. On my second morning with her we trotted along; the other horses gradually picked up a little speed—and then I was cantering. After the bone-rattling, bruising gait of the sitting trot, it felt exhilarating to leap through the air in a canter. Suddenly, I was no longer jolting—I was bounding, gliding, and flying. A potent burst of joyful energy flooded through me with a euphoric intensity. My skills may still have been limited in the extreme but, after all those years of childhood pining, here I was at last really learning to ride.

We were joined by Judith—a florist from Lincolnshire—and her twenty-something son, JP. We lunched on *asado* — an Argentine barbecue of huge, tender steaks, rich, bulging black sausage, and spicy chorizo cooked by the gauchos. The mere thought of all that meat piled before us would no doubt have given a nutritionist a heart attack, but it tasted fantastic and, with our appetites piqued by a morning of fresh air and dazzling sights, we cleaned our plates with voracious zest.

We rode some more, along craggy paths and earthen tracks. Sometimes we walked in single file but more often, in this spacious place, we ambled along in groups, side by side and companionably chatting. The others had far greater riding experience than I, but in this amiable world nobody seemed to care.

One afternoon we made our way through meadows of swaying grasses and bright wildflowers to the Cascada de los Cóndores—the condors' waterfall—where we tethered the horses to trees, then picked our way over a vertiginous path before dropping down onto a perfectly private sandy beach. Glistening water tumbled over the rock face into a small pool where we swam and dived from the jagged boulders. As we pottered gently back, kestrels and condors flexed their mighty wings as they hurtled about the hillsides. If I stayed close enough to José, I could just hear him singing gaucho ballads to himself as we weaved our way home.

One evening, a guitarist and singer named Charlie Ruiz drove up from the village and serenaded us before dinner. He was a big, grinning, dancing character with unkempt brown hair and a stubbly beard, who energetically made his way through Argentine folk songs and others that were more familiar: "Guantánamera," "La Bamba," and then a song that, with its opening chords, hurtled me back more than a decade in time to the year I spent living in Spain. That year, 1992, smoke-filled bars all over the country had pulsated to the tones of Joaquín Sabina and his song *"Y nos dieron las diez."* I found I still knew all the words and wondered why it is that my brain is so irritating in its selection process, remembering the lyrics to old Spanish songs but instantly forgetting useful things like appointments and telephone numbers. Still, it served some purpose. It was by singing along to this song that, all those years back, I had finally learned to roll my *r*'s, a prerequisite for pronouncing Spanish that I had long struggled to master.

That was the year that I really learned to speak the language. I'd been studying Spanish at school and university, but the classroom is no place to master expressions that live and breathe and curse. Then, for the third year of my university course, I was required to live abroad. I went to Plasencia, a town in Spain's western Extremadura province that sees few tourists. I worked as a teaching assistant in a local secondary school, shared a house with two Spanish girls, and expended tremendous energy investigating the after-dark aspects of Spanish culture. My language skills soon rocketed.

Charlie's rendition of *"Y nos dieron las diez"* drew to a close and he was joined in the sitting room by José, who had abandoned his customary knitted beret for the occasion and was instead wearing a traditional gaucho *panza de burro* (donkey belly) hat, with a round dome and flat brim, together with a red neck scarf. José recited a long gaucho lament that told the tale of the loss of a white-socked horse. When our cheering grew sufficiently loud and encouraging, he even consented to show us some traditional gaucho dancing. Amid much giggling, he grabbed one of the girls from

the kitchen as a partner—still in her apron and cap—and
together they capered and cavorted, stamped their feet and
waggled their legs in a dexterous display.

And then, the next morning, disaster struck.

I found José outside the tack room looking morose. His
usual beaming smile had been wiped clean from his face.
Now, his expression was distinctly doleful.

"Flopi está enferma," he said very sadly. Flopi is sick.

My first horrified thought was that I personally must
have finished her off. Clearly I had been too cocky over the
last day or two: Rather than making good progress as I had
thought, I had clearly made such a hash of my entry into the
equestrian world that I had sent my beleaguered mount
dragging her hooves to the sanatorium. But it soon transpired that poor Flopi's illness had nothing to do with my
own inadequate riding posture. José confided that he had
never seen anything like it but he thought she must have
been stung by the fierce African bees that swarm in these
parts.

"Come with me," he said, looking wistful. "Come and
say hello to Flopi."

I walked with him up to the corral where a mere shadow
of the former Flopi was tethered to a tree in one corner. She
was a desperate sight; her whole torso was distorted by
huge, lumpy swellings. Her upper legs and underbelly were
scarred by scabby, crusty welts that oozed yellow pus.

Robin had already telephoned the vet, who had said that
the prognosis for horses stung by bees was poor. He himself
had never managed to save one. Horribly discouraged,

Robin had rung a second medic; this one had been slightly more positive and recommended cortisone injections.

With Flopi in the infirmary, I was given Caradequeso—or, by his English appellation, Cheeseface. It didn't seem a very fair name for the horse—his face, after all, looked nothing like a cheese. That afternoon, I graduated to riding Gaucho, the same gray with whom Robin had demonstrated the basics on that very first day. I cantered some more and found the speed intoxicating.

But it was becoming increasingly apparent that my baseball cap was hampering the horsewoman image that I wished to convey. Judith was eager to make the journey down to the nearest town, Río Ceballos, to visit the woolly beret shop; we agreed an outing was in order. Teleri said she'd come with us (she wanted to buy Robin some new *bombachas,* the baggy cotton trousers that Argentines wear for outdoor work and riding) and advise us on gaucho style.

Río Ceballos's outdoor clothing shop was long and thin. Down the length of one wall, bombachas of all colors and sizes were piled onto shelves. There were black-and-white herringbone bombachas (apparently very fashionable at the time); there were plain cotton bombachas in gray and green and blue. There were even beautifully embroidered bombachas of the type that a well-turned-out gaucho might wear to a party. At the far end of the shop lay the hats: endless variations on the knitted beret, *panzas de burro,* and Texan-style leather cowboy hats. There were piles of multicolored *fajas,* the woven belts in which a gaucho carries his knife, tobacco, and other necessities, and cabinets full of silver-sheathed knives that twinkled in the light.

I tried on several pairs of bombachas. They seemed all right to me.

"Oh no," said Teleri. "They're far too tight. You must wear your bombachas baggy if you're going to spend all day on a horse."

The shop assistants agreed—there were five of them in all, and they were very eager to attend to us. Outside, on the street, the locals stood and stared through the plate-glass shop front at these ignorant, oddly dressed strangers.

I tried on another pair of bombachas—navy blue with red and green flowers embroidered down each outer leg. These were at the glamorous end of gaucho attire. They were real Saturday-night bombachas and, once they had been deemed suitably too-big, I bought them. Then, to complete my outfit, I purchased a leather hat, a striped *faja,* and a pair of half chaps. Judith bought a multitude of berets for the Christmas stockings of long-suffering relatives. Teleri bought a pair of herringbone bombachas for Robin that were breathtakingly *de moda.* And so, with our paper bags rustling in a very satisfactory manner, we made our way back to the farm just in time for dinner.

Newly attired, we rode the next day to a corral where the vet had arrived to inoculate a group of yearling horses that had not yet been broken in, and to test their blood for an equine form of AIDS. The gauchos had to herd these wild yearlings into the corral. Robin asked Charlotte if she'd like to help. She was thrilled by the opportunity to go off and ride with the real men and, with not so much as a backward glance, she disappeared off into the distance with an elderly gaucho named Luis.

Really, it had all the makings of a romantic novel: green-eyed girl on spirited gray mare meets grizzled gaucho on his weathered criollo workhorse. She holds her reins in soft gloved hands; he grasps a leather cattle whip with his calluses. Amid much whinnying and trembling of flanks, together they herd the horses.

"*Tu rancho o el mío?*" grunts the gaucho: Your shack or mine? (He doesn't for a moment imagine the truth—that she grew up in a castle.)

But then, just when I'd concocted this scenario, Charlotte and Luis returned looking none the sweatier, and we all sat down to eat at a table in front of one of the estancia's outbuildings. Robin laid out the lunch that a packhorse had generously carried there and poured us each a glass of wine. It was a warm, sunny day and it felt luxurious to sit for an hour or so eating and drinking in that paradisiacal place.

After lunch we watched the vet inoculate the horses. They didn't like it much; these were wild creatures that weren't used to being handled. But it was wonderful to see how the gauchos coaxed them, talking to them softly until they managed to slip the halters over their heads, and continually soothed them so that the animals, in most cases, were easily led. Even when one of them tried to vault a high wire fence and became trapped with its forelegs on one side and back legs suspended on the other, nobody raised a voice. The horse let out the most terrible guttural moaning but, within a few minutes, with total calm, the headman's son, Dani, had managed to climb the fence, lasso the horse's back legs, and hoist him to safety. Afterward, they tethered the trembling creature to a post so that they could treat his cuts and grazes, and the rest of the herd closed in around him, nuzzling and nickering in soft, horsy sympathy.

Toward the end of the week, we set out on a two-day ride. As we made our way to the boundary of the estancia, a graceful black condor glided overhead. On a fence to our right sat a pair of scissortails whose forked, feathered blades splayed out behind them. Flocks of tiny yellow goldfinches cheeped melodiously, then a many-colored rush-tyrant streaked by, flaunting its extraordinary multihued plumage. The sandy path sparkled as the sun's rays glinted on the finely ground mica. It was as though somebody had scattered gold and silver glitter to light our way like a trail of fairy-tale breadcrumbs.

It took us two hours to ride to the neighboring farm where we were going to camp for the night; it was a gentle journey of soft up-and-down undulations through the tussock. The owner of the land we now rode through was called Plomo—which means "lead" in Spanish. Plomo didn't seem very leaden to me, but Robin later revealed the reason for his strange name: As a child Plomo had been a particular pain in the neck and, one day, some houseguests staying with his family had commented that he was a real "plomo"—a terrible weight to be burdened with. As these things sometimes do, the nickname had stuck. We ate our picnic lunch on Plomo's terrace (he must have mellowed with the years for, despite his moniker, he was entirely charming to us), then climbed back on our horses and explored further afield.

Our afternoon ride was precipitous in places. The path was narrow and rocky, and weaved its way along a vertiginous cliff edge. A turkey vulture circled. I wondered whether it was watching. Perhaps it had spied that there was a novice rider picking her way over this perilous ground and had its beady eye on me. Maybe it was hoping that I might make a tasty feast if, as seemed likely, I soon met my demise.

"Lean well back here," Robin called out to me as we came to one particularly tricky part where the track descended in a series of terrifyingly steep, slippery steps. Then he paused. "Actually," he said, "it might be better if you just got off and walked."

That evening there was a total eclipse of the moon. We ate great plates of beef and rice stew that Plomo and his men had cooked over an open fire, then lay on the ground and stared up at the cloudless night sky. The southern cross sparkled across the celestial darkness. Orion's belt beamed bright and strong and Ursa Minor glimmered seductively. The moon, at first, seemed impossibly bright, like a single mottled pearl suspended in the dark navy sky. Its cratered surface glowed with a remarkable, marbled radiance. And then, chink by tiny chink, the earth's shadow began to creep across its face.

It was a slow process; we watched for an hour or more. But as bit by infinitesimal bit the moon was cast into the umbra, it became suffused with a faint, amber glow. I had always thought that an eclipse would mean total darkness. I had imagined that the moon would, to the eye's assumption, simply disappear. It didn't: The eclipsed part of the moon was still clearly visible—but it had changed its appearance entirely. Over its silken white mantle, it wore a coppery veil beneath which its mottling seemed to have seeped into creeping bloodred birthmarks.

We sipped our whisky *digestifs* and we took turns with Judith's binoculars, but mostly we just lay on the ground and stared silently upward at this mesmerizing extraterrestrial sight. Slowly, slowly, the moon passed into full eclipse. A single owl hooted. A wind stirred up and rustled the branches of the trees around us. And then we heard the pounding hooves of the horses galloping across the land.

I was supposed to leave Los Potreros after a week. On Saturday morning I was meant to make my way down to Córdoba city and to spend a couple of days there contemplating high-minded matters such as the seventeenth-century Jesuit architecture for which the town is famous. But then Robin very generously suggested I might like to stay a couple of days more at the estancia, indulge in a little more eating and drinking—and try my hand at polo. It wasn't a difficult choice.

We clambered onto our horses and made our way down the track that led to Robin's polo field. It didn't gleam with quite the same velvety texture as the lawns of Palermo, for this was a patch that was new to polo: Robin's laborious clearing of this piece of land was only just complete.

We players were all newcomers to the game as well, so Robin gave us each a stick and ball and told us to putt around the field on our own for a while. I was riding a horse called Pepino; apparently he had never played polo before, either, but he seemed to get the idea within a minute or two. He'd walk up to the ball and stop. He'd wait patiently while I hacked wildly at it with my stick. Then, when at last I'd managed to make contact and the ball had trundled a yard or two across the grass, Pepino would, with a resigned expression, amble toward it and stop once more. What poor Pepino didn't know was that, any minute now, we were going to play a heart-thumping, adrenaline-pumping, earth-shattering game.

The teams assembled. We lined up facing one another: Robin, JP, and I glared menacingly, eyeballs bulging, at our opponents—José, Charlotte, and Judith. Robin threw the ball into play—and we were off! Hopelessly, ineptly, but with an enthusiasm that suggested my life depended on the outcome, I spurred Pepino into action and we lolloped around the pitch. We bashed and we thrashed, we cheered and we groaned, we stuttered and muttered, and skipped and spun.

Judith mis-hit the ball—and for just a moment it lay abandoned, yards from where I stood.

"Come on, Pepino," I shrieked, and booted the unfortunate creature in the flanks in what, I should imagine, was a fair imitation of a belligerent Boadicea galloping against her foe. Pepino broke into a halfhearted canter; I swiped at the ball with such jaw-clenched intent that one might have imagined it was a Roman head. It trickled a very short distance.

Furiously, I swung again.

"Yes, yes, it's nearly there," I yelled. "One more, one more, and it should be there!"

And then, with one final triumphant clout of the stick, the ball very, very slowly, with all the speed and drive of a deflated football long discarded on the dump, dribbled through the goalposts.

A roar went up from the stands, the crowd cheered wildly, the gauchos ripped their shirts from their well-toned chests and . . . oh, all right, so it wasn't *exactly* like that. But I'm pretty sure one of the parakeets said something.

4

Northern Heights

Ω **Eventually, of course,** I had to leave Estancia Los
Potreros, the luxurious four-poster bed, the home-baked
cakes, the polo field, the waterfall, and the tussock-covered
hills. It was a wrench, but I'd completed my objective:
While I still might not have been the most stylish equestrian
in the world, I could now sit astride a docile horse without
falling off. I could trot and I could canter. I had negotiated
precipices and the polo field and I was still in one piece. It
was time to move on. And so, sadly, I said good-bye to
Robin, Teleri, and José and the delightful girls in the
kitchen. I bade farewell to Ídolo, Flopi (who, contrary to the
vet's dire prognosis, was recovering well—a snake was now
thought to be the culprit rather than bees), Cheeseface,
Gaucho, and Pepino, and made my way back down that unpaved road to the airport.

I was flying that day to Salta, in the far northwest of the
country, close to the Bolivian border: Argentina is a huge

territory—it's more than eleven times the size of the UK though it has less than two thirds the population—and, as I only had two months in which to see it, I'd decided to hop the longer distances by plane. I would travel round the Salta region for a week or so before making my way overland to Mendoza, the wine region that lies in the foothills of the Andes. From Mendoza I'd fly to Buenos Aires, the capital, then spend a few days up in the far northeast at Iguazú and the former Jesuit missions, before heading down south to Patagonia. I was planning to take advantage of as many opportunities to ride horses as I could along the way.

Salta was a pleasant place. The Plaza 9 de Julio's palm trees swayed gently in the breeze before the old colonial buildings and pastel pink church. I wandered around the streets—tranquil, puttering alleys and avenues—and stopped for a lunch of empanadas in a restaurant just over the road from the imposing plum-colored Iglesia San Francisco. Some of these tiny, crisp pastry packets oozed with a rich, runny cheese; others were filled with veal, spring onions, and potato. They were succulent, moist, and entirely delicious. The empty armor of an armadillo stared down at me from the wall above.

It was incredibly hot here in the far north, and tempers were sizzling, too. As I strolled back through the square, a demonstration was taking place. It seemed a relaxed affair when I walked by, but that evening's television news featured an uglier scene. Not long after I had passed, it seemed, the demonstrators had turned violent.

"*Hubieron incidentes*," reported the expressionless newsreader. There were incidents.

"*La gente tiene mucha bronca*," The people are furious, spat a female demonstrator, a middle-aged, stocky woman. She wore a thunderous expression; her eyes were fixed and steely. I wouldn't have wanted to be in the boots of the policeman who had to tussle with her.

Demonstrations are common in Argentina, where the disastrous effects of the economic crisis of 2001–2002 still blight the lives of many. For years, corruption has gnawed away at every aspect of Argentina's political system. Catastrophic economic mismanagement finally resulted in the devaluation of the peso in January 2002: the Argentine currency slid to a third of its former worth. People who had entrusted their savings to the banks saw the fruits of a lifetime's effort tumble before their eyes.

The peso had been pegged to the US dollar since 1991. The peg had been introduced to combat galloping hyperinflation in Argentina—at one point, inflation had been so rampant that supermarkets had to announce price rises over the PA system rather than continually relabel their goods. But while the peg had stabilized inflation, it had also made Argentina a horribly expensive country in which to live and do business. As the peg became increasingly unviable, manufacturers fell into bankruptcy and unemployment soared. The Argentine government defaulted on its rocketing foreign debt repayments and the International Monetary Fund refused to bail the country out.

In March 2001, President Fernando de la Rua brought Domingo Cavallo—the finance minister who had been responsible for the peg in the first place—back into the front line. Cavallo implemented draconian reductions in public spending, including a thirteen-percent pay cut for most state employees. Then, a few months later, it was announced that public sector workers in Buenos Aires would be paid a part of their salaries in government bonds. The Treasury simply didn't have the cash to remunerate them.

With economic collapse and the devaluation of the peso

looking inevitable, anyone who could sent their money abroad. Most people's mortgages and other loans had been taken out in US dollars: If the peso was devalued, their personal debt would be unmanageable. Billions of dollars left the country. Cavallo himself was reported to have moved his savings to the Cayman Islands.

By the end of the year, nearly fifteen million Argentines were reckoned to be living in poverty, with a further two thousand sliding beneath the line each day. Barter clubs took over from normal shopping. Crowds looted supermarkets, banks, and restaurants. Rioting at the end of December left twenty-seven people dead.

On December 20, President Fernando de la Rua resigned. Amid the political chaos, Argentina saw a succession of five presidents within a fortnight. Then, on January 7, 2002, the peso was finally devalued.

"We are devaluing. We are in collapse. Argentina is bankrupt," the new finance minister, Jorge Remes Lenicov, pronounced.

At the same time, he announced a two-day bank holiday— people's funds were quite literally locked away. Savings accounts were frozen; the Argentine people were told that those who held balances of up to $30,000 would not be able to access their money until June 2003. After that, they would only be able to draw it in eighteen monthly installments.

Meanwhile Carlos Menem, who had been president for ten years until 1999, was put under house arrest on arms trafficking charges. On top of that, he was reckoned to be guilty of the embezzlement of tens of millions of US dollars, and to have undeclared funds in Swiss bank accounts. The following year he would go into exile in Chile with his new wife, a former Miss Universe. (She was widely reported to be half his age but almost twice his height.)

Furious demonstrations filled the streets. Thousands stormed the banks, hurling eggs and destroying cash machines in protest. But their rebellion was in vain. The people couldn't take their money out of the banks because the banks were bust. Their savings had already been spent by a series of corrupt, lascivious, and incompetent governments. And this had happened in a land so rich in natural resources that, a century ago, it had been the seventh wealthiest country in the world.

Cable TV disappeared from the nation's screens, as the suppliers were unable to pay their bills. In the industrial city of Rosario it was announced on local radio that devaluation had sent the price of imported wigs soaring and one salon was making its own. Long lines formed as people rushed to sell their hair. A cattle truck overturned on its way to the market and hungry passersby descended on the carnage. This nation, so proud of its beef, so haughty in its refusal to consume anything but the best cuts, had been reduced to eating roadkill.

"It was daylight robbery, that's all you can say about it," said Gabriela, a woman I met a couple of days later on a day trip in an overland jeep. Gabriela owned a travel agency in Buenos Aires province and was on holiday in Salta. We were heading northwest following a famous old railway, the Train to the Clouds, which climbs up to the Chilean border. We'd left Salta at six A.M. and driven out of town in darkness. Then as dawn had broken, the hills that looked over the city had glowed pink in the soft, early morning light.

"During the crisis, it was terrible," she went on. It was fully light now and we were eating breakfast—*medialunas,* or croissants, and strong, hot coffee from Thermoses—by the railway tracks, waiting to greet the train as it hurtled past us packed with day-trippers heading up into the hills.

"Nobody had any money. Nobody had work. We couldn't go out to a restaurant, so we used to go to each other's houses and spend hours just chatting and laughing, and forgetting about it all for a while. We have big problems in this country, but the great thing about the Argentine people is that we also have solidarity among ourselves. In a village, if someone has problems, his neighbors will help him, no question. The government is terrible, but the people will always help each other."

The train arrived and we duly waved at its passengers, then our driver fired up the jeep's engine and we took to the road to follow in its wake.

The Train to the Clouds is considered to be a great engineering feat. The tracks' switchbacks allow it to forge steep inclines, and the viaducts and bridges span breathtaking gorges. But the train can only follow the tracks and then return to town. Our road trip by Movitrack jeep was going to take us much further afield. We'd drive through the puna, the high-altitude desert that Argentina shares with Chile and Bolivia. Then, at San Antonio de los Cobres, we'd leave the path of the railway and make for the salt flats. Finally we'd return to Salta through the remarkable rock formations of the Quebrada de Humahuaca and arrive back in the city at about ten-thirty that evening.

Movitrack was conceived by a German couple, Frank and Heike Neumann. In 1991 they spent their honeymoon driving in a jeep along the route of the Train to the Clouds and a part of Route 40, which runs from the far north to the deep south of Argentina. They were so struck by the stark beauty of the country's northern landscapes that they decided to set up a company that would re-create their travels for others.

The bright blue-and-yellow vehicle that we were riding

in had been designed by Frank himself. It could take eighteen passengers, and we had a full quota that day—about half of our contingent were Argentine, the rest were a mixture of British, German, and Belgian. Ten passengers traveled in the more spacious front section; partway through the day we swapped and those who had been at the front moved to the back. When it came to eating, the seats could be turned to face each other and tables were erected diner-style. During our stop by the railway our driver, Gabriel, and our guide, another Gabriela, had folded back the roof of the jeep so that it was now open-topped, giving its passengers panoramic views. Unfortunately, the newly arranged convertible also exposed us to the biting cold. Temperatures were low that morning and we soon started to shiver.

"The sun's just behind that hill there," we told each other, trying to sound upbeat as we hunkered with our hands in our armpits and our lips turning blue. "Any minute now, it will break over the brow and we'll warm up."

"The cold is all in your mind!" declared Gabriela the guide as she doled out thick, blanketlike ponchos in which we gratefully wrapped our frozen bodies.

Across the aisle from Gabriela the travel agent and me sat a British couple, Jeremy and Margaret. Margaret was a forward-thinking soul who had packed a hat and gloves for her day in the mountains. I, on the other hand, had not prepared so wisely: The sweltering heat of the city yesterday had fooled me into thinking that nothing more than a jacket and sweater would be needed.

Luckily for me, Margaret had bought a second set of woolens from a vendor at the clearing where we'd just stopped, and now she lent me her new purchases—a chunky brown-and-cream knit hat and gloves to match—for which I was profoundly grateful in the icy morning air.

Jeremy, it turned out, was a fellow writer; he specialized in wine. As a part of their Argentine tour, he and Margaret would be visiting wine trade friends in Mendoza. We compared itineraries.

"Well, we'll be in Mendoza at the same time," said Jeremy. We exchanged e-mail addresses and promised to meet up.

Wrapped in our ponchos, hats, and gloves, we stood up on our seats so that the dramatic Andean scenery rolled out in 360-degree splendor around us as we followed the route of the railway. The mountains rose rocky and grimly gray. The red-and-white train appeared to be in miniature, a small child's plaything, alongside these statuesque, supernal peaks.

To begin with, no vegetation flourished on these foreboding hills. Just the merest suggestion of green scrub lay smeared across their granite surface like a faint covering of algae. Then, after an hour or so, as we climbed higher, a new and exhilaratingly majestic plant leapt large from the hostile ground. Suddenly, we were surrounded by thousands of giant columnar cacti. It was as though an army of camouflaged militiamen had risen silently to their feet from their clandestine desert ditches. One minute, the land had lain lifeless. The next, an endless formation of these tall, prickly sentries kept watch as far as the eye could see.

These huge protuberances soared dramatically skyward. Some grew as single pillars, massive and erect; others branched out into high, prickly forks. The lower plants, which were pale and dusty green, blended in color with the rocky land. The higher trunks, though, towered along the hilltop ridges and stood out against the electric blue sky in stark silhouette. For mile after arid dusty mile, they dominated the land.

At the foot of one cactus, a single, morose-looking donkey stood tethered to a bristly bush, seeking shelter in the dappled shade while it waited for its owner to return. Its coat blended perfectly with the spartan sepia landscape.

Sporadically, tiny patches of lush green grass and swaying poplar trees burst out from this arid environment. In these pockets water somehow must have found a way to trickle. Occasionally we passed another vehicle, but this was a remote spot and there were few passersby. And then we arrived at the puna.

The puna was stark, sparse, enormous—and stultifyingly brown. Immense expanses of low, desiccated scrub stretched on and on toward the mountains. We were high now and the hills no longer appeared so tall and craggily sculpted. Instead, the flat earth seemed to sweep smoothly toward a ring of distant low summits that enclosed the plains like the rim of a crater.

"It's incredible," I murmured to Gabriela, "but I wouldn't want to get lost out here."

"Or to live here," Gabriela agreed.

Every now and then herds of llamas, colored brown and dirty white like everything else, scratched their sustenance from spiky, stunted shrubs. What kind of meager life could those creatures eke from this environment? I wondered. Day after day, month after month, they must just root around in this malnourished earth subsisting on tiny mouthfuls of hard, prickly foliage.

Once, we passed a smattering of squat adobe huts the color of a stale, dusty toffee found behind the bed. A single tractor sat in silence. A lone boy stood stock-still in the dirt and stared. Distinct from the dun, a tiny, white-rendered church with twin domed bell towers whispered hoarsely of hope and glory—but to me this seemed a godforsaken place. A person living in this settlement would need to pray. A short distance from the settlement, a cemetery sprouted crucifixes that suggested the dead were more numerous than the living in this bleak land.

Jeremy was starting to look faintly queasy. We were at about thirteen thousand feet now and the altitude, he said, was affecting him.

"Would you like a coca leaf?" Gabriela asked him, passing a plastic bag half filled with dried green leaves in his direction. Gabriela herself had been chewing through its contents for some hours now. "It's the local cure for altitude sickness. It really works," she declared, her own chipper mood standing as testament to the cure. "The Andean people use the leaves to make tea. It gives them energy."

Nobody seemed to have been drinking any coca-leaf tea on the puna that morning, though. The landscape was eerily empty. Its utter lifelessness was faintly terrifying—in the middle of this huge dusty void, we provided the only speck of color as we trundled along in our blue-and-yellow jeep. In our multihued clothing—red, green, pink, and purple— we crawled along like tiny alien life forms on this immense, drab plateau.

Yet, at the same time, the puna was a strangely beautiful place. We were truly in another world up here. The sense of isolation was intimidating. It was oppressive. The idea of living as the inhabitants of that village did—year after year, decade after decade, with the dust and the desolation, with minimal human contact, with the overwhelming *nothingness* of the puna and the dark, stony granite of the Andes pressing down beyond—all this made my heart constrict. But the sheer size of this wilderness, its inhospitable soil, and its utter bareness were enthralling in a spine-chilling way. It was almost as though one's senses had sniffed danger in this despondent spot, and the veins had filled with a stirring dose of adrenaline in response. And because, perhaps, of the emptiness, the puna seemed suffused with a great serenity. The air was thin but, above the desperately monotone earth, the sky was rich with color. It reached seemingly forever, bright royal blue and turquoise blending into a darker indigo above, and all smeared with light white clouds. It was intoxicating to be out there—but I was happy that the Movitrack jeep assured me of a safe route home.

We drove on and arrived for an early lunch at San Antonio de los Cobres. This was a simple town whose economy revolved around copper mining and the knitting of llama and alpaca socks, gloves, and hats for those who climbed off the Train to the Clouds when it stopped here. Two boys posed with their goat and asked for a peso; when I gave them one, they demanded one each. A little girl held a lamb in her arms and hung around our vehicle hoping for handouts.

One of the Argentine women in our group winced and turned away.

"It's so sad. I want to help them, but there's nothing I can do," she said. She talked about the collapse of public funding since the economic crisis, and the government's failure to properly finance rural schools.

"In Buenos Aires, you see very rich people, very glamorous, wearing good clothes. And then there's this," said Gabriela. "That's the problem with Argentina. It's a country of extremes."

The town's only dining room was expecting us: Movitrack took their customers there several times each week. We ate a simple meal—a thin but tasty soup in which tiny cubes of vegetables floated, followed by very straightforward meat and potatoes—then climbed back into the jeep and ascended to our highest pass of the day at 13,600 feet. Gabriel stopped so that we could admire the view, but we weren't allowed to leave the vehicle as customers on previous outings had fallen ill when they'd tried to walk around in the thin air. Then we pressed on toward the Salinas Grandes, the great salt pits.

The salt plains were visible from miles away. They looked at first to be a thin strip of white that cut through the earthen surroundings. Then, as we slowly drew nearer along the rough, unsurfaced road, they appeared to seep and spread until, when our jeep eventually drew up on the salt itself, these crystalline flats seemed to stretch to infinity.

I later found out that the Salinas Grandes covered nearly eight hundred square miles—that's to say they were only slightly smaller than the entire country of Luxembourg. They were dead level, utterly horizontal for mile after mile until, in the very far distance, the hills rose once again—but the mountains now lay so far away that they created nothing more than a shallow, undulating sliver squeezed between the salt and the sky.

The packed salt was not pure bright white. It was more like the shade of very weak tea with too much milk. It had formed into encrusted hexagons: Low walls about an inch high pushed up from the flat surface and divided this extraordinary pallid expanse into geometric shapes each roughly as wide as a man is tall. Not a twig, not a leaf, not a mound marred their endless pattern.

We climbed out of our jeep and for half an hour or so we walked on this singular terrain. The crystals were packed firm and crisp; only the low crusts crunched slightly under-foot. The sun reflected off the salt's pale skin and, for the first time that day, we felt truly hot.

We drove on, down the Cuesta de Lipán toward the tiny

village of Purmamarca. We were back on asphalt now and the road curled, an inky thread twisting and twining down the hillside. It was late afternoon; the sun had begun to dip. The grasses gleamed golden; a few puffy, fluffy clouds hung in the valley below. With our roof open, we stood on the seats and just stared at the remarkable, natural world that enveloped us. We were the only people out there. Gabriela, the guide, pumped the stereo up high and the theme tune from *The Mission* throbbed from the jeep's speakers. I felt a real high—it could have been the scenery or, perhaps, a sudden oxygen rush as we descended from altitude. Slowly, slowly we wound our way downward toward the real world until we reached Purmamarca where the face of the "seven-colored rock" blushed in the rosy evening light. The minerals that tint this hill its astonishing hue correspond to sediments from the Mesozoic period—which, in layman's terms, meant that this rock dated back to dinosaur days.

We climbed back into our truck once more for the final long haul back to Salta. It had been a long but terrifically exhilarating day. It seemed incredible that, in just a matter of hours, we could have seen such a variety of astonishing landscapes—the carved, forbidding Andes with their soaring cacti; the remarkable emptiness of the endless puna; the salt flats and the ancient multicolored rocks of Purmamarca. We were ready, now, just to sit back in our seats and try to let all those myriad wonders settle in our minds. But our guide was having none of it.

"Let's party! I have champagne! *Salud!*" hollered Gabriela. The cork popped from the bottle and she started to pour.

5

"The Horses Have Gone Out and Have Not Come Back"

The mummy sat huddled in a fetal position. It looked female, though with its skin shrunk tight over its cheekbones and its eyes sunken, it was hard to tell. It was dressed in rough cloth and wore a flat fur hat. With its skeletal arms and knees drawn up to its chest and its head slightly askew, the preserved corpse stared through its lifeless eyes from its glass box at the museum visitors who stared back. There was no signboard to tell us who this person was or what era he or she had lived through. I wondered what kind of life this mummified creature might once have known in this high, desiccated land.

I was now in a tiny village called Tilcara, halfway between Salta and the Bolivian border. I'd been intrigued by the remarkable pink and orange rocks I'd seen on my Movitrack trip, so I'd decided to jump on a bus heading north and spend a few days exploring the villages of the Quebrada de Humahuaca in more depth.

Salta's bus station had hosted a scene of tranquil bustle. The concourse had been lined by perhaps twenty or thirty booths belonging to the different bus companies. Each route was covered by particular firms; to buy a ticket, one had first to find out which *colectivo* serviced that journey. Hexagonal kiosks sold snacks and drinks. Between the booths and the bus bays a line of green-painted benches stood neatly; upon them sprawled passengers and their luggage.

This had been my first trip on an Argentine bus and I hadn't allowed my expectations to rise too high. But the double-decker had turned out to be a luxurious affair with air-conditioning, generous upholstered seats, and low-grade American videos.

We'd crawled through every dusty pueblo—General Güemes, Perico, and Palpalá. They'd been parched, parsimonious places. Single-story sand-colored buildings had lined the road and, in front of them, stallholders had peddled fruit and terra-cotta cooking pots.

There had seemed to be *incidentes* in Güemes, just as there had been in Salta a few days earlier. A demonstration had blocked the main road and the bus had been diverted. As we'd turned off, I'd looked toward the protesters and seen piles of burning debris on the tarmac.

The road had bridged extensive dry riverbeds where just the narrowest veins of water trickled through. In occasional pockets of green, oxen, goats, sheep, and horses had grazed. Then, suddenly, the landscape had become truly dramatic. To the right of the bus, cliffs had towered in remarkable colors—terra-cotta, yellow, and pink. Great, prickly, columnar cacti had soared before them. It had been an incredible, almost dreamlike sight.

The indigenous tribes of bygone days must have woven wonderful legends to explain these gaudy colors, I'd mused as the bus had glided past the flashy formations. In precolonial times, the Andean northwest was the most heavily populated region of what is now Argentina—archaeologists reckon that indigenous tribes began to settle here as far back as 10,000 B.C.—and still today this is the only region of Argentina that has a strong indigenous population.

I wondered how old that mummified figure in the museum that flanked Tilcara's town square could be. Its taut, fragile skin and vacant glassy eyes gave away nothing to my inexpert eyes, but according to the leaflet handed to me with my ticket it was unearthed in Chile's Atacama desert; other mummies from that area have been dated and found to be around three thousand years old.

Three thousand years ago, this area would have been peopled principally by hunter-gatherer tribes. I wondered how the mummy who sat hunched in front of me would have passed her days: sweeping out the family cave? Trying out a new recipe for freshly speared llama? Indulging in some prehistoric interior design by daubing pictographs on the wall?

I came out of the museum and into Tilcara's town square. It was late afternoon but the sun still beat down baking hot. Dark-skinned stallholders sat sleepily behind piles of handicrafts that suggested other tourists ought to be present, but there were none to be seen. The vendors made no attempt to sell. It was just too hot. And in any case, who would want a woven poncho or a llama-wool bobble hat in this broiling heat?

Skinny, listless mongrels lay sprawled in whatever shade they could find, their eyelids half closed, their tongues lolling. Battered old cars sat motionless by the curb. In a café that faced onto the square, a very old man sat all alone and, painstakingly slowly, licked around and around an ice-cream cone.

I walked down the main street toward the *pucará,* the fortress for which Tilcara is famous. The street was scorched, desiccated, and deserted. It was eerily quiet. The few people brave enough to venture outdoors moved silently like slow-motion, overheated shadows.

The *pucarás* of this region were built from about A.D. 1000 until 1430, when the Inca empire came to town. They were large, densely populated settlements, with stone houses and terraced, irrigated fields. The people who lived here were shepherds and farmers. They grew corn, potatoes, beans, and pumpkins near the banks of the river Grande. They bred llamas, which helped them work the land as well as providing meat and wool for clothing. But a little more than a hundred and fifty years after these tribes had been assimilated into the Inca empire, the Spanish came a-conquering and swallowed up the lot of them.

Spanish inroads into Argentina followed two routes. The earliest explorers came by sea. In 1516, a group sailed from the Atlantic coast up the Río de la Plata toward modern-day Paraguay, but their intrusions weren't welcomed by the Querandí tribesmen, who butchered them. It wasn't until a couple of decades later, in 1535, that the first Spaniards arrived in the territories where I was now, via an overland route from the north. Still, the conquistadors didn't find much here to interest them and it wasn't until ten years after that, when the Spanish struck silver in Potosí (in current-day Bolivia), that they forged south in earnest, hoping that further riches might lie in this sandy ground. By the end of the sixteenth century, twenty-five towns had been founded in what is now northwest Argentina.

In 1594 the Spanish claimed Tilcara for their king. They arrested the *curaca,* the tribal chief of the *pucará,* and ruled the people by the Spanish *"encomienda"* system which governed these northern Andean parts for more than two hundred years, though it never took hold in the rest of Argentina. *Encomienda* translates as "protection" or "patronage": The idea was that a group of indigenous people was entrusted to a Spaniard who would teach them Catholicism and tend to their most basic material needs. In return, the Indians had to provide the *encomendero* with labor. Needless to say, the *encomenderos* were prone to prioritize the fattening of their own purses over the nourishing of their wards' souls, and the cruelties committed by the Spaniards against the indigenous population became the stuff of legend.

One early crusader to rail against the conquistadors' brutality was Bartolomé de las Casas. Las Casas came from good adventuring stock: His father, Pedro, had sailed with Christopher Columbus on his second voyage to the New World in 1493. He had brought back with him a novel gift for his son—a young Taino. The Taino boy only stayed in Seville for a couple of years, but this acquaintance furnished Bartolomé with a sympathy for the Indian race that would affect the direction of his future life.

When he grew old enough, Bartolomé accompanied his father on a colonizing expedition to the Caribbean island of Hispaniola, where he was given an *encomienda* of his own, but some years later he surrendered this and spent his time instead traveling around the Caribbean and the South American mainland recording his compatriots' savagery toward the Indians. He subsequently dedicated his life to protesting the barbaric behavior of his countrymen, and to publicizing the atrocities he had witnessed. In his *An Account, Much Abbreviated, of the Destruction of the Indies* he quotes the words of a Franciscan friar who worked in this southern part of the Spanish Empire.

"I do declare that I myself saw with my own eyes the Spaniards cut off the hands, noses, and ears of male and female Indians, with no reason save that they desired to do so, and in so many places and parts that it would be too long to tell. And I saw that the Spaniards would turn dogs on the Indians, to tear them to pieces . . . Likewise it is true that they seized suckling babies by their arms and threw them as far as they were able."

Many of Las Casas's claims were wildly exaggerated, but at the time they were written they were as effective as a conquistador's most deadly rapier. His work was translated into English, and the fury it inspired in the Protestant world gave rise to the Black Legend writings which portrayed the Spaniards as greedy bloodthirsty monsters who had desecrated an innocent Utopian civilization.

There wasn't much happening at the *pucará* the day I visited, though. The descendants of those flesh-tearing dogs hadn't the energy even to break into a waddle. The settlement had, apparently, been substantially restored, but still the tumbledown piles of stones and sandy paths gave little more than a suggestion of how this village would once have looked. Nowadays, the ancient settlement was inhabited solely by cacti who had set up house where human homes would once have stood. Wearing bold white-and-yellow flowers around their tips like exotic turbans, this new population swarmed the place, sucking at the dry soil.

I made my way back to my *pensión,* a former neocolonial house that now welcomed paying guests. It was almost spookily silent. When I walked across the perfectly polished wooden floors my shoes squeaked and, in that noiseless place, every footstep seemed amplified like screams of over-heated anguish.

Built in the 1930s, the house seemed to retain many of its original features: a huge bathroom with a capacious porcelain basin, black age-spotted floor tiles, and a gigantic metal weighing scale. Strangely, it smelled old-fashioned too, of that rather bitter disinfectant that they used to use in the bathrooms at school. My bedroom was dominated by two brass bedsteads covered by floral bedspreads. The curtains were made from matching fabric with ruched tiebacks. Between the beds hung a small wooden crucifix and a painting of the Virgin Mary with her child in a thick gilt frame. A llama was tethered in the garden.

The current owners of the house were, as it happened, also the proprietors of the only horse-riding operation in town. It had been almost a week since I last rode a horse, and I was experiencing serious withdrawal. It was odd, really. A month ago I had lived what had seemed to me to be a perfectly full and happy life that hadn't involved horses at all. But now, after a bit of cantering around in the hills of Córdoba, a few days without them felt like a terrible privation.

I asked the *dueña* if it would be possible to ride the following day.

"Maybe, and maybe not," she replied, before going on to explain: "*Los caballos han salido y no han vuelto.*" The horses have gone out and they have not come back. They might come back tonight. On the other hand, they might not.

The weather cooled fast as evening drew in. I strolled up the packed-earth lanes past squat adobe houses, looking for any kind of entertainment. Upon the hill that overlooked the village, somebody had carved in large, ironic Hollywood-esque capitals: "BIENVENIDOS A TILCARA." Welcome to Tilcara.

I came to the village cemetery. The dead had the best view in Tilcara, looking out over the mountains and valleys. The tombs were richly decorated. Bulky bouquets of gaudy paper flowers were interspersed with generous bunches of real blooms. These brash bursts of color leapt out at the visitor; they almost seemed to sing with life in this resting place of the dead. They were brilliantly vital, a vibrant polychromatic palette in this town so big on brown.

Back at the village square, I sat in a bar and ordered a bottle of local black beer. It was thin and frothy but full of flavor. The town was coming to life now that the temperatures had dropped. Figures began to emerge from the low mud-brick houses and suddenly the streets were buzzing with chatter. The little bar began to fill up. In the distance, a church bell started to toll. As darkness fell, the landlord brought around candles for each table.

To begin with, I thought the candles were simply an atmospheric touch. But as the room became darker and darker I began to wonder: Were the candles quaint ornamentation—or were they, more prosaically, a basic necessity in a town where the electricity had been cut? It grew darker still. There didn't seem to be any light in the street either or, when I looked, in any of the surrounding buildings.

"Is there a problem with the electricity?" I finally asked the girl behind the bar.

"Yes." She sighed. "It's because there's a storm. It's coming this way from Perico. Somewhere along the line, the power's gone out."

I sat for a while longer. Finally, I tired of waiting in the blackness for the light to return and went to try to find some food.

"Is it possible to eat here?" I asked the waiter of the next-door restaurant. He was standing out on the pavement, smoking a cigarette and watching the shadowy world go by.

"What? You want to sit here all alone in the dark?" he asked, and laughed.

I decided that perhaps I didn't, and made my way back to my lodgings. I had an apple and a couple of cereal bars in my rucksack that would serve as a meager meal if they had to; in any case, I'd eaten a good lunch. The storm was closing in now. I picked my way uncertainly along the uneven cobbles, which were lit only by the almost continual strobe effect of lightning and the headlights of the occasional car. Tilcara was lively in the blackness. It seemed to be populated by dark, nocturnal creatures who, like bats or vampires, emerged only into the night. Back at the house, the *dueña* was waiting with candles.

"*Han vuelto los caballos?*" I asked. Have the horses come back?

"*No. Todavía no.*" No. Not yet.

The electricity came back in the middle of the night, which was more than could be said for the horses. As riding was off the agenda, I went instead to Humahuaca, a town an hour's bus journey north.

This local bus was a rickety, rattling old thing, a far cry from the luxury of yesterday's long-distance transport. The seats were worn and cranky; the windows were covered by tattered, faded red curtains.

Astonishing rock formations floated past the window—amazing, Technicolor, geological works of art. Spectacularly hewn formations of yellow-tinted amber and gold, layers of flame and russet, then vermilion and carmine red stood solid as they had for millennia, while we juddered on by in our bus.

Every now and then we passed a tiny settlement of adobe houses. These homes were basic constructions, and hutlike in appearance. Perfectly rectangular, with very slightly sloping flat roofs, they each had an oblong door and, usually, a single neatly squared window. The people in this area were still designing their houses as their ancestors had done: They say the mud bricks keep their homes cool in summer and warm in winter, though realistically it's unlikely that these rural folk could afford to buy modern, high-tech building materials. Still, against the breathtaking backdrop of the multihued cliffs, the utter simplicity of these houses was attractive.

In none of these settlements was there a soul in sight. Occasionally, in the fertile valley before the hills, a solitary worker toiled with a hoe while his donkey waited patiently, tethered to a tree. And then, in the middle of nowhere, there was a school whose playground leapt with childish vitality. Perhaps twenty or thirty small boys tore around a yard chasing a soccer ball. They seemed oblivious to the blistering heat. As our bus passed, a small scrap of a child executed a skillful high kick, his puny leg soaring up toward his ear.

The bus pulled into Humahuaca. This was a larger town than Tilcara, but it seemed to be more traditional. Street after dusty street was lined by those same squat clay constructions. Old women sauntered through the narrow lanes in typical Andean garb—heavily gathered skirts and traditional trilby hats. In the bus station groups of them sat and chatted, surrounded by huge, brightly woven shopping baskets.

A little before midday, I made my way to the town square ready to witness Humahuaca's most happening event: At twelve o'clock daily a mechanical figurine of Saint Francis Solano slid out from his enclave high in the wall of the *cabildo,* the town hall, and blessed the congregation.

His disciples that day were many. The plaza was packed with Argentine tourists who seemed to have been bused in to Humahuaca just for this occasion. Local women and girls worked the crowd selling jewelry, tiny wooden dolls wearing lurid knits, and trilby hats which they piled high on their heads like stacks of concave pancakes. Despite the heat, these vendors were wearing knitted sweaters.

As the minute hand ticked ever nearer to twelve, the atmosphere in that tiny square became tense with anticipation. With one minute to go, necks craned upward and all eyes were fixed on the spot from where Solano would emerge to greet us. Then, at last, it was time. The clock set to with its ponderous chimes—*donngg . . . donngg . . . donngg*—and a pair of rounded wooden doors in the white-rendered wall slowly rolled open. A wooden robed friar wielding a white crucifix skated haltingly out and raised his mechanized arm in clunky benediction.

It was a bizarre attraction, but an interesting one. Saint Francis Solano passed through Humahuaca during his incredibly long walk from the coast of Peru to the Argentine city of Tucumán in the late sixteenth century. He covered a distance of over two thousand miles—and he journeyed barefoot.

Solano was born in Andalusia, in Spain; he was educated by Jesuits but subsequently joined the Franciscan order by whom he was ordained in 1576. Thirteen years later he left his homeland for missionary work in South America.

He was clearly a devout character, perhaps even a masochist. He was tremendously keen on pain: It is said that when novices under his instruction were found guilty of some misdemeanor, he preferred to do their penance for them under the pretext that he himself must have been to blame. He ate little, and his self-imposed privations were such that he was frequently in poor health.

Solano was also big on miracles—curing the sick, walking on water, and so on. He mastered many indigenous dialects, but they were perhaps unnecessary as it was said that he had the "gift of tongues," which worked like a kind of reverse-action Babel fish: When he spoke, people of all tongues could understand him. And whatever it was that he said, it was clearly effective: He was once reported to have converted nine thousand natives with a single sermon. He was also a staunch defender of the indigenous peoples' rights and spoke out vociferously against the conquistadors' plundering.

Solano had finished doing his thing, and I walked back to the bus station. School seemed to have finished for the day and the streets were full of children carrying bags and books. Across Argentina the schoolchildren wore the same uniform white cotton overcoats. When they walked to and from their classes, it seemed as though the streets had been taken over by a multitude of miniature biochemists.

Back in Tilcara I ate *locro* for lunch—a rich and tasty local dish of stewed beef and corn. The restaurant was advertising llama trekking. Given the absence of horses, I thought I might attempt a caper with these long-necked beasts instead, but when I inquired I was told that Santo, the guide, had gone out and not come back.

I went back to my *pensión* and tried, one final time, to locate the horses.

"*Han vuelto los caballos?*" I asked, ever hopeful.

"*Todavía no.*"

6

"The Horses Are Fully Booked Until Wednesday"

I must have been riveted by the screening of *Bruce Almighty* on the bus back to Salta the following morning because, somehow, I managed to miss the biggest event of the journey—our detention by a military roadblock. I was sprawled out on my comfortable second-row seat, my head craned backward, gazing up at the unlikely antics of Jim Carrey and Jennifer Aniston, when it dawned on me: We had stopped. Turning around I found, to my very great surprise, that two men in uniform were marching up and down the aisle. One of them politely asked a woman sitting across from me if he could check inside the bundle of blankets on her lap; once he had ascertained that they contained a real live baby and not a few pounds of cocaine, he thanked her very sincerely. And then he and his colleague left.

Nobody on the bus seemed surprised in the slightest by this intrusion. I was soon to discover why: Roadblocks in Argentina are common occurrences. The military and the police use them to check that drivers' papers are in order and to search their vehicles. This particular road, the main route down from Bolivia, was of particular interest as drugs were frequently trafficked from the north. Still, the soldiers hadn't actually seemed to do an awful lot. The bus was jam-packed with luggage, but the only bundle that I'd seen them search was the baby across the aisle. They were delightful, friendly, affable men—but when it came to sniffing out narcotics, I'm afraid they weren't a patch on a spaniel.

In fact, the Argentines were turning out to be a friendly lot in general. Everywhere I went, the people were unfailingly polite. They weren't just courteous to me—they treated each other well too. As the bus trundled along its way again, the soldiers and the driver having exchanged hearty smiles and had a little chat, I had to consider: During the whole time I'd been in Argentina so far, I hadn't encountered a single raised voice. Yes, there had been the *"incidentes"*—but the Argentines seemed to save their rancor for the authorities. Among themselves, and to their visitors, they were entirely charming.

I changed buses at Jujuy and had to wait for an hour on the concourse. Two little girls, aged perhaps three and five, sat with their mother on a bench. They had perfectly braided, sleek ebony hair and nibbled on sandwiches that their mother handed to them. Between mouthfuls they leapt repeatedly from their seats to chase a solitary pigeon, then hooted with unrestrained laughter as it waddled away from them with an awkward, high-speed gait and flapped its raggedy gray wings.

Vendors walked up and down carrying trays of sweet biscuits and boxes of fizzy drinks. Little gaggles of people waited with their bundles; others formed short lines before the ticket booths of the various bus companies: Balut, Veloz del Norte, Cotta del Norte . . .

Back on the main highway, we drove through a plateau whose landscape alternated between ploughed earthy fields and scrub with a smattering of trees. To our right, the great, gray Andes loomed.

It felt cold today. The temperature had dropped dramatically overnight. In Tilcara it had been chilly and a fog had settled over the hills. Back in Salta, the receptionist at my hotel told me the temperature had been eighty-six degrees yesterday. Today it was fifty-nine. I suspected that in Tilcara the difference had been even greater. I asked her if this kind of change in weather was normal here in Salta.

"No," she said, and shivered. "It's not normal at all."

I washed my hair before going out in the evening and, given the chill outdoors and the fact that I wasn't carrying a hair dryer, I paid special attention to toweling it vigorously. Sadly, my toweling hand slipped so that my thumb went in my eye, and within minutes the flesh around it started to turn a telltale purple. It seemed a ludicrous injury. I'd survived rocky rides and polo, I'd traveled over the deserted puna, I'd bypassed *incidentes*—and then I'd washed my hair and given myself a black eye.

Feeling sorry for myself, I treated myself to a good dinner in a charming little restaurant just off the square.

"Are you traveling alone?" asked the very friendly waiter as I ordered steak, fries, salad, and half a bottle of red wine.

"Ah, it's the best way," he said with a sigh when I told him that I was. "You have the freedom to do exactly as you choose. You don't have to worry about anybody else. You can just get up in the morning and go where the mood takes you. *Ay qué suerte!* How lucky you are, señorita."

He came back a few minutes later bearing a bottle of red wine, then a succulent slab of red meat, hot, potatoey fries, and the small side salad that I'd ordered just to assuage my conscience. The food in Argentina was turning out to be outstanding, I considered as my knife slid effortlessly through my fillet. I'd worried before I'd left home that I'd be eating meat, meat, and more meat and that my stomach would soon rebel. But that wasn't turning out to be the case. Everywhere I'd traveled so far, there had been a wide variety of dishes on the menus, many of them containing no meat at all. A large percentage of Argentines are of Italian descent, and their heritage could be seen in the food: The restaurants produced crisp pizzas and excellent pasta dishes of countless varieties—and, when I did decide to order steak, it was always perfectly cooked and deliciously tender. My stomach, instead of grumbling, seemed entirely delighted.

My alarm woke me from a deep sleep at six o'clock the following morning, and I headed back to the terminal to catch the seven o'clock bus to Cachi. I would have liked to travel later, but it was Sunday and this was the only service running—and I was eager not to linger another day in Salta because, according to my guidebook, there was a horse-riding operation in Cachi. After my failure to find horses farther north, I was determined that now, at last, I would ride some more.

Despite the early start, I knew I had to stay awake through the journey: The road from Salta to Cachi was reputed to be one of the most magnificent in the whole of Argentina, and I didn't want to miss the scenery. The route takes in the famous Cuesta del Obispo. They say that the views from this road are so breathtaking that the locals hold screaming babies to the window and the infants are instantly quiet. To be sure of a good view, I'd bought my ticket well in advance and I had the best seat on the bus: I was in the window seat behind the driver so I could see both out of my own window and through the front windshield.

Every few minutes the bus stopped to allow more people to board. They were all dressed up in their Sunday clothes and seemed to be heading out of town to spend the day with friends or relatives living further afield. Soon there were passengers standing in the aisle. A little while later, even the aisle was packed.

"A seat for the *abuela*," the shout went up as a phenomenally old woman boarded the bus with her daughter. "Can anyone give up their seat for the granny?"

The man next to me stood up and the old woman was maneuvered into the tiny space he had vacated. She was a scraggy, skinny character wearing a floral cotton dress and a head scarf, and looked as though she were at least a hundred years old. She sat down next to me, legs apart, with both wrinkled hands clutching the walking stick she had planted firmly between her knees. Every now and then, she fell forward, doubling over and resting her head on her hands.

"Good Lord," I thought, "what if she drops dead?" I was the person sitting next to her, after all. Her daughter was squashed into the mêlée somewhere behind. If the old woman expired on the bus, surely I would be the one who ought to do something about it.

Thankfully the *abuela* stayed with us, for the duration of that journey at least, and with no deaths or other diversions the bus made its way through the striking Quebrada de Escoipe gorge. It was amazingly, incredibly green. Willows

wept, poplars stretched, and streams babbled. Rectangular
patches of vegetables glowed richly emerald. Tall plumes of
grasses twisted in the breeze. It was verdant and lush; this
fertile land sprouted and shot vegetation. After the stark,
arid landscapes of recent days, the change filled the senses.
It was as though the chlorophyll were reaching out to the
sunlight and joyfully sucking in its energy so that it could
wildly, willfully, wonderfully propagate some more.

Little by little, the people alighted from the bus. With
great Sunday-morning jollity, with the optimism of knowing there's a whole day ahead of food and drink and socializ-
ing, they bustled through the crowded aisle until they
arrived at the door, where a jovial conductor helped them
down the steep step.

"Hasta luego, que lo pase bien." Good-bye, have a good one,
he called, beaming cheerfully at each of them as he waved
them on their way.

We stopped for a fifteen-minute break against a backdrop of meadows while the driver mopped out the bus.
When we piled back on, the old woman and her daughter
had left.

The man who had given up his seat came back to his
place. He was in his late forties and wore a cotton sun hat, a
check shirt, and a blue tank top. He was a pleasant, benign
character.

"Time for a maté." He sighed happily. He took out of his
bag a rounded gourd and an ornate silver pipe with a bulbous, perforated bottom. He poured chopped green leaves
into the gourd until the cup was half full, then added hot
water from a pink-patterned Thermos. He offered me some:
It is the custom when drinking maté always to share. Then
he sat back and started languorously to sip through the pipe.
And to chat.

The problem was, he talked extremely quietly. What with the battering of the bus over the unsurfaced road and Bonnie Tyler's "Total Eclipse of the Heart" blasting out from the driver's radio, it was very hard to make out what the man was talking about. Perhaps it was his accent—though I wasn't, in general, finding the Argentines difficult to understand. Their speech is less drawled than that of many South American countries; it's closer in that respect to Castilian Spanish. There are some slight differences in pronunciation: For example, the South Americans don't "lisp" as the Spanish do, and the *ll,* pronounced in Spain either as we say the *lli* in million or as a very soft *j,* becomes in Argentina a strong *sh* so that *calle,* meaning street, is pronounced like the English "cachet"—but I was finding these nuances simple to adapt to. There were some vocabulary disparities that were causing more of a headache—the most nerve-racking for me, and probably for all Spaniards visiting South America, was the verb *coger.* It's one of the most commonly used words in Spain, where it means to take, or to fetch, or to catch a bus. In South America, on the other hand, it means to fuck. But beyond the odd horrific mishap, when I'd told some poor, innocent soul that I was going to fuck the bus and then frozen speechless when I'd realized what I'd said, I was finding it easy to communicate with the Argentines. I was enjoying being able to order food easily, to ask for directions, and just to sit and chat effortlessly to people about their lives, their country, and their opinions. Until now.

From the low mumbling, I could just about understand that the man was telling me his life story. I smiled in what I hoped was an empathetic way. It seemed to be the right reaction—the man smiled back and settled more comfortably into his seat as he continued his story. After a few minutes, he seemed to be reaching some kind of climax. I still had no idea what he was saying, but obviously some kind of response was required. I let out a little chuckle.

"Well, really, it's no laughing matter," he suddenly barked.

I agreed that it absolutely was not, and assumed a less cheerful expression.

I never did find out what tribulations had so marred my fellow passenger's tale. It dawned on me later that perhaps he hadn't been telling me his life story at all but had been regaling me with a little local history, for, contrary to what one might expect from such a natural paradise, there was a period when these Calchaquí valleys through which we now traveled must have appeared to be perilously close to hell.

It was in these valleys that the indigenous population put up some of the fiercest resistance to Spanish rule. In the 1630s, the Spanish got it into their heads that gold lay in the depths of these scenic hills; they therefore attempted to impose forced labor on the Diaguita people who inhabited the region. The native people fought ferociously but were ultimately defeated.

Less than twenty years later, though, the native tribes rose up again, this time under the command of a renegade Spaniard named Pedro Bohórquez. But once again, the Spanish proved stronger than the indigenes. Once they had regained control, they executed Bohórquez and expelled the Diaguita people from their own land, sending them to provide labor for distant Spanish communities.

We arrived at the famous Cuesta del Obispo and climbed up and round. Hairpin bends gave onto sheer drops over a vertiginous cliff edge. The views were outstanding.

"When it rains, all that there"—the man next to me pointed at the sandy ground above us—"that all falls down onto the road."

I felt grateful that today was dry.

"And in winter, the road freezes over, and the bus goes like this." He wiped his hands about in a sliding motion.

"We are lucky today," he said. "The weather is good."

The bus arrived in Cachi at eleven-thirty. I checked into my *hostal,* then went straight out to hunt for horses.

"Todos los caballos están reservados hasta miércoles." All the horses are booked until Wednesday, said the woman at the other end of the phone with the peremptory tone of one who knew her coffers were filled.

"Todos . . . hasta miércoles?" I found myself weakly parroting her words.

Today was Sunday. Wednesday was three whole days away. How was I supposed to wait that long? How was I meant to entertain myself in this tiny pimple of a no-horse town until *Wednesday?*

What was the matter with these people, anyway? Here I was in Argentina where children learned to ride before they could walk, where they galloped to school, for goodness' sake. This was a country whose veins pumped to the pounding of horses' hooves. And I was unable to find a single old nag to so much as take a limp on.

I sat in the town square and sulked over a beer. A couple of boys, who looked to be aged about eight and ten, trotted by bareback on a pony, hooting with giggles as they jiggled up and down on their good-natured mount. I glared at them.

Cachi was a pretty place. It was quiet and leafy; small but perfectly serene. The center of the tiny plaza had been carefully planted with trees and flowers. The church that flanked one side had a simple magnolia facade that rose into delicate cornicing at the roof. Above, three bronze bells hung in a line of arches within a smoothly curving cupola. The side streets were cobbled and lined with old buildings that bellowed of Spanish colonization: intricate stonework, portentous wooden doors whose paint now peeled, and stone pillars in relief. But delightful as the place was, there was nobody here who would hire me a horse and so I felt annoyed with it.

In the end, I took drastic action. I drained my beer, then marched off to the public telephone *cabina* at the end of the street. Throwing my budget to the wind, I called El Molino, an old mill that its owners had transformed into a luxury guesthouse. It was expensive, but it was only a few miles down the road—and according to my guidebook, the people there kept horses.

"Are you good at riding horses?" asked Nuny, the señora, as I explained my predicament to her over the telephone.

I had to admit that I wasn't exactly *good* at it.

Nuny sounded doubtful. "The horses in the village are a lot more docile than ours," she said a little nervously.

"But all the horses in the village are booked till Wednesday," I told her fretfully.

In any case, I no longer cared about the temper of the horse. I had come to Argentina to ride, and in recent days I hadn't so much as trotted around the block. I'd enjoyed my time up north, for sure—but now I was becoming restless. In the mood I was in right then I didn't feel I'd be greatly bothered if I mounted a rearing, frothing, bucking bronco, just as long as it had four legs and a tail.

"Well, we'll see you tomorrow then," said Nuny. "I'll try to find you a horse that's tame!"

With a small smile of optimism, I put down the phone.

But little did I know as I did so that I'd have a terrifying animal-related experience before I got near kicking distance of Nuny's mill.

As the afternoon temperature started to drop, I went out for a walk. There was supposed to be a pretty village, La Aguada, a little less than four miles away. The road that led there was a rough track that gave onto views of the lush vegetation of the valley and the craggy mountains beyond.

I passed the church. In a side room, children stood behind desks and recited their religious lessons. It was still warm and the door had been opened to let in a breeze.

"Santa María, madre de Dios, ruega por nosotros pecadores ahora y en la hora de nuestra muerte..." Holy Mary, Mother of God, pray for us sinners now and at the hour of our death ... The words, low and rhythmic, emanated as a hypnotic thrum through the tepid evening air.

A little farther down the street an outdoor bar was packed with a very different following. Scores of men, leaning forward in their chairs, fists clenched with rapt concentration, watched soccer on a television in the corner of the courtyard. Every now and then their raucous cheers and jeers rocked the Sunday-evening stillness.

As I left the village behind and started to walk down the dirt path toward La Aguada, a man cantered past me. He was riding bareback and his horse's hooves threw up clouds of pale dust. I walked happily for an hour or two, past more of those low adobe buildings and fields of geometrically planted vegetables overshadowed by poplars and willows. Bushes of bright yellow flowers burst riotously from the earth, their delicate, deep red tendrils stretching for the blue sky. Occasional cacti sprouted and branched with flow-ers blossoming from their tips.

When I had walked enough, I turned for home. I negoti-ated my way through a group of hot-blooded young men drinking beer in a clearing after a game of soccer. And then, as I passed a house on the outskirts of the village, a pack of about five dogs scorched out from a yard, barking fiercely. I scarcely had time to flinch before the leader of the pack, a bony black mongrel with evil in its eyes, sank its fangs into my leg.

The dogs' owner ran in hot pursuit, shouting and curs-ing the animals, but he was too late. For a couple of seconds which stretched suspended in time I stared, appalled, at that abominable hound's jaws clamped viselike around my calf.

I felt no pain; my only sense was one of horrified disbe-lief. The dog released me; he and his fellow antagonists bolted back to their yard. The owner disappeared and I was left to inspect my wound.

I was wearing shorts so the dog's teeth had pressed straight into my skin. At first, though, I thought I'd been lucky. It wasn't a serious bite and, to begin with—although my flesh was marked with deep indentations which were fast turning purple—I thought it hadn't broken the skin. But then, as I walked, two tiny droplets of blood welled up, rich and red, on my leg.

Just how much blood does an animal have to draw be-fore you're at risk from rabies? I wondered in trepidation. The chances had to be small—the dreadful mutt hadn't been a stray, after all—but I hadn't been inoculated against the disease. You have a window of a couple of days after be-ing bitten in which you must administer the rabies vaccine: Given that I'd never be too far from a hospital, I had chosen not to have the shot before I'd left home.

I limped back down the path toward the village. Visions of an ugly, saliva-frothing death played before my eyes. I wondered how long it took for the symptoms to set in, and which of them would strike first. Convulsive twitching? Lockjaw? Hallucinations? There was nothing else for it. I was going to have to find a hospital.

My shock quickly turned to fury. I had spent days searching for horses in vain. At last I had found some, I was booked in to ride them in the morning—and a hideous, vicious, malevolent demon of a dog had hurtled out of its house and sunk its teeth into me. Now, it seemed, I had to cancel my booking at El Molino and, instead, journey the next morning all the way back to Salta to seek medical attention. I was going to miss my riding. It was as though there was some kind of mean spirit out there, some kind of mischief-making monster who had deemed that I should not be allowed to ride horses.

I went back to my *hostal*. I relayed my terrible news to Pablo, the floppy-haired boy who seemed to do all the work in the place and who at that moment was sweeping the floor.

"Ay, qué horror!" he gasped.

I asked him his views as to the local dogs' health. Did he think I ought to see a doctor?

"Oh yes, definitely," he said, with a fervency that I found deeply discouraging.

I went down to my basement room and took a shower. I looked through my copious medical supplies and found that, despite the weight of the first-aid bag I'd been lugging around for weeks, I had somehow omitted to pack antiseptic ointments of any kind. Back upstairs, I asked Pablo if the *hostal* was better equipped. It wasn't.

"But why don't you just go to the hospital?" Pablo queried. "They'll clean it for you."

The hospital? A tiny light flickered in the murky gloom of my dark, distressed mind. This village only had four streets. Surely, *surely*—it couldn't stretch to a hospital? That would mean I wouldn't have to go to Salta after all.

It did, and the *guardia*—two blue-pajama-clad women, a wooden table, and a medicine cabinet—was open and ready to receive the wounded at eight o'clock on a Sunday evening. In fact, because it was eight o'clock on a Sunday evening and every self-respecting inhabitant of the town was seeking a more spiritual healing in the tiny, bell-topped church, I was the only person up there.

The two women looked up gleefully as I entered.

"Anti-rabies injections?" the younger of the two asked. She looked suddenly rather sad. "I don't think we have those—do we?"

The older woman confirmed that they didn't.

"We can give you the one for tetanus!" she piped brightly. I had the impression that she was eager for something to do.

"No, it's all right, I've already had that one," I told her glumly. Then it occurred to me—if they didn't have rabies injections here, might that be because they didn't have a problem with the disease? After all, I was quite sure I wasn't the first person that brute of a dog had bitten. His enthusiasm for sinking his fangs into my leg had been such that I rather suspected he had a munch at everyone who passed by—yet the hospital didn't seem to be packed full of patients in the convulsive throes of a rabid death.

"Oh no, we don't have any rabies here," chirped the younger pajama girl. "But why don't you come over here and sit down? Then I can wipe some iodine on your leg."

The brown ointment duly applied, I walked back toward the plaza and my room. I was feeling calmer now and was deeply thankful for two things at least: First, the likelihood of death by rabies seemed to be reassuringly small, and, second, at least I had been able to talk easily and coherently to the *guardia* in their own language. I thanked my twenty-one-year-old self for having put in so many arduous hours of language-learning in the late-night bars of Plasencia all those years ago. My evening would have been considerably worse if I hadn't been able to speak Spanish.

Mass was still being celebrated in the church. The congregation, unable all to squeeze inside, spilled out into the square itself. I stood among them for a while, soaking up the soothing, repetitious rhythms of religion. We exchanged the peace. I wondered if anybody might take the trouble to explain the concept to that belligerent black dog.

7

Perfectly Groomed

During the night, I developed a raging sore throat and a slight fever. I was fairly sure these weren't the symptoms of rabies—they felt like the signs of a perfectly ordinary cold—but still, I was a little worse for wear when I arrived the following lunchtime at El Molino flushed and rasping, with a freshly bitten leg and a fading black eye.

Nuny, on the other hand, was impeccably dressed with stylish sunglasses and flawlessly coiffed hair drawn back in a clip.

"Welcome!" she said, politely ignoring my mangy look. "Let me show you around the house."

Nuny and her husband, Alberto, had been living at El Molino for thirteen years. Their house was an immaculate, elegant place. Flowers bloomed perkily in terra-cotta pots. Polished silver—trinkets, bowls, and tiny pillboxes—adorned every surface. On the hall table, a thick pile of gleaming photograph frames paraded the family in their more glorious moments: graduations, weddings, and get-togethers. They seemed to be perfectly pedigreed, all-smiling, eternally beautiful people.

In the living room, sofas and armchairs the color of English mustard sat plumply beneath oil portraits of portly types, while rugs with something of the heirloom about them lay draped over shining terra-cotta floor tiles. A broad arched picture window gave out onto the poplar trees of the orchard beyond and bestowed upon the room an over-whelmingly vibrant, yet deeply peaceful sense of green. Down a stone staircase lay the cellar where the wine from El Molino's own vineyards awaited consumption.

Outside, the terrace with its green-painted furniture and carved wooden balustrade looked down onto the gar-den. Between the trees, two hammocks were strung. Every-thing was spotless.

The old mill was still running in the breakfast room, grinding corn that belonged to a neighboring farmer.

"My daughter is an architect," Nuny told me. "She helped us to design the house around the mill."

A gray, circular slab rotated slowly above a second stationary stone; it was powered by water that tumbled through a narrow chute running down the hill above the house. The yellow nuggets of corn filtered gently from a wooden funnel above the millstone, and, as they were crushed, fine yellow powder spilled out from the stones' sides to create a landscape of small golden dunes.

I started to suspect that, under her delightful, decorous exterior, Nuny must have been panicking slightly at the thought of allowing such a grungy creature as myself into her establishment. I wasn't sure that I quite met El Molino's usual standards: Apparently, Nuny and Alberto were some-times visited by European royalty. Félix Luna, the renowned

Argentine historian, had stayed here. Once, Nuny said, they had been descended upon by a paparazzi photographer looking for a famous model who never arrived. She showed me the visitors' book with its signatures from the great and the good.

In a bid to explain my shabby appearance, I regaled Nuny with the tale of my canine trauma.

"She's been bitten by a dog!" she exclaimed in horror to Alberto, who had just materialized from his office. "Just in the road out here. A pack of dogs ran out from a house and one of them bit her!"

"Which house?" Alberto demanded with some consternation. "What was the people's name?"

"I don't know. I didn't stop to talk to them. I was so shocked I just walked away."

"Of course, of course," they murmured soothingly.

"The girls have turned down your bed for a siesta," Nuny announced a few minutes later, clearly thinking I looked in need of a rest. "We'll sort out the horse-riding in the morning. The *peón* can go with you."

"There aren't many horses around here," Nuny told me the next morning, soon after breakfast, as we walked up from the house to where the animals were tethered. "They're very expensive to keep because the land is so dry you have to buy in feed. We keep five horses here, but they cost us a fortune."

So that was why I'd been having such difficulty finding any.

The *peón*, whose name was Rubén, had saddled up a criollo mare called Alenia for me to ride. She was a

delightfully docile creature; I had to wonder if the horses in
the village ever shifted out of a plod if they were any gentler
than this.

Rubén, a dark-skinned man in a white cotton shirt and a
battered navy blue hat, seemed to have been given strict instructions to walk slowly with me and to expose me to as
little danger as was humanly possible. We set off at a prudent
adagio along the unpaved road to the neighboring villages of
La Aguada and then Las Trancas.

"He's very shy. He doesn't talk much," Nuny had warned
me in a loud whisper as we'd left the house, but once I had
figured out the vagaries of his valley accent we had quite a
chat. He was born here in the valley, he told me. He'd lived
here all his life. He learned to ride before he learned to
walk. He'd worked for Nuny and Alberto for eight years.

We meandered along past more adobe houses. I was
happy with the easy pace. I was feeling better today, but I
wasn't particularly eager for outlandish acts of fortitude and
daring. What's more, this was my first day away from
Robin's gratifyingly substantial military saddles, and I was
riding with a couple of leather rings for stirrups. To one side
of the road, the land was arid and sparse, but to the other it
was verdant and fertile.

"In the summer, will it all be green?" I asked Rubén.

"Oh yes," he said. "It will be completely green, everywhere."

A man tending a vegetable patch called out to Rubén in
greeting. We rode past a school where kids in their uniform
white coats kicked around in a yard. After a while, we felt
relaxed enough to trot, and then my horse broke into a
beautiful smooth canter. It felt glorious after the jerky sitting trot—but when I turned round, Rubén had stayed behind. I took the hint: Cantering was not in his mandate. It

seemed unkind to land this affable man in any kind of trouble so I pulled Alenia up and we trotted gently on. We turned off the road and wended our way down a rocky track and over a stream before heading for home.

It felt wonderful to be back on a horse. I was surprised by the way I had taken to riding. The soft scent of the animal, the way it twitched and rotated its ears, alerting me to every sound and smell, the gentle swaying motion as we ambled along, all these things enchanted me. So much for my fears that I might loathe horses: On the contrary, each time I rode, the more I loved them.

I devoured a three-course lunch on the terrace at El Molino. A very short while later, Nuny presented me with a tray of tea, scones, and jam because, she explained, this is what the English eat in the afternoon. I found space for the scones, then lay fatly in one of the hammocks and read. My sore throat seemed to have vanished.

I ate dinner that evening with four other guests who had arrived during the day. Tomás and Agustina were a recently married couple from Buenos Aires. Tomás was a lawyer who had taken a postgraduate degree at Harvard and had lived in New York for a time; Agustina was in the process of changing jobs. The other couple were middle-aged Austrians.

"We only stayed in Buenos Aires for two days because we hated it," the Austrian Herr pronounced, gutturally, almost as soon as we had sat down on our ornately carved chairs at the long, polished dining table. Above us hung heavy crystal chandeliers. A wooden cabinet against the wall harbored an extraordinary number of glasses of all conceivable shapes. "All that graffiti. I thought it was very ugly."

"Yes, it was awful," brayed the Frau. "So we left. But now we are outside the city we are always getting lost because the tourist offices in Argentina give us the wrong information. They are hopeless." She gave a hefty shrug.

Tomás and Agustina nodded sincerely and politely, alternating sympathy and horror at the visitors' predicament.

In a bid to move the conversation on, I asked them where they had been since leaving the capital.

"We've driven today from the south. Last night we were in Cafayate."

"Ah, I'm heading there next," I told them. "It's supposed to be very beautiful, isn't it?" Cafayate was a town well known for its wineries.

"Well, yes, the scenery is good," conceded the Herr, swilling his red wine and siphoning it down his sagging throat between sentences. "But the roads are really dreadful! We were supposed to be here yesterday but the roads were so bad that the journey took twice the time we expected."

Tomás and Agustina expressed consternation and regret, and we lapsed into a strained silence while we chewed on our beef.

And then, with a conversational masterstroke, Tomás changed the subject.

"I'm afraid I have never been to Austria," he said, smiling sweetly. "All I know of the country is *The Sound of Music*."

The Austrian Herr let out an agonized roar.

"Oh no, but really, I liked it very much," said Tomás with an earnest sincerity that Maria von Trapp would have struggled to match.

In vain, I fought the urge to laugh.

We all left El Molino the following morning. The Austrians climbed into their rented car and continued north along the roads they so despised—although they had declared over coffee last night that they were intending to return next year to Argentina and to stay for longer.

"Why do you want to do that?" I had blurted. I was astounded: After their dinnertime diatribe, I had assumed that they would never deign to set foot in the country again.

"Because I like it here very much," the Herr had replied, equally surprised that I could have asked such a stupid question. I shuddered to think what observations he kept for countries he hated.

Tomás and Agustina were continuing their journey toward Salta as well. We exchanged telephone numbers—they insisted I ring them when I arrived in Buenos Aires so that they could show me around and, hopefully, ensure I went away with a better impression than the Austrians had—and they kindly agreed to drop me at the Cachi bus station. From there I was planning to make the journey south to Cafayate.

We drew up in the shabby clearing that served as Cachi's terminal. It was deserted except for a good-looking girl in her twenties who was sitting on a step with a couple of rucksacks for company.

She looked up as I unloaded my luggage from Tomás and Agustina's car.

"Are you going to Angastaco and Cafayate?" she asked as they drove away.

I was. Cafayate lay only a hundred miles from Cachi but the road, as the Austrians had observed, was tortuous and public transport was patchy. The bus ran only once a week, at eleven-thirty on a Wednesday morning, and to get to Cafayate one had to change at Angastaco. Today was

Wednesday and I'd been assured, when I'd asked the woman at the ticket counter a few days previously, that the bus would arrive in Angastaco shortly before the connecting service would leave. But this girl, whose name was Luciana, had different information.

"My boyfriend and I are trying to go there too," she said with a tight, tired smile, "but I don't think we can make the connection in one day. My boyfriend has gone to phone the bus company to find out."

A few minutes later, Federico, the boyfriend, came back from the *cabina*. From the end of the street, we could see him shaking his head.

"No," he said as he trudged up to us. "It's impossible to do the whole journey in one day. The bus leaves from Angastaco before the one from Cachi arrives. You have to spend at least one night in Angastaco."

We looked at each other glumly. Angastaco wasn't a place any of us wanted to be stranded.

"Or," said Luciana, turning to me, "if you like, we can all share a taxi."

The taxi office lay on the other side of the forecourt; dividing the cost between three of us, we'd only pay fifty pesos each. A few minutes later, we were loading ourselves into a battered white car.

"How long will the journey take?" Luciana asked the driver.

The driver shook his head and let out a long, breathy sigh. *"La ruta es muy fea"*—The road is hideous, he replied. "From here to Cafayate it usually takes about five hours."

We set off over the rough *ripio,* or unpaved road. The narrow track fell away into sheer drops on our left, and cut around tightly curling blind bends that hugged the hillsides to our right.

We crawled and clattered along. Pebbles flicked up from the stony surface and smacked sharply on the windscreen, which was already lined by a number of meandering cracks. After a while, the precipitous descents flattened out into spacious plains of sandy ground smattered with scruffy, scrawny bushes. This was a titanic panorama that rolled and swept with impressive grandeur toward its distant horizon.

The sky was heavily overcast, but from the chinks in between the slate gray cloud, jets of sunlight broke through, illuminating the land with a golden gleam. The yellow of the soil here was intense: It looked almost identical in color and form to the milled corn that had flowed from the stones in El Molino's breakfast room.

We weaved around the twists and coils, rendered speechless by the sheer scale of the vista that opened up about us. The occasional cactus poked up from the vast, flat plain and rose tall and thin above the low, leafless scrub.

Federico, sitting in the front passenger seat, broke the silence. "This is awesome," he said.

"Yes," said the driver in a noncommittal tone that suggested he'd greatly prefer a polluted urban highway.

We stopped for a few minutes at a village called Molinos. We wanted to buy sandwiches to eat on the journey, but Molinos was a dried-up, dead-end kind of place that didn't stretch to such luxuries. The best we could find was a pot of yogurt and a bottle of water. Lunch, it seemed, would have to wait.

As we rolled off down the road once more, the hills began slowly to encroach on the plain and we entered a new, more varied terrain. And then our surroundings became more remarkable still. In place of the gray mountains to which we had become accustomed, strangely sculpted sandstone formations curved and twirled around us. These were nothing like the multihued mountains north of Salta. These were a uniform ocher in color, and much more intricately crafted by the elements.

The soft, pale tan stone had been carved into terra-cotta peaks, arrows, caves, and crevices. Spires shot and buttresses flew, and ornate cloisters stretched between them. In places, smoothly rounded boulders appeared to be piled high, like columns of globular chalices piled one on top of another. Rows of cylindrical columns towered like mighty basilicas from behind which wispy choirboys in billowing gowns might at any moment appear. Overhead, ponderous black clouds weighed heavy, casting a strange luminosity on the scene, but there was no rain. This was a strikingly arid world. For an hour or more we saw no water, no trees, no leaves. It seemed as though we had stepped out of our world of greens and blues and into a coppery biblical wilderness.

And then, magically, the land turned lush. The road, for the first time all day, was now surfaced with tarmac. Still full of the astonishment our journey had provoked, we seemed almost to levitate along this smooth highway, through the fields of cultivated vines, until at four o'clock in the afternoon we arrived in the oasis of Cafayate.

8

Picaflor's Protest

Picaflor was a spirited horse, and he didn't seem enthusiastic about the next day's excursion. There was something about the way he kept stopping dead in his tracks, turning around, and heading for home that suggested that, maybe, he would rather be munching buttercups in a meadow than jogging along with a hard-bottomed novice bouncing up and down on his back.

As soon as I'd arrived in Cafayate the previous afternoon, I'd headed to the office of the town's horse-riding outfit in a street just off the plaza.

"Tomorrow, yes, no problem," the man behind the desk had replied with soothing simplicity when I'd asked if I could book an excursion for the next day. "Come back here in the morning at, let's say . . . nine-thirty? I'll just give Freddy a call."

"Separate the reins, pull hard on one side, and give him a big kick," shouted Freddy now, laughing as Picaflor and I

pirouetted in tiny circles in the middle of the road: I pulled
Picaflor around to face forward, then he spun off backward.
As soon as I'd turned him again, he skipped toward home
once more.

I did as Freddy said; poor Picaflor got the message and
bolted down the road toward him.

"Ay, Picaflor, qué te pasa?" Oh, Picaflor, what's the matter
with you? Freddy murmured as we drew up level with him.
He fondled the horse's ears and sighed lovingly. Freddy was
clearly very fond of Picaflor.

Picaflor was a black *peruana* gelding with white socks.
His name meant "hummingbird" in Spanish and, like his
avian namesake, he was pretty and flittery yet he flew along
with a fabulously smooth gait. Freddy was riding a chestnut
criollo called Payador, meaning Minstrel. As for Freddy's
name, it didn't sound all that Argentine to me.

"My father once had a very good friend—he was an
Englishman and his name was Freddy," Freddy explained
when I asked him. "One day, this friend had to return to his
homeland and my father never saw him again. So when I was
born, he called me Freddy as a way of remembering his
friend."

Freddy was from Cachi but he'd been living here in
Cafayate for the last eighteen years. He had three children
aged seventeen, fourteen, and nine, and ten horses. During
the daytime, he took tourists out riding. Then, in the
evenings, he taught folk dance at a local music school.

We rode out of town and through expansive green
countryside. We stopped at an old mill that dated from
Jesuit times—the priests used to have a mission here until
their order was expelled from Argentina in 1767. The room
in which the mill still stood was entirely bare; its flagstone
floor was spotlessly clean. Where once monks and their

Indian protégés would have tended to the grinding of corn and quinoa, a solitary octogenarian now kept watch.

We climbed back on our horses and headed up a sandy track where Freddy showed me a large flat rock into whose surface were burrowed bowl-shaped indentations, like a great gathering of mortars. This was where the women of the Diaguita tribe used to squat to grind and prepare their food while their menfolk fished and hunted.

"What are you doing this afternoon?" Freddy asked. I told him I was planning to visit one of the bodegas: The Cafayate area is famous for its white wine produced from the Torrontes grape.

"Would you like to ride out there on horseback?" Freddy asked. "I can take you if you like."

And so we agreed that we'd meet again at three o'clock and I could tour the vineyards with Picaflor, Payador, and Freddy.

There was a long, flat dirt road leading back into town.

"You want to canter?" Freddy asked with a grin. We kicked the horses on and, adrenaline surging, hurtled toward Cafayate in a cloud of dust.

At three o'clock I was sitting in the appointed spot, perched on the edge of a pavement under a tree, when I heard the furious hammering of hooves on tarmac. From around the corner, Freddy and his nine-year-old daughter appeared, roaring with laughter as they rattled down the street at a sprightly trot. They pulled up in front of me and Freddy's daughter vaulted off her horse with the agility of a leotard-clad gymnast who somersaults from a beam. I wondered wistfully if I would ever be able to dismount with such style—and had to conclude that, almost certainly, I would not.

The Finca Las Nubes toward which we were heading didn't open until four-thirty, so we first rode out over sandy terrain to see the cave paintings of guanacos. Having tied the horses to a tree, we climbed up a steep, rocky incline. Some minutes later we arrived, short of breath, at a large overhanging stone beneath which a group of Diaguita people used to live a long, long time ago. We stooped to clamber beneath the sloping roof that the angle of the rock created and there, on the far wall, images of guanacos were daubed clearly in white.

"What did they paint with?" I asked. It looked like chalk, but chalk etchings wouldn't last a year, let alone the centuries that these drawings had endured.

"We don't really know," said Freddy. "It seems to be some kind of plant extract. But nobody knows exactly what it is."

We rode back to the vineyard and trotted along a driveway between rows of ordered green vines until we reached the main house. Beyond the stripes of vegetation, the rocky gray of the Andes loomed, for these were high-altitude vines—Cafayate lies at nearly 5,500 feet. Outside the bodega's main building, a group had congregated.

"Look, there's a tour that's just started," said Freddy. "Why don't you go and join them while I tie up the horses."

As he suggested, I bounded off toward the throng that stood around a guide on one of the nearer terraces.

The woman around whom the group was gathered turned to me as I approached them. "If you like, you can go down to the house and another guide will show you round."

"Oh no, it's all right, I'll just join in from here," I said, lingering at the back of the party and eager not to create a scene.

It wasn't until a few minutes had passed, when I'd caught my breath and composed myself a little, that I realized: There was something unusual about this particular troupe. All except two of those who surrounded me were younger than I was by at least twenty years. They were behaving themselves a little too well. They weren't chatting subversively while the guide explained the intricacies of grape varietals, yet their eyes wandered shiftily and they shuffled in a way that suggested they were bored. A couple of the teenagers turned around and gave me a slightly funny look. With horror, I realized what I had done. I'd attached myself to a school trip.

It was only now that I saw that one of the older members of the party, whom I had imagined to be an innocent tourist but whom I now took to be the teacher, was carrying a video camera. She was filming the entire expedition. Presumably, then, the class was going to review the lesson in the vineyard once they arrived back at school. What were they going to say about the peculiarly clad foreigner—I was fully kitted out in cowboy hat, gaucho's bombachas, and brown suede half-chaps—slouching about in the furthest recesses of their screen? I felt quite certain they would howl with derision. The bodega's irrigation system could surely provide no entertainment equal to the delights of weeping with laughter at the weirdo in the hat, and although I wasn't going to be present when my self-respect was ripped to smithereens by shrieking adolescents, somehow the prospect of their contempt still made me shrink inside with a peculiar nervousness.

When the group moved into the main house, ready to

go down into the cellars, I grabbed my chance and slid sweatily away.

"It was a school trip," I muttered, blushing, to Freddy when I rejoined him and the horses.

"Ah, I see!" His cheeks turned rosy with mirth beneath his nut brown tan.

We indulged in a good hard canter on the way home. We streaked along, the wind rushing in our faces, the adrenaline pumping through our veins. The horses picked up their hooves and flew through the air—but just as we were thundering through the dust like the favorites on Derby day, Picaflor chose to assert his personality for one last time. Suddenly, in the middle of the charge, he dug his hooves into the dirt and executed a spontaneous emergency stop. I stayed on—but this sudden change of pace came as something of a surprise.

Freddy pulled up on Payador and hooted with laughter.

"*Ay, Picaflor.*" He sighed once more, shaking his head and smiling fondly at his horse. Then he turned to me. "You see, sometimes I bring him to this field here and let him eat the grass. He really likes it in there. He just wants some grass to eat."

He gazed lovingly at Picaflor, and chuckled some more.

The two llamas I met the following day had greater fortune than poor Picaflor—they were allowed to snack all they liked, and nobody booted them in the flanks or tugged on their reins. Standing beneath a cactus on top of a wide stony terrace, they reached high with their long brown necks and languidly savored its sprouts. They ate with their mouths partly open and chewed in a comical circular motion.

Between morsels, they watched me with a perpetual half-smile, as though they were somehow amused that this foreigner should have paid good money to drive out here and look at a few piles of old rocks.

I was at the Quilmes ruins, thirty-seven miles south of Cafayate. It was here that the last bitter battles of the Calchaquí Wars were played out as one lingering pocket of Diaguita fiercely resisted Spanish rule. The Spanish finally overcame the tribes of Quilmes in 1667, a full ten years after Pedro Bohórquez had been defeated and the other Indians in these parts subdued.

It was a harsh, hot day. Low dry-stone walls spread across the flats and up the hillside terraces. The walls rose only to about knee height: From a distance, the pattern they threw upon the sandy ground seemed to mimic the architect's floor plan of an unfathomably large, sprawling edifice. The layout of the buildings in which the Quilmes had sheltered was clear to see.

In between the walls, cacti presided, dignified and august. Small, sparse green bushes hunkered beneath them. *"No destruya las plantas,"* Don't destroy the plants, instructed a bold signpost rooted in one particularly arid and plant-free spot.

The Spaniards defeated the Quilmes in the end by starving them out. They barricaded this barren settlement so that the people were unable to gather the food they grew on the fertile plains below, or to fetch water to drink—for this wasn't the original town of the Quilmes but the fortress to which the people withdrew when the Spanish started to attack them. But the Quilmes held out defiantly till the last: When they eventually surrendered, not one able-bodied man remained to sling his stones. The captured were all wounded, women, and children.

The llamas continued to chew, still savoring their cactus sprouts, unaware of the terrible dramas that had been played out before their time. A lizard darted at my feet, scorching from one terrace to another. It was the same beige color as the ground and it moved hyperfast, performing its own desperate retreat into the safe haven of the stones.

I climbed the steep incline to the former village's highest point. The sun was searing; at the top, I needed to stand and gather my breath on this lofty plateau. On its far side, the hill dropped sharply away. I wondered if this was where the Quilmes mothers had come to end their children's suffering: Legend has it that, rather than watch their babies die a slow and tortuous death by starving, the mothers threw them from the cliff tops.

Once his victory was secure, the Spanish governor of this province was determined to prevent any further uprisings and so he decreed that the Quilmes people should be expelled from their native land and forced into labor a long way from home. After they had surrendered, therefore, the emaciated, weak survivors were made to march a gruelling nine hundred miles over mountain ranges and rough terrain to the province of Buenos Aires. The majority of them died along the way.

The few who completed the journey called their new town Quilmes in memory of their native land. Somewhat ironically, given that its namesake tribe was defeated by thirst and hunger, Quilmes is now known principally for its brewery. The company that manufactures the "Quilmes" brand has an eighty percent market share of the beer trade in Argentina and bottles tens of millions of liters of cool, refreshing, life-giving liquid each year.

The day I visited, the former Quilmes settlement was

silent. It was producing nothing more than a couple of prickly cacti. Scarcely another soul had come to visit this ghostly mass of dry-stone walls. The distant mountains were hazy in the midday sun, and I stood for some minutes just staring at this impressive, austere fortress town and thinking about its desperately cruel demise.

I rejoined my driver and we descended the steep dust track that linked the ruins to the main road of the modern world three miles away. Back in Cafayate, I sat on a restaurant terrace in the leafy plaza overlooked by a graceful church the color of clotted cream. Cafayate was a lively little town, its square lined by cafés, ice-cream shops, and craft stalls. I was comfortable and happy just to sit there for an hour or two, to watch this world go by and to drink a bottle of Quilmes beer in some kind of misguided recognition of those tyrannized and tormented people after whom it was named.

9

"The Horses Are Lost in the Fog"

I had difficulty breaking out of my *hostal* at five-thirty the following morning. It was pitch-dark and everyone else was asleep.

I'd told the proprietress the previous evening that I'd be leaving early because I wanted to catch the six o'clock bus to Tucumán. I'd paid my bill, and she'd given me a set of keys with which to open the main door and then the iron gate that gave onto the street. Clearly she wasn't planning to be up at such an ungodly hour herself.

I crept through the blackness from my room toward the outside door. My rucksack hit a chair, which crashed at terrific volume. I had no idea where the light switches were, so, in the dim shadows of the entrance hall, I battled with the unfamiliar keys in vain. None of them seemed to fit. Deciding I would have to dedicate both hands to the difficult business of opening the door, I very, very gently placed my luggage on the ground. It thudded resoundingly.

A tiny surge of panic bolted through me. What if I really couldn't get out? Would I miss the bus? Or would I have to stampede through the building making all the noise I could until everyone was awake and some bad-tempered, freshly roused soul came and quite literally kicked me onto the street?

Fortunately, after some minutes' fumbling, I finally found the right key so I was able to break free without having to resort to such extreme measures, and at five-forty-five I was standing in a lonely, unlit backstreet. The bus stop was designated by a stick, jabbed in the ground by a tree, and topped by a circle upon which the words "Aconquija Parada," the Aconquija stop, were painted.

I had a long journey ahead. This bus would arrive in Tucumán at twelve-thirty. Then I'd have seven hours to while away, wandering about town, until at seven-thirty in the evening I'd catch a sleeper bus bound for Mendoza. It would arrive there at ten o'clock the following morning.

I waited for a few minutes, all alone. Then, through the darkness, a great block of a coach loomed, its headlights bright and fierce—and it drove straight past. I had started off up the road in horrified hot pursuit when *"Ya vuelve, ya vuelve,"* It'll come back, it'll come back—a languid, disembodied voice echoed out of the shadows. I squinted across the road in the direction from which the voice had come and there, sitting on the step of the doorway to the public library, were two men whose presence I hadn't even noticed.

Over the next few minutes all manner of other shadowy creatures appeared. A boy on a bicycle kissed his girlfriend good-bye. Two farmers in straw hats strolled up lugging sacks. A mother and a father bid their daughter farewell. And then, when a good gathering had amassed around the stick in the ground, the bus reappeared and we all climbed on.

I fell back to sleep as the bus made its way out of town. When I woke up, the sun had risen and Argentina's scenery had changed dramatically once more. We were riding high now, at about ten thousand feet. Clouds nestled in valleys beneath us. On both sides, rolling hills undulated out over great distances, covered with just a thin layer of green-yellow grass on which horses and cattle grazed.

I unwrapped the Cafayate *artesanal* biscuits that I had brought for breakfast. They turned out to be like million-aire's shortbread, coated in chocolate and with a *dulce de leche* filling. The sugar zinged and tingled through my early-morning veins.

We wound our way down through the clouds. Wisps of mist hovered ethereal just above the land around us, imbu-ing the scene with a celestial, incorporeal air.

A young man sprinted down the roadside to catch the bus, which stopped for him. He climbed on, pink-faced and perspiring.

"Nearly missed you!" he panted, laughing. "I can never get it right. Either I nearly miss the bus, or I stand there for an hour waiting."

We descended into the town of Tafí del Valle, then started to climb once more, but through completely differ-ent scenery. Now an almost jungly verdancy surrounded us. Great fronds of bracken shot up from the hillside. Dense crops of long, luscious grass cascaded down, while ebullient bunches of wild fuchsia threw flushes of deep, wanton pink onto the green palette. The rocks were now clothed in pro-lific swaths of bright, moist moss. The hills above were en-shrouded in mist; beneath us, a stream weaved along its gleaming bed of pebbles.

Up and up, then down and down we drove until, finally, we descended onto flat plains of orchards that, in turn, gave onto the town of Tucumán.

I took a cab to the Plaza Independencia, Tucumán's main square. Tucumán is said to be the most important city in the north of Argentina. It was one of the first settlements to be founded by the Spanish—its wealth originally came from the production of sugar—and it was here that Argentina's independence from Spain was formally declared in 1816. Perhaps in response to its anticolonialist tendencies, most of its grand old buildings have now been torn down and a humdrum modern mishmash stands in their place. Seven hours here was going to be quite sufficient.

"Is it hot or is it hot?" asked the taxi driver.

I said I really didn't know: I'd only just arrived, but the weather looked fine to me.

The driver was in his early twenties and seemed an exuberant soul.

"So, what do you make of the men here in Tucumán?" he asked, getting to the point with breathtaking directness.

"Well, given that I only arrived at the bus station a couple of minutes ago, I haven't seen many yet," I replied. "In fact, the only man I've seen so far is you."

The taxi driver preened himself a little in his rearview mirror and sat up slightly straighter in his sagging upholstered seat.

"*Y como te parezco?*" And what do you think of me?

"*Bien.*" Fine, I said in my stoniest, least seductive tones.

We talked briefly about my journey—the places I'd been and where I was heading next.

"Never in my life have I met anyone like you before," said the driver. "I'd like to take you out for a meal so we could chat more."

What was this? Wasn't he taking idle cab chat a little too far? All I wanted was to go to the plaza.

"Oh well, what a shame," I said in a tone of voice that suggested that, perhaps, it wasn't a shame at all. "I'm only here for a few hours and then I'm leaving for Mendoza, so we won't be able to."

I was feeling grungy after my journey and I still had a long way to go. My plans for Tucumán involved such quotidian chores as eating lunch and checking my e-mail. I wasn't in the mood for a date, hot or otherwise.

"Oh no!" proclaimed the very desperate driver. He sighed wistfully. "If I had a guitar, I would sing you a song."

A guitar? A song? What on earth was the matter with this man? Were there no women in Tucumán for him to woo? Could things here really be so bad that he felt the need to serenade the first gray-faced, sleep-deprived, travel-weary tourist who collapsed into his cab?

"Well, you haven't, so you can't," I said, heartlessly bludgeoning his tacky attempts at romance to a pulpy, bloody demise.

"No, I haven't," lamented the driver and then, to my very great relief, we arrived at the Plaza Independencia and bid each other adieu.

The Tucumán town center was packed. It was a Saturday lunchtime and most of the restaurants had no tables to spare. I ate a tasteless sandwich in an establishment that, tellingly, was almost empty and then, at one-thirty on the dot: *ker-thump*. The shop doors closed. *Kkkkkkk*. The iron grates came down. *Clunk-click*. The keys turned in the locks. It was siesta time in Tucumán. Within minutes, all those strolling, smiling people had evacuated the town center with a speed that most populations reserve for an act of chemical warfare.

I now had six hours left to kill in Tucumán. A brief recon revealed that three places remained open: the bookshop, the Internet café, and the ice-cream parlor. Duly, I bought books, sent e-mails, and ate ice cream.

I sat for a while on a bench in the square. Two little children begged for small change. *"No pisar el cesped,"* Don't walk on the grass, insisted a sign stuck into a patch of baked, brown, grassless earth.

The seven-thirty bus to Mendoza finally left at eight-thirty, but despite the delay it was a comfortable journey. The spacious seats reclined almost to flat. The bus attendant served dinner: breaded cutlets reheated to just lukewarm that all but leaped from their plastic containers singing of salmonella. I was grateful to have brought along an emergency stash of cereal bars.

The movie, dubbed into Spanish, was entirely lousy. When it finished at ten o'clock, I put on my airline eye mask and slept, with only occasional interruptions, until eight o'clock the next morning when we made a brief stop in the town of San Juan. There, I jumped out of the bus to scrub my face and brush my teeth in the station washroom. Then our journey continued.

San Juan seemed an unremarkable place. From the bus window, at least, there were no striking monuments, there was no spectacular architecture. That was presumably because many of the town's older constructions were razed to the ground by the catastrophic earthquake that struck in

January 1944. But the buildings weren't the only ones to quiver. The aftershocks of that seismic wave gave rise to a tremulous love affair that rocked the whole of Argentina— for it was at a gala held to raise money for its victims that Colonel Juan Perón met the actress Eva Duarte.

Perón, at the time, was the military regime's Secretary of Labor. He had been assigned the task of administering the government's relief effort for the San Juan earthquake victims, and so he organized a fund-raising event in which actors and actresses would walk through the Buenos Aires streets with collecting boxes. It was at the festivities that followed this occasion that he met his future wife.

Evita—as she became known—had already catapulted herself from her humble beginnings with breathtaking verve and ambition. Life hadn't started well for her: Born in the dusty, dead-end pampas town of Los Toldos, she was the illegitimate daughter of an already married farm manager who abandoned his second family when Evita was less than a year old. But Evita refused to accept her lot.

Showing herself to be a veritable paragon of self-advancement, Evita made her way to Buenos Aires. Popular legend has it that she seduced the tango star Agustín Magaldi, and forced him to take her to the city, though this is disputed by some people who point out that there is no record of Magaldi's having visited Evita's hometown that year. In any case, she arrived somehow in the capital and once there she employed her own particular blend of naked determination and generosity in love to survive the early years. (One apocryphal tale surrounding Evita relates a story in which she, by then the President's wife, shared an elevator with a retired general. Having overheard another occupant of the elevator use the word *puta,* meaning whore, she exclaimed in outrage to the general, "Did you hear what he called me?" "Don't worry about it," the general is said to have replied. "I left the army years ago and still people insist on calling me 'General.'") But, whatever wiles she employed in her bid for success, by the time she met Perón at the San Juan fund-raiser, Evita was one of the most sought-after radio actresses of her time.

Just a couple of hours after leaving San Juan, my bus drew up in Mendoza. It was Sunday and the town—a gentle, serene place, best known for its wine production—was quiet. I wandered down the main street and sat with a pastry, coffee, and a newspaper in the sun.

The main street here, I noticed, was called Sarmiento after Domingo Faustino Sarmiento: He was Argentina's president from 1868 to 1874 and was born in nearby San Juan. Sarmiento was powerfully pro-European. He insisted throughout his career that education was the solution to Argentina's problems and his advocacy of state schooling for both boys and girls, with an emphasis on science and physical exercise, stirred up heated debate.

I was beginning to observe that the street names in Argentina were always the same whichever town I went to, and that they all referred to roughly the same period of history. Every town seemed to have a road or a square called "25 de Mayo," May 25, which referred to the day in 1810 when the town council in Buenos Aires declared independence from the Spanish viceroy. Most towns also had a street called "9 de Julio," July 9, which was the day in 1816 that the Argentines made their formal declaration of independence in Tucumán. Then particular towns had named specific streets according to dates that were important to them:

Tucumán, I'd noticed, had a September 24—the date in 1685 that the city was moved to its present site (previously it had been located on the Pueblo Viejo River, which was prone to flooding). It seemed an interesting way to name the streets and, I should have thought, one that ensured the people knew the vital dates of their country's history. Just imagine how well informed we could all be if, in every town in Britain, there was a street called October 14 relating to the Battle of Hastings, or a square named November 3 after the date in 1534 that the Pope's authority over England was abolished. How clever would we all look then?

In Argentina, when the streets weren't named after dates, they tended to be named after presidents and revolutionary heroes. There were many streets called Sarmiento, for example, or San Martín, who was one of the greatest independence fighters of South America and who right here in Mendoza trained the army that liberated Chile. Every rundown huddle of a hamlet seemed to have a Calle Mitre—Bartolomé Mitre was the first elected president of a united Argentina, as well as an important poet and historian, and the founder of the newspaper *La Nación*. There was usually a Belgrano—a military leader in the war for Argentine independence—as well.

Mendoza itself was named not after Pedro de Mendoza—he who tried to found Buenos Aires but ran away leaving his horses behind him—but Captain General García Hurtado de Mendoza, the Chilean governor, who in the early 1560s sent Pedro de Castillo over the Andes to found a city on the other side.

Nearly two hundred years later, Charles Darwin rode over the cordillera following much the same route. When he arrived in Mendoza, he didn't much like what he found.

"To my mind, the town had a stupid, forlorn aspect," he

wrote in his diary on March 27, 1835. (His journal would later be published as *The Voyage of the Beagle*.)

To my own mind, the town had a delightful, relaxed aspect. I sat and drank my coffee, and read my paper, and watched the world go by. My coffee hour moved seamlessly into lunch—a light dish of tagliatelle with perfectly al dente vegetables—in an outdoor café on the pedestrianized Avenida Sarmiento. Later, I walked through the Plaza Independencia. In the sultry evening warmth, the square was filled with fountains and flowers, trees, jugglers, and stalls selling jewelry, belts, and hats. There was even one stall dedicated solely to the sale of dog collars, which I assumed must be something of a niche market. A man played soccer with his son while couples sat and chatted on the wooden benches that encircled the fountains.

Life in Mendoza hadn't always been so peaceful, however. Back in the early nineteenth century, the province was governed by a very sanguinary monk named Félix Aldao.

Aldao had been a wayward, belligerent child: His parents enlisted him in the priesthood in the hope that religion might restrain his dissolute impulses. It didn't. In a bid to get close to the lustier side of things, Aldao joined up as a military chaplain and, in 1817, when independence fighters were still battling the Spanish in the Andes, a curious incident occurred.

"A strange figure dressed in white, like some phantom, was dealing blow after blow with wild ferocity," wrote Domingo Sarmiento in his essay *Life in the Argentine Republic in the Days of the Tyrants*. Sarmiento went on to explain: This was Friar Aldao, the division's chaplain, who had in the heat of the moment abandoned his duties to the dying and, taking up the sword, had added to their number instead.

"That evening's combat had revealed his natural instincts in all their strength, proving how little fitted he was for a profession requiring mildness and brotherly love; he had felt the pleasure in shedding blood which is natural to those who have the organ of destructiveness strongly developed; war attracted him irresistibly; he wished to rid himself of the troublesome gown he wore, and to win the laurels of the soldier in place of the symbol of humiliation and penitence."

Suffice it to say, Sarmiento didn't like Aldao much—but not everybody loathed the militant monk with quite Sarmiento's intensity. Aldao was a Mendoza man (though he had taken his vows in Chile); San Martín thought sufficiently highly of him to make him a captain in his army of liberation, and he was popular among both his soldiers and the civilian poor.

But that didn't stop Sarmiento's savage pen. His bloodlust unleashed on the battlefield, Sarmiento related, Aldao sought out those other vices that he had so longed for: drink, gambling, and women. In time, he fell violently in love with a girl from a respectable family but his priestly vows excluded him from marriage. The two therefore eloped to the other side of the Andes; the Church was scandalized and forced Aldao to return to Mendoza to face the ministerial music.

The couple lived in relative obscurity for a while, but when political unrest broke out, Aldao joined his two soldier brothers in warfare once more. The trio traveled through the land, slaying some and manipulating others, and gained considerable influence. However, the day came when "el fraile"—the friar, as his enemies called him—took one drink too many.

Following victory in battle, Félix Aldao's brother
Francisco was in the enemy camp completing the treaty
with the surrendering officers when an intoxicated Félix ordered that cannons be discharged into the very place where
his brother was standing. Francisco was killed—and Félix's
grief was such that, instead of accepting his own part in the
tragedy, he ordered that the defeated officers be slain.

"Thus the evil propensities, which had been for a time under restraint, broke forth again; and revenge for his brother's
death was an excuse for every excess. He had caused the officers to be put to death on that uncontested battlefield; the
next day he ordered the execution of all the sergeants, and on
the next the corporals. Every time he became intoxicated
his thirst for blood returned with redoubled fury," wrote
Sarmiento.

Argentina's gaudy history progressed. Power shifted,
Félix went to jail (popular legend has it that as he was arrested he shouted, "Don't touch me. I'm a priest and I have
the body of Jesus Christ in my hands!"), and the second
brother was assassinated. But in 1832 Félix Aldao returned
to Mendoza and soon became the most powerful man in the
province: The nominal governors were so afraid of him that
his most casual comment became law.

"His harem had been increased by the acquisition of new
mistresses; and the immoralities and scandal of his private
life formed the common topic of conversation, where the
shameful rivalry of these degraded women was openly exposed; they not only taunted each other with their degrada-
tion, but laid violent hands on one another in the streets,"
Sarmiento continued. "Highwaymen became numerous,
schools were closed, trade languished, the administration of
justice was given up to stupid or ignorant men."

Finally in 1845, at the age of fifty-nine, Félix Aldao died from "a cancer on his face, which ate into his nose and eyes, until he became partially blind; while the odor was so offensive that his companions at the card-table could hardly endure it."

Sarmiento was not an impartial biographer—and his ire was no doubt inflamed by the fact that he was forced to write his book in exile as Aldao and his fellow caudillos threatened his life—but whichever side one was on, it's clear that Aldao was colorful to the last.

I had arranged with Jeremy and Margaret, the couple I'd met on the Movitrack trip in Salta, that I would meet them first thing on Tuesday morning and join them on their tour of some of the local bodegas: Jeremy was writing an article for a wine magazine and had generously invited me along on his research trip. That left the next day, Monday, free for a horse-riding expedition high into the Andes.

On this particular trip, I was part of a group. There were seven lads from Birmingham, only one of whom had ever been on a horse before. There was a British girl called Fiona. And there was one unfortunate Argentine woman who spoke no English.

Our guide's name was Cecilia. Cecilia was a wholesome, athletic creature with very long, very blond hair tied into a French braid and pink cheeks that blushed from many hours spent in the fresh air. She wore a clean white shirt with a navy V-necked sweater, alluringly well-fitting olive green bombachas, and a pair of stylishly battered black riding boots. Accompanying her was Abel. He too was outrageously good-looking with dark chocolatey eyes and unblemished tan skin that puckered into a dimple when he smiled beneath his wide-brimmed gaucho hat.

We drove out of town and up through meadows covered in thousands of fluffy dandelion heads. They cast a light, white mantle on the grass that echoed the wispy clouds above.

We were heading into the Quebrada del Cóndor; we would be riding at an altitude of roughly ten thousand feet, which qualified as the fully fledged, authentic Andes. But the weather was starting to look distinctly turbid. As we climbed higher, the scattered woolly clouds flocked together to form a dense, impenetrable fleece and, before long, we were engulfed in fog.

At eleven o'clock we arrived at a tiny wooden house in the hills. A shed outside was packed full of goat kids with floppy velvet ears and strangely smiling mouths. The brume was thick around us now and the temperature had plummeted. At the last moment, leaving my hotel room, I'd thrown gloves and waterproof trousers into my rucksack and, here in the hills, I was profoundly thankful that I had. The weather up here was nothing like the warm sunshine of Mendoza yesterday.

We went inside to wait while Cecilia and Abel saddled up the horses. The owner of this hut had ornamented his wood-paneled walls with the skin of a puma and a pair of flimsy old snowshoes. There were five bunk beds, a table, a stove, and a fireplace whose hearth that glacial morning was the most popular spot in the house. Somebody brought us some breakfast—*medialunas* and instant coffee—which we ate and drank. And we waited. And we waited some more.

The saddling of the horses seemed to be taking an awfully long time. Finally I went to investigate. The murk outside seemed impervious now: I could scarcely see three feet in front of me as I tentatively picked my way down the path toward the corral. Then Cecilia hurtled by on her horse. She was in a blistering bad mood: The horses, she hissed, were lost in the fog and the men couldn't find them. It was one o'clock before, finally, we were ready to go.

"There is to be absolutely no cantering," commanded Cecilia. She was still angry and none of us quite dared to question her. "If one horse goes off, they all follow."

Most of the people in our group had never been on a horse before in their lives; we were riding in thick fog; we were going to proceed very slowly indeed. In case we hadn't fully absorbed her point, Cecilia proceeded to regale us with hideous tales of past calamities.

"One time, a tourist cantered fast between two rocks. The horse got its foot stuck, fell, and broke its leg," she said. "It had to be put down."

We contorted our faces into suitable expressions of horror.

"And that wasn't the only disaster," Cecilia carried on. "Another woman went too fast, and she fell off her horse and broke her arm."

There was something in Cecilia's tone that suggested she hadn't been altogether sorry to see the woman suffer.

I was riding a dun mare called Larita. We trooped with the calm obedience of a royal parade out of the corral and along a narrow track through the hills. The mists were trying to rise now, and were hovering and eddying about us. As the air began to clear and the visibility improved, we passed a condor perched on the dark face of a craggy outcrop of granite. The mighty bird flexed its powerful wings as we passed. It was huge and muscular, an awe-inspiring vision. The rock upon which it sat was smeared with a rust red oxide deposit. It looked like the daubed-on blood of that vo-racious bird's prey.

In one meadow, a small pile of bones lay like a skeletal cairn. Nearby, larger bones were scattered. Tufts of brown flesh and hair still clung to them in places. I briefly won-dered whether these might be the mortal remains of a fool-hardy tourist who had cantered into the formidable force of Cecilia's ire, but apparently they were the bones of a bovine cadaver.

"That cow was killed two years ago by a puma, but it has been mummified by the cold," said Cecilia. One or two of the Birmingham boys must have looked nervous beneath their brawn because, after a pause, she added, "But don't worry, the pumas only come out at night." Her mood, it seemed, was softening.

We rode over streams, and up and down stony paths. Then, after three hours, we returned to the hut. The fire was burning. We clustered around; by now, we were all frozen through. Cecilia and her colleagues brought us jugs of red wine and plates of freshly grilled *asado,* which we de-voured with carnivorous relish.

I met up with Jeremy and Margaret at their hotel the next morning. Jeremy's expertise was Spanish wines—he used to be the director of wines for Spain's Wine Promotion Agency and has since written a number of books. But now that he was in Argentina, he was investigating the grapes on the other side of the pond.

"It's only really in the last two or three years that this area has been producing so many wines of such high quality. In the next few years, there's going to be an explosion of

Argentine wines on the international market," Jeremy told me as we glided out of town in the navy Mercedes his hotel had rented him for the day. At the wheel sat an impeccably well-dressed, ridiculously attractive driver called Sebastián. The wine industry was one of the sectors least affected by Argentina's economic crisis of 2001–2002: high levels of foreign investment in the 1990s, when the peso was pegged to the dollar, meant that the Argentines were able to import the best technological advances from abroad. By the time the peso was devalued in 2002, Argentine wines competed in quality with those from the rest of the New World and, with devaluation, they became good value abroad. Their export potential therefore greatly increased.

Jeremy's first appointment that day was at Dolium. The owner was Mario Giadorou, a charming man in his early seventies with bushy gray eyebrows over laughing blue eyes. Mario was born and raised in Italy. He had worked as a mechanical engineer in his homeland, then moved to the USA in 1959 when a job opportunity arose there. He had relocated to Argentina in 1961 and had lived in the country ever since. When he was sixty-five, Mario had retired from engineering and had conceived the Dolium brand.

"You have two possibilities when you get older," he told us in almost perfect English as he smiled and leaned back in the chair behind his desk. "The first is to be a retiree with a larger television set, but that was not really my cup of tea. I wanted to be active, so I started this. But before starting I took my normal approach—to go as deep as possible into the technology so that I can have the best design. So I designed this winery in a different way from everyone else."

It soon became apparent that the pistons of Mario's engineering background pumped through every high-tech bottle this bodega produced. Dolium was the first underground

winery in Argentina: the subterranean temperature is lower
and more constant so one doesn't have to rely so heavily on
artificial cooling and ventilation.

"I know Argentina very well." Mario grinned. "Already
in 1998 I was thinking: In Argentina there will be a terrific
energy crisis. So I prepared for that. I use very little energy.
And I put a generator in my design so that I could be independent."

We went downstairs and tasted the young wines from
his underground barrels; we went upstairs to the light and
airy top floor where walls of windows looked out over the
vines, and tasted some more mature, deliciously rounded
vintages.

Running slightly late now, we jumped back into
Sebastián's very smooth car and made for Terrazas de los
Andes, a much bigger, more corporate winery—it's part of
the Chandon group. Moët et Chandon, the French champagne house, opened an operation in Argentina in the 1950s
to make sparkling wines. In the 1980s, they expanded to
still wines and created Terrazas to produce high-quality varietals. We toured the winery, where I learned that the wine is
filtered through egg whites, then tasted some more. And
then we climbed back into the car for our main appointment of the day—Bodega Enrique Foster.

Harry and Lois Foster were friends of Jeremy and
Margaret's and were the principal reason they had traveled
to Argentina at all. They were vibrant, energetic New
Yorkers who seemed to have business concerns across the
globe. Following many years of interest in Argentine
Malbec, they had set up the bodega three years previously
with the intention of making the best Malbec in the world.

The Malbec grape originated in southwest France, but
the French climate doesn't allow it to ripen properly. In

France, therefore, it's grown principally to be blended with other grape types—but in Mendoza, the conditions for Malbec are perfect.

The pièce de résistance of the Enrique Foster bodega is not the Argentine sunshine, however, but a vast "gravity-flow" crane contraption that means the wine doesn't have to be pumped from one stage of its production to the next. The previous owners of these vineyards had no winery—they had simply sold their grapes to other local enterprises. So when Harry and Lois bought the land they had to set about constructing their own plant. After some research in Californian vineyards, they decided that the high quality that could be achieved by using gravity flow would be worth the extra cost, and so they introduced the crane, which doesn't pump but lifts and lets flow.

We chatted to Mauricio, Harry and Lois's vintner. He was a big, swarthy man with an easy smile and a relaxed manner. He had wine-making interests outside Enrique Foster, and he invited Jeremy to taste a Cabernet Sauvignon. Jeremy found the results very interesting.

"I almost thought I could taste gooseberries," he remarked with delighted astonishment.

"No," said Mauricio. "What you can taste is sweet pepper. You know when you roast a pepper on the barbecue and it becomes slightly sweet? That is the flavor."

At this point, I knew I was out of my depth.

Fortunately, the only tasting I was involved in was a pleasantly relaxed affair: We sat at tables on the terrace overlooking the vineyards, ate piping hot, crispy empanadas and salad, and drank Enrique Foster wines with our meal. I'm no expert, but I thought them quite fantastic.

We left at three-thirty, and I later joined Jeremy and Margaret and Harry and Lois for supper.

"What have you done since you left us?" Lois inquired. She was a bright character with a tremendous zest for life. She told me that at the age of sixty-four her greatest fear was of dying before she had done everything she wanted to do. She therefore looked after herself fastidiously.

"In New York," she said, "I limit myself to one glass of wine a day. But here, of course, it's impossible."

The two of them, it transpired, had attended an appointment every hour that afternoon. I felt entirely inadequate at having to confess that I'd gone back to my hotel and taken a nap.

10

Stick and Ball

I was spectacularly unhappy at having to haul myself out of bed at seven o'clock the following morning, even after my siesta of the day before. Lois and Harry had probably been up for hours and completed several engagements by now, I considered as I wearily dragged my luggage down the stairs and checked out of my hotel. But there was no time in my schedule for tiredness, for that morning I was flying east to the nonstop, bar-hopping, tango-dancing capital. "God is everywhere," they say in Argentina, "but if you want to talk to him, you have to make an appointment in Buenos Aires."

Buenos Aires was not always the hyperelegant, superenergetic center that it is today. In fact, its origins were decidedly downbeat.

The first European to explore the area was Juan Díaz de Solís. In 1516 de Solís sailed up the Río de la Plata with his merry band of men, who promptly ceased being merry when they were butchered by the Querandí tribe. Four years later, Ferdinand Magellan loitered briefly around here wondering whether the Plata estuary was the entrance to the fabled strait that cut through America.

In 1526, Sebastian Cabot roved considerably farther: He sailed up the Río de la Plata and some way along the Paraná River. Even better, he managed to stay alive and returned to Spain bearing a few silver trinkets. It was he who named the Río de la Plata—the River of Silver—and, safely back in Europe, he regaled his fellow adventurers with wild tales of tribes laden with riches. His successors—like their compatriots to the northwest—were hell-bent on finding this bonanza and determined to explore the area further. They finally founded Buenos Aires ten years after Cabot's jamboree: Pedro de Mendoza erected the first tents in 1536. The settlement didn't last long, though—the Querandís forced the Spaniards to retreat and it wasn't until 1580 that Buenos Aires was definitively established by Juan de Garay.

Unfortunately for these early explorers and settlers, there turned out to be no precious metals piled up on the banks of the Río de la Plata—and once the conquistadors discovered that Buenos Aires was not sitting on a silver mine, they lost interest fairly fast. For the first decades, the population of Buenos Aires was minuscule: Only a few hundred people lived there. The Spanish Crown had backed the town's refounding because it wanted to establish a military garrison that would protect its new lands against pirate and privateer attacks from the Atlantic, but it refused to subsidize the new settlement. Forced to fend for themselves, the inhabitants depended for their survival on the arrival of registered ships, but Spanish shipping regulations were stringent: registered ships docked in Buenos Aires only once every year or two. Most goods had to be transported overland from Lima, which dramatically inflated their cost.

The only way the *porteños,* the "port people" of Buenos Aires, could survive was through smuggling. They paid for contraband goods with cattle hides. Like the horses left by Pedro de Mendoza, cattle—which had also been introduced by the conquistadors—had been reproducing at a phenomenal rate on the pampas. These cattle were slaughtered solely for their skins. Their carcasses were left on the plains to rot.

Little by little, though, Buenos Aires gained status in South America. When in 1776 the viceroyalty of the River Plate was created with Buenos Aires at its head, the city gained power and freedom to trade. The population boomed. Cattle ranches were set up in the surrounding pampas and the export industry took off.

The British briefly attempted invasions of the city in 1806 and 1807, but they were quickly quelled by the criollos (South American–born Spaniards). It was this victory that, in part, gave the criollos the confidence to seek independence from Spain and led to the revolution of May 25, 1810; formal independence was declared in 1816. By the time Darwin arrived in Buenos Aires in September 1833, the city was fully established (though it wouldn't officially become Argentina's capital until some years later). He described his impressions in *The Voyage of the Beagle:*

"The city of Buenos Ayres is large; and I should think one of the most regular in the world. Every street is at right angles to the one it crosses, and the parallel ones being equidistant, the houses are collected into solid squares of equal dimensions, which are called quadras. On the other hand, the houses themselves are hollow squares; all the rooms opening into a neat little courtyard. They are generally only one story high, with flat roofs, which are fitted with seats, and are much frequented by the inhabitants in summer. In the center of town is the plaza, where the public offices, fortress, cathedral, etc., stand . . . The general assemblage of buildings possesses considerable architectural beauty, although none individually can boast of any."

The naturalist W. H. Hudson gave a childlike perspective of the city in his memoir *Far Away and Long Ago*. Hudson was of British descent and was born on the Argentine pampas in 1841. His first memories of Buenos Aires dated from when he was about six years old. He recalled the washerwomen congregating each day on the banks of the Río de la Plata, and the tremendous noise of cartwheels clattering over the large, round cobbles of the city streets as the drivers galloped their horses home at night. His auditory recollections continued with descriptions of the night watchmen's calls.

"When night came it appeared that the fierce policemen, with their swords and brass buttons, were no longer needed to safeguard the people, and their place in the streets was taken by a quaint, frowsy-looking body of men, mostly old, some almost decrepit, wearing big cloaks and carrying staffs and heavy iron lanterns with a tallow candle alight inside. But what a pleasure it was to lie awake at night and listen to their voices calling the hours! The calls began at the stroke of eleven, and then from beneath the window would come the wonderful long drawling call of *Las ón-ce han dá-do y se-ré-no,* which means eleven of the clock and all serene, but if clouded the concluding word would be *nu-blá-do,* and so on, according to the weather. From all the streets, from all over the town, the long-drawn calls would float to my listening ears, with infinite variety in the voices—the high and shrill, the falsetto, the harsh, raucous note like the caw of the carrion-crow, the solemn, booming bass, and then some fine, rich, pure voice that soared heavenwards above all the others and was like the pealing notes of an organ."

Hudson also describes in gruesome detail the *"saladero"* or butchering ground that lay in the south of the city during the nineteenth century. Each day, farmers from the pampas would bring their livestock—cattle, sheep, and horses— here to be slaughtered. Some were killed for their meat, but most were butchered just for their hides.

"The blood so abundantly shed from day to day, mixing with the dust, had formed a crust half a foot thick all over the open space: Let the reader try to imagine the smell of this crust and of tons of offal and flesh and bones lying everywhere in heaps. But no, it cannot be imagined . . . The reader can only take my word for it that this smell was probably the worst ever known on the earth . . . travellers approaching or leaving the capital by the great south road, which skirted the killing-grounds, would hold their noses and ride a mile or so at a furious gallop until they got out of the abominable stench."

But the carts, the night watchmen, and the cattle carcasses were long gone by that Wednesday lunchtime when I arrived in Buenos Aires. I checked into my hotel and then walked out along the nearby Calle Florida, one of the city's main pedestrian shopping streets. There was a buzz here that implied the entire city was tripping on a caffeine overdose. The narrow thoroughfare was packed, elbow to elbow, with shoppers and office workers on their lunch breaks. They strode and marched, dodged and skipped, chattered, bellowed and laughed. Shoe shiners squatted on low stools on the edges of the street before their antiquated, painted advertising boards. Brushes with black- and brown-daubed bristles lay in neat rows at their feet alongside tins of "Inmortal"—immortal—shoe polish. Having been in sleepy little towns for the last few weeks, I found this sudden onslaught of energy quite overwhelming.

I was hungry for lunch, but the first few cafés I passed seemed so chic and bohemian that I didn't quite dare go in. It was strange; I'd been away from city life for less than a month but already I felt out of my depth in such fast-moving establishments. I felt dowdily dressed. The sheer vigor of these places frightened me. In the end I forced myself through a doorway and timidly ate pasta and salad served by flurrying black-clad waitresses.

I spent the whole of the next day walking. For seven or eight hours, I tramped around the city streets, breathing in their atmosphere. Once I'd recovered from my shock at the sight of so many people, I adored Buenos Aires.

I walked up toward Recoleta. Young men in hoodies and knee-length shorts strutted through the streets enmeshed in a tangle of dog leads. These were professional dog-walkers: Respectable *porteños* liked pedigree dogs to adorn their apartments and, to aid their physical and mental welfare, they enlisted them in the canine equivalent of day care. Each morning these dog-walkers collected their charges and took them to play in the park. The dogs were elegant creatures: long-haired retrievers, German shepherds and red setters, collies and Labradors all trotted toward the city's wide green spaces, perfectly groomed, perfectly shaped, perfectly well behaved. Each dog-walker strode along with a small horde of these canines—the most I counted was eighteen dogs with one man. It struck me as odd, in a city full of apartments, that the *porteños* should have a taste for such large breeds of dog—but this is a town where appearances count and perhaps a dog, like so much else, confers greater status if it's big.

The buildings were well groomed, too. The apartment blocks' elegant stonework was impeccably smooth and immaculately clean. Weighty slabs of wooden doors boomed of power, wealth, and immutability, while each great brassy globe of a doorknob shone like the rising sun itself. It was springtime and the jacaranda trees were in bloom. The city was awash with pale purple blossoms adorning branches that stretched before windows with magnolia-painted shutters and wrought-iron balconies. On the pavements, pools of these bluish petals encircled the tree trunks like outsized chinoiserie dinner plates that had faded with age.

I walked up to the Plaza Alvear and went into the Recoleta Cemetery, whose vaults had harbored whatever corporeal matter remained of the great, the good, and the downright awkward of Buenos Aires for the last two hundred years. This place was like a small, terrifically ornate city. It had streets and buildings—but the only people who lived here were the dead.

A plethora of stone crosses of all shapes and styles topped the domes, pyramids, and columns that sheltered the vaults below. Intricately carved winged angels beamed beatifically. The bust of a bearded colonel topped the rigidly geometric, unyielding gray edifice that held his crumbling remains. Nymphs, cherubs, and countless statues of the Virgin Mary stretched, reclined, swanned, and sauntered.

I peered with morbid fascination through dusty windows and padlocked grates. Inside, marble floors and shelving held the coffins of several generations. In some, carved granite steps spiraled into a basement beneath which, presumably, still more corpses slowly moldered. Some of these tiny edifices were spotlessly clean and adorned with freshly cut flowers, prayer books, and cushions for kneeling. Others were grimy, untended, and dismal.

It struck me as an odd place to leave one's granny, and more bizarre still to come and kneel with one's prayer book alongside her decaying skeleton. There was something curious about incarcerating a corpse in a coffin and leaving it, aboveground, amid all this marble and stone. There was nowhere for the rotting matter to go. There was no soil for it gradually to nourish. There was no sense of a return to the earth. Instead, for endless centuries, these privileged people's mortal remains did just that: They remained. They stayed right here, sealed in a sepulchre, stared at by tourists.

Following the crowds, I found myself in a narrow alleyway where a gathering of people—some respectful, some gawping, some merely bemused—congregated before a black vault whose doorway was threaded with flowers. This was the most visited tomb in the whole of the Recoleta Cemetery. It was the resting place of Evita Perón.

Evita died of cancer in 1952. She was just thirty-three years old, but even at that young age she was the most idolized woman Argentina had ever known.

After meeting Perón at that famous earthquake fundraiser in 1944, Evita had lost little time. She had moved in with him within weeks: The story goes that he had another, very young mistress when Evita came on the scene and that, one morning when Perón was at work, Evita dispatched the girl and her belongings and moved into Perón's apartment in her place. Perón knew nothing about it till he came home for his siesta and found Evita comfortably installed with her suitcases unpacked.

They married in October the following year; four months later, amid considerable political turmoil, Perón was elected president. If Evita had been prominent as an actress before, now she positively rocketed into the public eye. She bombarded the land with her own special brand of love in her bid to conquer the hearts of downtrodden Argentines. She shot glittering jets of compassion and showered teardrops like tracer fire. Tirelessly, unstintingly, unflaggingly she promoted herself and her husband—and their adoration of the common Argentine man and woman.

The *descamisados,* the "shirtless" majority, revered Evita. (The oligarchy, meanwhile, detested her.) When the poor began to visit Evita and ask for her aid, she helped them, and in 1948 the Eva Perón Foundation was created. Funding came partly from government handouts, trade unions, and taxes on lottery and cinema tickets, but most of the Foundation's money was raised through donations. Argentina was rich. Many were happy to be generous—and those that weren't recognized that it was unwise to refuse a request from Evita Perón.

The Foundation soon became a mammoth governmental love machine. It financed hospitals and houses for the poor. It even built a "children's city" for the offspring of the most poverty-stricken families. But most memorably, Evita used to receive the poor in her office, and she personally granted them the material goods they required.

The system was this: Those in need would write to Evita and explain their situation. The Foundation would then send an invitation card stipulating the date and time their meeting with the great lady would be held. Even Che Guevara once wrote to Evita in his prerevolutionary days, though his request could not have been entirely serious as Guevara came from a well-to-do family—and his "need" was for a jeep in which to make a seemingly unnecessary journey through South America. (She never replied and he never made his jeep trip; instead, he and his friend Alberto

Granado took off the following year on Granado's motor-bike to make the journey that would be recorded as *The Motorcycle Diaries*.)

Accounts from contemporary journalists describe the chaos, the noise, and the stench of those gatherings. The *descamisados* who had made their way from their slums to make a request of the sparkling *señora* would be ushered into a waiting room where they sat, ragged and reeking, until their turn was called. Babies bawled; mothers babbled. And through it all, for hours on end, Evita would sit resplendent amid her jewels and her immaculate peroxide-blond hair, and bestow compassion on the common man and woman. She gave each visitor two fifty-peso notes and wrote out chits for the items they needed: clothes, houses, sewing machines, beds, cooking pots, mattresses, food, jobs, and money. She was young and beautiful. She worked long, grueling hours for her devoted public, missing meals and arriving home at dawn. She kissed the syphilitic and stroked the leprous, and she convinced the stinking she loved them. And then she contracted cancer and died.

Evita passed away at eight-twenty-five P.M. on July 26, 1952. The evening news broadcast would subsequently move its slot from eight-thirty to eight-twenty-five to mark the importance of that hour to the Argentine people.

"Although no instructions had been given to this effect, the entire city and the entire country instantly went into the deepest, most heartfelt state of mourning. Cinemas stopped their movies, theaters interrupted their plays, restaurants, bars, and *boîtes* immediately showed customers to the door, their shutters slamming down over suddenly darkened street-fronts. Within a matter of minutes the city was silent and dark," was how Nicholas Fraser and Marysa Navarro described the scene in their book *Evita: The Real Lives of Eva Perón*.

The restaurants, shops, and cinemas stayed closed for days. Flags flew at half mast. Huge pictures of Evita were erected at traffic junctions. The crowds flooded to pay their respects: The crush was such that more than two thousand people had to be treated for injuries in the twenty-four hours after the First Lady had breathed her last. But if Evita had played a starring role in life, the drama that would envelop her in death would be more lurid by far.

Just three years after Evita died, Perón was overthrown by a military coup. He fled into exile. Evita had not yet been properly buried: Her body had been embalmed so that she might be gazed upon in perpetuity, but, while the preservation process was complete, the grandiose tomb that was to be her final resting place had not yet been finished. Evita's embalmed corpse was therefore still lying in a government building in Buenos Aires.

The new government was determined to break up the Peróns' popular following. It banned all photographs of the couple, and even forbade the very pronouncement of the word *"peronismo."* Obviously, the completion of Evita's tomb—a monument that would instantly become a place of pilgrimage for her devotees—was out of the question.

The body had to be disposed of—but how? While the embalmer's ministrations had left Evita's cadaver smelling sickly-sweet, the question of what to do with it now that she had fallen from grace threatened to create an almighty stench. The Catholic Church ruled out cremation. The authorities tried to bury her remains in an unnamed grave but, somehow, the news of where she was to be interred was leaked before the coffin arrived and the plans had to be shelved. Finally, the government decided that Evita, like Perón, must be banished from the country altogether. They went to unimaginable lengths to throw her disciples off her

formaldehyde-enriched scent, even sending coffins full of
ballast to a number of foreign embassies so that nobody
should know which box contained the actual body.

Finally, an Italian priest crept quietly away with the real
coffin. Some weeks later he reappeared before the president
of the day, Aramburu, and handed him a sealed brown envelope: Inside were the top-secret details of Evita's whereabouts. Aramburu chose not to open the envelope but
handed it to his lawyer with instructions that, after his
death, it should be passed to whoever had succeeded him as
premier; that person could choose to open the envelope or
not as he thought best.

And so Evita was shipped out of the country and finally
buried. That, the authorities hoped and prayed, would be
the end of the ghoulish tale. But perhaps they should have
known better than to mess with the ghost of Eva Perón—
for she was yet to come back to haunt them.

By 1970, the power of the military government was on
the wane as guerrilla groups waged an increasingly bloody
war against the incumbent regime. On May 29, former
president Aramburu was kidnapped and executed. When his
body was discovered, his lawyer, as instructed, passed the
envelope to the then president, who thought the question
of Evita's whereabouts had poisoned Argentine politics for
long enough. He therefore opened the envelope and ordered her grave to be traced.

Evita was found to be buried under a false name in
Milan. She was disinterred, then driven in a hearse up into
France and then on to Spain; just outside Madrid, the coffin
was transferred to a plain van and driven to the mansion of
Juan Perón, who now lived in exile in the city with his third
wife, Isabelita. Upon inspection, Evita's nose was found to

be rather squashed and her forehead slightly disfigured, but other than that, she was in exactly the same state as she had been when she had first been embalmed. In a further grisly detail—as if this story needed more—when they opened the coffin, Isabelita apparently ran her fingers through her dead predecessor's braided hair, lovingly removing the dirt that had gathered between her dyed platinum locks. And then, more bizarrely still, Perón and Isabelita stashed the coffin in an attic.

Juan Perón returned to government in Argentina in 1973, but Evita's cadaver didn't follow him until after his death the following year—and by the time the faithful had agreed on the design of a second great tomb in which the couple should lie (goodness knows what they were planning to do with Isabelita—perhaps upon her death they'd all indulge in a rather rigid threesome), another military coup had ousted the Peronists once more. Finally, on October 22, 1976, Evita's body was given back to her family and they buried her, hopefully forever, in the Recoleta Cemetery.

It was macabre to think that a few feet away from where I stood, a well-traveled corpse now resided. She was well and truly locked in—she lay, apparently, in a compartment beneath a trapdoor, beneath another compartment with another trapdoor—and there was only one key, which the Duarte family was said to keep, so neither escape nor kidnapping was likely.

I wondered what kind of state the cadaver was now in. My knowledge of embalming was rudimentary in the extreme but I should have imagined that, if the preservation had been successful for the first fifteen or so years until Evita had been dug up in Italy, it ought to have been more or less effective thirty-odd years after that.

Nicholas Fraser and Marysa Navarro described the embalming process in their book. The work was carried out by an expert named Dr. Ara.

"Incisions had been made in the heels and below the neck, by which the body had been drained. It was then placed in a bath of 150 liters of acetate and potassium nitrate, weighted with the coffin lid to keep it submerged. Then it was injected and reinjected with mixtures of formol, thymol and pure alcohol, dipped in bath after bath, month after month, reinjected each time and finally coated with a thin but hard layer of transparent plastic, so that it could be displayed and touched."

It was a gloriously gruesome process to contemplate: All that submerging of the body in the bath had a sinister element to it. The whole gory saga blended something of the *film noir* with the genre of the "madwoman in the attic." And yet this was no work of fiction. Evita was here, lying right beneath my feet. Just a little spadework away rested the preserved flesh of that ultimate femme fatale: She had fallen victim to life's cruelties yet had ultimately reigned victorious. She had been utterly despised and, at the same time, totally revered—and, whatever her shortcomings, her cadaver still embodied the most glamorous legend that Argentina had ever engendered.

I emerged from all this murkiness and walked next door to the church of Nuestra Señora del Pilar, which gleamed brilliant white in the sunshine. El Pilar is one of Buenos Aires's most elegant oratories, the worshipping ground of the upper classes that Evita so despised. The blue mosaic tiles of the bell tower's dome gleamed beneath an ornate black crucifix. In front, neatly fenced gardens bloomed with well-tended yellow flowers. Inside, above the altar, a huge, ornate, gilded retable centered upon a statue of the Virgin Mary with her child. In surrounding alcoves saints with pious expressions stood and wilted, their sorrowful heads hanging bereft, their skeletal hands wringing in variations of agony and regret. The ornamental stucco that surrounded these figures was breathtaking—great swirls of gold curled around in the shapes of crowns and unfurling leaves. Marble pillars shone. In another alcove, amid more golden stucco whorls and winged angels, Jesus bled bright red beneath his crown of thorns.

At the back of the church was the reliquary. A collection of human skulls, presumably the craniums of good people long gone, lined up in hollow-eyed judgment of us modern-day sinners.

I stopped for a fortifying coffee at the famous café La Biela, which hummed with activity beneath a gargantuan gum tree whose branches weaved like long-reaching tentacles across a space that might have housed an entire city block. Tourists in sneakers with backpacks at their feet drank long, thirst-quenching Coca-Colas. At neighboring tables, the city's best-shod sipped on espresso amid piles of paper shopping bags carrying that week's style. It was difficult to marry this bustling scene of prosperity with the agonies of less than three years ago, when the people of Buenos Aires were reduced to barter because they weren't allowed to access their cash—as, indeed, it was difficult to imagine this same illustrious café thirty years back: During the chaos and violence of the 1970s, La Biela was a popular meeting place for young, politically minded people of both left- and right-wing sympathies. As a result, it was frequently bombed by both sides.

During the late 1960s and early 1970s, Argentine politics descended into chaos. Public anger with the incompetence of the ruling regime exploded: Strikes, political kidnappings, and bank robberies governed the country. Antigovernment guerrilla groups popped up left, leftish, and slightly less to the left, and their members began to abduct and murder government sympathizers—and, sometimes, each other.

When in 1973 the government relaxed its prohibition of the Peronists and Juan Perón returned from exile, huge numbers of people—some accounts say half a million, others double that—traveled out to the airport to greet him, believing that he held the answers to Argentina's desperate plight. At the airport, infighting broke out between his followers and scores were killed.

Perón was elected president, but within nine months of taking office his heart gave out and he died. His widow, Isabelita, assumed the presidency. She was inexperienced and inept. Her advisers, with the police, responded to the disorder by retaliating with kidnappings of their own.

"Buenos Aires became a city roamed by unmarked cars, usually Ford Falcons, supplied on a fleet order to police, but preferred by all for reliability at high speed and relatively low running cost. The cars were parked outside Government House, without a license plate to mar the bumper. They sped through the city ignoring lights; they were feared by the public . . . Inside these cars sat men in dark glasses and half-open shirts, holding machine guns, wearing half a dozen chains around their necks, with Saint Christophers, crucifixes, and Virgin Marys," wrote Andrew Graham-Yooll in his book *A State of Fear*.

Graham-Yooll was news editor of the English-language *Buenos Aires Herald,* one of the only newspapers to dare to report both sides of the political conflict, to attempt to compile a list of the dead of both the left and the right, and to print writs of habeas corpus in the names of those abducted by the security services.

"In a matter of a couple of hours, women lost their men and children; middle-aged couples lost their three sons; a child was left alone; a man aged overnight, his eyes bulged, his cheeks sagged, his hair went dusty gray and brittle, as those he had cared and worked for all his life were torn from his home in the small hours of an ordinary day. Men in masks or without them, shouting or wordless, brutal or polite, destructive or charming, stormed a home and carried away a sought victim, and perhaps one or two others as well, because they were there.

"Whole lifetimes became smothered dreams, destroyed in minutes by murderous nightmares and evil characters out of the most horrifying fantastic literature."

Some parents were so terrified of repercussions, they didn't even make serious efforts to find their children again. Others were too ashamed.

"A middle-aged couple had sworn their children to secrecy about the 'disappearance' of their elder brother. Once a month, the parents wrote a letter to themselves, on blue paper, telling the news of an eldest son who was writing from Spain. They circulated the letter among his aunts, for they could not bear the embarrassment it would mean to the rest of the family to know that one of their nephews had been abducted by the security forces on suspicion of being a member of a guerrilla cell."

The guerrilla war boomed. Inflation spiraled and when the government tried to curb it with devaluation and a limit on wage increases, the unions mustered a general strike. Suffering from nervous exhaustion, Isabelita disappeared increasingly from the public stage. Finally, in March 1976, the army staged a coup, overthrew Isabelita, and replaced her government with a military dictatorship under General Jorge Videla.

Videla's military junta was determined to quash guerrilla resistance. It instigated a "Process of National Reorganization," sometimes called Argentina's Dirty War; its chosen method was the abduction, torture, and "disappearance" of anyone suspected of harboring the slightest sympathy toward the left. Human rights organizations now consider that Videla's government was guilty of the deaths of about thirty thousand people, but nobody knows the figure for sure.

Whatever the exact number, the political landscape soon became enmeshed in a labyrinth of violence. Such was the lust for destruction among both left-wing guerrillas and right-wing paramilitaries that sometimes they targeted the same person simultaneously.

"During my journalistic career, I received countless threats," wrote Jacobo Timerman, former editor of the liberal newspaper *La Opinión,* in his book *Prisoner Without a Name, Cell Without a Number.* "One morning two letters arrived in the same mail: One was from the rightist terrorist organization (protected and utilized by paramilitary groups), condemning me to death because of its belief that my militancy on behalf of the right to trial for anyone arrested and my battle for human rights were hindrances in overthrowing communism; the other letter was from the terrorist Trotskyite group, *Ejército Revolucionario Popular* (ERP)—the Popular Revolutionary Army—and indicated that if I continued accusing leftist revolutionaries of being Fascists and referring to them as the lunatic Left, I would be tried and most likely sentenced to death."

Timerman was subsequently arrested and tortured. He spent two and a half years imprisoned and under house arrest without ever being charged. On his release, he was stripped of his Argentine citizenship (he had lived in Argentina since the age of five) and deported to Israel.

Graham-Yooll, too, was arrested and held very briefly. He subsequently took advantage of his dual British-Argentine citizenship and, six months after the 1976 military coup, he went with his family into exile in London.

I walked away from La Biela and back through the streets of Recoleta. A couple of well-dressed women in their fifties wore expensive-looking sunglasses and carried paper shopping bags containing new clothes wrapped in crisp, crinkling tissue paper. These two would have been in their twenties during the 1970s when those atrocities rent Argentine society. Which side had they been on? I wondered. Or had they tried to have no opinion at all—did they just keep quiet in the hope that they and theirs would stay safe? Did they ever think about it now? Were their dreams ever invaded by nightmarish visions of Ford Falcons harboring murderous men in black?

I was making my way across town now, heading southeast to the Plaza de Mayo. It was Thursday afternoon; at three-thirty, the Madres de la Plaza de Mayo—the women who still campaign for information about the disappearance of their children and demand that the perpetrators be brought to justice—would be making their weekly demonstration outside the Casa Rosada, the pink-painted presidential palace.

As I arrived at the square, I found roads closed, scores of police in riot gear, and police vans barricading the way. But whatever protest had been vented there, it seemed to have finished now. The police were clearing up, stacking their metal barriers and piling them into their vans. Groups of men in navy blue uniforms stood around and chatted with a relaxed, end-of-shift air. Their time up, the last lot of demonstrators had clearly been sent on their way—and nobody seemed to think it necessary to provide security for the Madres de la Plaza de Mayo.

Slowly, the women gathered in small huddles. Most of them were middle-aged or elderly now. Their children had vanished thirty-odd years ago. They would have ended their days, after a period of torture, encased in cement on a muddy riverbed, or perhaps abandoned in the boot of a burned-out car, charred until their corpses were unrecognizable. They were long gone, but their mothers still gathered every Thursday, photographs of their children pinned to their chests, demanding that today's government investigate the crimes of the previous regime.

Memoria. Verdad. Justicia. Memory. Truth. Justice, proclaimed the letters, stark black on white, on one woman's chest. This woman was not so old. She looked as though she might be in her mid-fifties. She had auburn-colored, professionally set hair and large round sunglasses that gaped like the black holes into which so many had vanished. I wondered whether this woman had lost a child—if so, it must have been a tiny mite—or whether, perhaps, a brother or sister had gone. Or perhaps she had just come along to lend her support.

A row of older women paraded behind a long, white banner: "30,000 DESAPARECIDOS," the lettering proclaimed. Thirty thousand disappeared. They shuffled along, wearing over their graying hair matching white head scarves embroidered in blue cross-stitch with the names of the children they had lost. It was a warm spring day; they wore light jackets in herringbone and plaid, or cable-stitched cardigans and light chiffon neck scarves. Behind them, groups of younger men and women strolled, holding flags that asserted their loyalty to this desperate cause.

Sometimes pregnant women had been abducted. Their babies had been born in secret detention centers, taken from their mothers (who had then been murdered), and given to military families. These children grew up in their adoptive worlds knowing nothing of their true origins. Today, an organization called Abuelas de la Plaza de Mayo, Grandmothers of the Plaza de Mayo, is active in searching for those men and women, now in their twenties and thirties, who were abducted as newborns. So far, almost eighty have been reunited with their true families—but the trauma of finding out the circumstances of their birth and adoption must be unbearable.

One woman turned and smiled at me. I was sitting on a bench, on the side of the square. She was a small, round character and wore a chunky, bloodred cardigan. A picture of a girl with dark hair was pinned to her chest. What painful memories had brought this woman here today? Had that daughter really been involved in left-wing guerrilla activities—or had she just been unfortunate, in the wrong place at the wrong time, as had so many of those who disappeared? Was she picked from the street by men in an unmarked car? Or had the security forces come to the house in the dead of night? Had there been a struggle? Had this

mother in her warm, hand-knitted woolly witnessed the abduction of her child? Had she run to the police, to be told
that there was no record of the arrest, then to one of those
rare liberal newspapers—*La Opinión* or the *Buenos Aires
Herald,* perhaps—and wept as she pleaded with the editor to
print her story in the mistaken belief that it might do some
good?

What had her daughter screamed—pleas or promises?—
as she was blindfolded and stripped, tied to a table, doused
with water, and tortured with electric shocks? I remembered Jacobo Timerman's memoir: "At night, the torture
sessions take place, and music is turned on to block out the
cries." I wondered what music, if any, the interrogators had
chosen to accompany the agony of that woman's child.

The mothers chatted amicably among themselves. A
couple of them turned and beamed toward me. They didn't
show any overt bitterness; they appeared rent with neither
anger nor grief. They pottered rather than marched. Their
demonstration had the air of an activity they were squeezing
in between bridge and bingo. I couldn't hear what they
talked about, but the atmosphere of the place suggested it
might have been last night's installment of a soap opera, or
the scandalous fact that Beatriz, daughter of Mario, was
pregnant out of wedlock and that scoundrel from the gas
station was thought to be the father though nobody quite
knew, not even Beatriz herself.

These women seemed resigned; their protest seemed
almost to be an act arising from habit. Yet, still today, members of both the Mothers and the Grandmothers groups are
harassed. Just a few years ago the home of the president
of the Abuelas de la Plaza de Mayo was attacked by gunmen.
The Madres de la Plaza de Mayo have been the victims of

threats to blow up their headquarters. Clearly there are still people out there who don't like them to delve too deep.

In any case, the wider population of Argentina didn't seem to want to be involved. When I mentioned to a couple of people that I'd been down to the square to see the Madres de la Plaza de Mayo, they looked surprised.

"They don't do that anymore, do they?" they asked. And when I said yes, they did, they said, "Oh, they must have started it again." And that was the end of that.

"All that stuff—it's not something we think about very much," one man told me. "We were very small when it happened. We can't remember."

The man was in his early thirties; he would have been born just a couple of years before the disappearances reached their horrific apogee. He would have had friends in that age group now targeted by the Abuelas. What would it be like, I reflected, to look around a gathering of one's peers and wonder: Are any of them not who they think they are? Maybe this man was right. Maybe it was better not to dwell on it too much.

11

Eight Thundering Mounts,
Two Stuffed Steeds,
and a Virgin Who Was Teeny Tiny

Luján is Argentina's most important pilgrimage site: In 1630, a statue of the Virgin was being transported through the town on its way to Santiago del Estero when the cart it was traveling in stuck fast in the ground between two churches. The statue's owner took this as a sign that the Virgin had decided she'd like to set up home here, so he built her a chapel and here she remained. Now, five million devotees come to pray to her each year.

I was setting out on a rather different pilgrimage, though, as I climbed onto the bus the next day to travel to this town that lies forty miles west of Buenos Aires. In keeping with the equine theme of my journey, the objects of my devotion were not religious relics but a couple of embalmed, rather moth-eaten steeds who stood on display in the town's Transport Museum. I was going to visit the two most famous criollo horses of all time: Gato and Mancha were the companions of Aimé Tschiffely, who, in the 1920s, made one of the most extraordinary equestrian expeditions ever.

Tschiffely was Swiss by birth, but he lived in Argentina and worked as a teacher at St. George's, one of the top boys' schools in Buenos Aires. (Robin Begg's grandfather had been a pupil of Tschiffely's and one of his textbooks, which Robin kept at Los Potreros, was embellished in a margin with a cartoon drawn and signed by the teacher.) After several years confined to the classroom and the antics of teenage boys, Tschiffely decided to throw in the chalk and to see if the company of horses would prove any more amenable. He would endeavor, he proclaimed, to ride ten thousand miles from Buenos Aires to Washington, D.C., with two Argentine criollos.

Everyone told Tschiffely that he was mad, that he could never make the distance. "I felt strongly tempted to quote to them the saying, 'Let fools laugh; wise men dare and win,' but a doubt assailed me as to which of us was really the fool, so I refrained," he wrote in his subsequent account, *Tschiffely's Ride*.

Tschiffely successfully completed his journey and arrived in Washington after two and a half years in the saddle. He had crossed mountain ranges and deserts; he'd encountered tribesmen and ambassadors; he'd slept in sleazy, rundown villages and lofty historic cities whose finer establishments had at first turned him away because he looked such an unholy mess. Clearly, Tschiffely was a man of great courage and determination. But above his own adventuring spirit, Tschiffely credited his achievement to the incredible resilience of his two criollo horses.

"Great were my feelings of relief when we left the Matacaballo desert behind us and, in spite of my already high opinion of the horses' resistance, I admired the splendid behavior they had shown during so long and trying a journey—a journey that would have killed most horses unaccustomed to such conditions," Tschiffely wrote of crossing the ferocious Peruvian desert that the locals called the "Horsekiller." The trio had crossed this arid wasteland in a single twenty-hour journey; convinced that the burden of carrying water would hinder the horses more than their own thirst, Tschiffely had taken no refreshment for the animals and had carried just a tiny ration of lemon juice for himself.

After their long, long ride, Tschiffely and his horses returned by ship to Buenos Aires and, from there, Gato and Mancha retired to live out the rest of their days peacefully munching grass on an estancia in the pampas.

Tschiffely himself never returned to the classrooms of St. George's; instead, he went to live in London when his equestrian journey was complete. He took up writing full-time and became a sought-after fixture on the 1920s London lecture circuit. Then, more than ten years after his initial odyssey, Tschiffely returned to Argentina with the intention of traveling around Patagonia—this time by car. Before he headed south, though, he stopped off at the estancia that was now Gato and Mancha's home. He recorded his reunion with the two criollos in his book *This Way Southward*:

"Within the circle of stout posts I at once recognized my horses' familiar forms and colors. Although still some fifty yards away, I shouted: 'Mancha, Gato!' Immediately both turned around and stared at me, their heads held high, ears pricked up, and nostrils dilated . . . I spoke to the animals, and they slowly came toward me. When I touched Mancha's broad forehead, both sniffed me all over."

Many years had passed, but Tschiffely's horses had never

forgotten the man with whom they had traveled ten thousand miles—and I was both intrigued by and delighted at the prospect of meeting them myself.

I arrived at the bus stop and walked the few hundred yards to the town square where the ticket office was situated.

"Sorry, the Transport Museum is closed," said the ticket-selling woman from her tiny kiosk.

"Closed? Until when?" I fervently hoped the curator had just trotted out for a coffee, or perhaps an early lunch.

"For at least a couple of weeks. They're preparing the carriages for a procession."

I was aghast. I'd trekked all the way out here especially to see Gato and Mancha; in a couple of weeks I'd be hundreds of miles away. There was no chance I could return. I explained all this to the woman behind the counter and she tutted with sympathy.

"Well, why don't you go next door to the police station and explain that to them. Maybe they can let you in."

I'd had no idea that the police wielded such power over the museum world, but I did as the woman suggested. I explained my situation to a mustachioed officer at the door who took me through to a back office. There I related my tale once more to two round, perfectly permed women who perched behind their desks like fluffed-up pom-poms.

"No problem at all!" said the woollier of the two women. She swept the telephone receiver up from its cradle, jabbered a few words, and instructed the policeman to escort me back across the street to the museum. "And while you're there," she called after me, "make sure you go to the library, where they have a lot of information about Gato and Mancha."

The policeman and I walked back toward the museum, which fronted onto the adjacent side of the plaza; I muttered effusive thanks. The formerly impenetrable wooden door to the museum swung magically open and a genial, gray-haired caretaker escorted me inside. We walked past rows of ornate carriages, a gleaming railway engine, and several lines of very cranky-looking cars. And then, at the far end of the very furthest room, we came to Tschiffely's noble steeds.

To be truthful, they looked slightly out of sorts—and very out of place. Their surroundings didn't sing of their heroic deeds. It perhaps didn't help that the museum was closed, but it seemed to me to be a lackluster sort of place (though one with an immensely kind staff). It didn't seem right that these two horses, even in death, should be enclosed in a glass box in this characterless rectangular room with its dull concrete floor, and that they should be surrounded by, of all things, motorcars.

"I grew to hate automobiles," wrote Tschiffely; "the drivers showed very little consideration for me and seemed to delight in seeing the horses rear and plunge when they passed us. They were my pet aversion from the beginning of the trip to the end, and if all my wishes had been carried out, Hades would be well supplied with motors and motorists."

Some years after he wrote *Tschiffely's Ride,* Aimé Tschiffely penned a second memoir about his journey, *The Tale of Two Horses*—but this time the story was told from Gato and Mancha's point of view.

"If it hadn't been for thousands of speeding cars, we might have enjoyed ourselves," narrates Mancha toward the end of the story, as the trio rides through the United States. "Oh, how I hated some of those nasty motorists!"

The horses' wide eyes stared glassily from the box at the automobiles that now surrounded them. Their ears pointed high and perky; their coats lay laced with the patchwork stitches of a taxidermist's needle. On their backs, saddles and packs spoke of their journey. Gato and Mancha were aged thirty-six and forty when they finally turned up their hooves and trotted off to the equine heaven where the grass is always lush and the horse forever young—Gato died in 1944 and Mancha on Christmas Day in 1947. Given the time that had passed, they weren't actually as mangy as I'd expected (though I later discovered the pair had been treated to a little "restoration" in the 1980s). But they were rigid and static in their box. They stood stock-still with no suggestion of so much as a whinny between them. It seemed a sad end, somehow, for those doughty horses who had shown such spirit in traveling so far.

I left the museum. A few doorways down there was affixed a plaque inscribed with the word *"Biblioteca."* This was the library. I rang on the bell and waited. After some delay, the door creaked open and there stood an astonishingly tiny old lady. The hallway that squeezed behind the door was tight and thin, its walls covered in white Formica shelving that was packed with piles of old papers. The minuscule woman directed me to the right, up a narrow staircase, and into a room on the left where a small collection of books lined the walls.

"Take a seat here." The librarian gestured toward a brown plastic chair at a beige melamine table. "I'll get you the papers about the horses."

She tottered into an adjacent room and returned a minute or two later with two folders piled high with documents of all manner of shapes. There were newspaper cuttings, letters, and, perhaps most interesting of all, the original correspondence relating to the horses' preservation.

When Tschiffely returned from the United States, he gave the horses back to Dr. Emilio Solanet, the man who found Gato and Mancha for him in the first place and owned Estancia Cardal, where they would live out their days. Some years later, in 1933, it was suggested to Solanet that the horses' fame and popularity were still such that the public might be interested in seeing them preserved after their deaths and kept as museum exhibits.

"Posiblemene serán suficientes los cueros (y los cascos?)" Will the hides (and the skulls) be enough? Solanet wrote in elegant cursive script to the taxidermist. "In which case, it would be easier to send you the hides dried and conditioned in the normal way we'd treat any other hide . . . skinned and put out to air twenty-four hours after death and then sent, well salted, either to you or to whomever you instruct."

Many years elapsed. Then there was a telegram, sent on February 18, 1944, from Solanet to Dr. Enrique Udaondo, the director of the Museo Colonial e Histórico de la Provincia de Buenos Aires.

"Ha muerto el caballo criollo Gato Cardal que hizo raid B Aires Nueva York con Tschiffely. Tengo el cuero preparado para enviar al taxidermista que Vd me diga ateniendome a lo convenido en el año 1933." The criollo horse Gato Cardal who made the journey B Aires New York with Tschiffely has died. I have the hide ready to send to whichever taxidermist you indicate as agreed in 1933.

And so the horses were stuffed.

The rest of their remains were buried on Solanet's estancia—and, finally, in 1998, Tschiffely's ashes came to join them. Tschiffely had died some years earlier at Mile End

Hospital in London—he turned up his own hooves in 1954—and his ashes had subsequently been interred at Buenos Aires' Recoleta Cemetery. But in the 1990s a letter from Tschiffely's widow was discovered at the Estancia Cardal, which was still in the hands of Solanet's family. The letter explained that Tschiffely had wished his ashes to be buried alongside those of his horses, and so the casket containing the horseman's remains was taken from its Recoleta vault and escorted to the pampas. Now Tschiffely and his horses together enjoy the abundant grass—from a few feet under.

I left the library and crossed the square to the basilica. I wasn't planning to come back to Luján any time soon, so, while I was here, I thought I had better pay a visit to the Virgin. She'd worked plenty of miracles in her time, and I had to consider that it might be wise to keep on good terms with her.

The basilica was a glorious, lofty edifice. Built in 1887 from light ashlar, it was constructed in neo-Gothic style— inspired, apparently, by Notre Dame in Paris. Two magnificent spires whirled toward the heavens. They were so tall that they seemed almost to disappear into the skies themselves. They seemed to me like an ornate stone dual carriageway that shot high into the ether, its sides ever converging in the eyes of us mere earthlings until, finally, it disappeared into a celestial vanishing point.

I ventured through the imposing doorway and made my way down the wide, monumental nave. At the end of this walkway, just in front of the altar, a small troupe of worshippers gathered around a priest. They seemed to be greatly in awe of something rather small that stood just before the altar. I couldn't see what they were looking at, so tentatively I squeezed round the side of the group to have a closer look. There, behind them, was a very, very tiny statue. At first I thought this must just be a replica of the Virgin—but if that was the case, why were they attending to her with such reverence?

"Touch her dress! Touch her dress!" a matronly woman hissed at her son, who was aged about nine. The boy's face screwed up in an expression of panic mixed with distaste. "Go on! Touch her!" The mother gave him a shove in the direction of the effigy. He whipped out his hand, poked at the blue mantle with one squeamish finger, and hastily retreated.

So this was the Virgin! She was *minuscule*. This statue that attracted five million devoted worshippers each year, this patron saint of Argentina, was not just averagely small. She was *tiny*. She was the merest slip of a thing. She was a snip, she was a wisp. She was—and I apologize for the blasphemous comparison—not much taller than a Barbie.

The devotees congregated more closely around the priest now. He was holding some kind of water-filled holey contraption and as he walked down the nave among them, he flicked his wrist so that the liquid sprayed them lightly. The crowd surged around him, pressing closer, desperate to be anointed. As for me, well, I'm afraid I've long harbored an irrational fear of religious pageantry, and so I ran away.

The following afternoon the inaugural fixtures of the Argentine Open polo tournament were scheduled. Polo is an ancient sport—it's thought to have originated in either

China or Persia more than two thousand years ago. It's reckoned to be the oldest organized ball game in the world, though how it can be that people thought of bashing a ball with a stick from the back of a galloping horse before they thought about kicking one around with their own two feet beats me. Anyway, as the Moguls and their horses swept through the Indian subcontinent in the 1500s they took the game with them, and it was in India that the British learned the sport: army officers and tea planters first swung their sticks there in the 1850s. They introduced the game to England, and English expatriates in turn brought it to Argentina; the first official polo match was played on Argentine soil on September 3, 1875. But since then the Argentines with their wide open spaces and great affinity for all things equine have far surpassed all other nations at polo—and at the Argentine Open, the very best players in the world take to the turf.

Given the great popularity of polo in Argentina and the tremendous prestige which the Argentine Open commands, I was concerned as to whether I'd be able to buy a ticket easily. There was something about the awe in which the tournament is held in the polo world that suggested to me I would only get in if I sidled up to a sponsor, or perhaps canoodled a groom. I'd therefore asked several people how I should go about it.

"Oh, just turn up and buy a ticket at the door," they'd said. I'd talked on the phone to Tomás, whom I had met at El Molino in Cachi—he who had professed his love of *The Sound of Music* to the unhappy Austrian. I was planning to meet him and his wife, Agustina, for dinner after the polo, and he had offered some words of advice.

"The best place to sit is the Dorrego Central. That's

where all the young people go. It's much livelier than the other stands."

And so I rolled up at the Palermo polo ground at about three o'clock. I stood in a short line before the ticket booth and bought my ticket for the Dorrego Central for the grand sum of ten pesos and, by ten past three, I was in.

The second game of the day was going to be the big one—Indios Chapaleufú versus La Mariana—but it didn't start in the main stadium till four o'clock. So I wandered around the ground for a while and checked out the white marquees that sold saddles and sticks and baseball caps. I wandered onto the sidelines of the second, outside pitch, where an earlier match was under way. And then, at five to four, I took my place on the wide concrete step of my allotted stand.

My fellow spectators seemed to be a cordial, gentle bunch, a mixture of men and women of all ages. Some chatted into cell phones; others called out, waving, and greeted friends. Surrounded by such good cheer I sat happily soaking in the scene and admiring the dazzling deep green of the lawn that unfurled before me.

Unveiled for its first match of the tournament, the pitch shimmered in velvety perfection. It was mown in rigid stripes like the Regency wallpaper that might, perhaps, have adorned the high-class drawing rooms of those earliest players. Each blade was cropped to uniform height; neither buttercup nor daisy dared flaunt its colors among them. It was the kind of lawn that would usually sport little notices forbidding one to walk on the grass. It seemed unthinkable that, any moment now, a horde of eight horses would gallop wantonly across it and sully this pure, impeccable canvas with churned-up earthen clods. I wondered whether the groundsman was among us today, whether he had stayed to watch the destruction of his backbreaking labor—or whether he had taken refuge somewhere private, to be haunted by the heavy drumroll of hooves.

Then the players rode onto the field to warm up—and the divots flew from my mind. These men seemed effortlessly graceful as they cantered smoothly in their tight white jodhpurs and team-colored tops. Their horses were beautiful creatures. Their muscles rippled; their coats quite literally gleamed. Their lower legs were bandaged in their respective team colors and their tails were tied up into stiff little bunches.

The match began, and the tempo increased. Now these modern-day warriors hurtled up and down the pitch like dashing knights in days of old. Brandishing sticks instead of swords and with polished leather knee pads for armor, they hurled themselves into combat, jousting fearlessly against their foe. Their horses thundered beneath them like the steeds of a charging cavalry brigade, leaving in their wake a trail of dusty little powder puffs. The noise was terrific: a sonorous booming shook the stands as the animals' hooves smashed into the ground again and again.

Just yards away from me one of the La Mariana boys galloped in gallant pursuit of his opponent. His horse's legs curled tight underneath its belly as it launched itself powerfully from the ground. For a fraction of a second, the horse seemed to soar through the air. And then once more its rear hooves slammed into the trembling earth, then stretched backward as the front hooves pounded down. Its gluteal muscles bulged and heaved, and at breakneck speed the horse propelled its rider toward his grail.

The players whipped their sticks around in dexterous circles, elegantly clipping the ball so that it glided in a faultless arc. When the other team took possession, the riders spun their horses as though on a five-centavo bit and careered off once more.

I remembered my own efforts at playing polo with Pepino all those weeks ago at Robin's estancia: my fumbling attempts to clout the ball so that it moved a yard or two, the aching in my wrist from raising the stick just to hip height, my walking-pace goal which had left me so euphoric. My efforts had been light-years away from this.

Leaning out of the saddle, these professionals executed superhuman backhand swipes that I knew for certain would dislocate my own joints if I tried them. They rode off each other with breathtaking strength and speed. As two bold combatants pressed against one another, flank to galloping flank, I noticed that the Chapaleufú player was leaning so far forward out of his saddle that his legs were no longer anchoring him at all. His thighs pointed directly downward, and his knees were bent so that his lower legs lay horizontally, just perched on top of the horse's spine—and he was positioned like this while scorching along at a full gallop, piling the entire weight of his horse against the heaving rump of his opponent's. And still he didn't fall off.

Maybe such skill lay in these men's genes. Looking at the sports section of that morning's newspaper, I had discovered that polo is a clannish pursuit. Most of the members of each team seemed to have the same noble blood coursing through their veins: Of the Chapaleufú team that I was watching now, three out of four players shared the surname Heguy. Chapaleufú also had a B team, and three of its four members were Heguys too. It didn't take much to figure out what the Heguy family must talk about over Sunday lunch.

The La Mariana team enjoyed a similar familial bond: Three of their players were called Merlos. And the La

Aguada team that I had briefly seen playing on the outside
pitch earlier consisted entirely of the Novillo Estrada family.
I wondered what would happen if some poor boy were born
into one of these firmly entrenched polo families and discovered a deep-rooted desire to become, say, an accountant
or an architect. Or a ballet dancer. What would they do to
him? Disown him? Or simply strap him to a galloping horse
and send him off over the horizon, never to be seen again?

Back in the Dorrego Central stand, the battle was reaching its climax. By the beginning of the last chukka the score
was dead even—14–14—and tension was running high:
The crowd wanted Indios Chapaleufú to win. Then, with
one minute to go, Chapaleufú scored. Their fans went wild,
screeching with jubilation—and then, moments later, disaster struck. With just fifteen seconds left on the clock, La
Mariana was awarded a penalty.

The disapproving whistles of the onlookers cut through
the stadium like the screams of a damsel in distress. The La
Mariana player lined up and took his free shot—and missed!
The crowd roared with delirious delight. The whistle blew.
Indios Chapaleufú had won.

12

Before a Fall

At **Iguazú's airport** elderly vacationers struggled with suitcases so large that, had one slotted three or four of them together, an undemanding family of four could quite possibly have set up home inside. Of course, what with their hernias and bad backs, these white-haired folk couldn't actually lift their luggage, not even when wearing sensible soft-soled shoes. And so they dragged their reinforced, steel-plated blocks off the carousel and hauled them on wheels toward the exit, gaily bashing themselves, crashing into one another, and generally bludgeoning any poor fool who ventured within striking distance. Going on vacation, I reflected, must constitute a serious threat to these people's health.

I was now in real tourist land. The morning following the polo match I'd flown up to Iguazú in the far northeast where, amid torrid jungle and lashing white waterfalls, the Argentine border meets Brazil and Paraguay. The Iguazú falls are one of Argentina's most spectacular attractions and are rewarded with a place on every sightseer's agenda. I wasn't just planning to visit the falls, though; I was intending to spend a few days up here so that I could travel deeper into the province of Misiones and see the ruins of two of the mission settlements that the Jesuits had built in the seventeenth century.

On this first day, though, I visited none of these wonders because, by the time I had escaped death-by-Samsonite in the airport arrivals hall and fled to my hostel in the tiny, sleepy town of Puerto Iguazú, there wasn't a lot of the day left. Still, Puerto Iguazú seemed a charming little place. All the package tourists were securely stowed in the big, brash hotels on the road to the falls, leaving the town itself laid-back and quaint.

It was a one-story kind of place. Tiny restaurants and *pensiones* straddled the rust red road; the rich ocher of the soil contrasted dramatically with the vibrant emerald of the trees whose leaves glowed almost luminous beneath the fierce subtropical sun. I wandered for an hour or so in an idle, Sunday afternoon way along the rough cobbled roads and a short distance out of the village. There the settlement's sleepy overtures to civilization were riotously outbid and the jungle ruled, a luxuriant forest of abundant green.

I strolled back into town past shops selling trinkets—T-shirts, balsa-wood toucans, and pottery figurines of gauchos sipping maté. Occasionally, a flat-faced bus painted yellow, red, and blue loped by smearing brash shocks of color onto this already florid scene. A few thirsty souls sat and sipped chilled beer at plastic tables under a white awning adorned with red cursive lettering: *"Pizzas. Hamburguesería. Pastas."* I was warm after my walk in the searing sun, and I sat down to join them.

Nervous of the battering I might have to endure in the line for the National Park the next morning, I got up at six-thirty, left my hostel shortly after seven, and by seven-twenty-five was safely on the first bus of the day to the falls. When the gates swung open at eight—the time at which most of the tour groups would just have been tucking into their eggs and bacon—I bought my ticket and climbed onto a little open-sided train that would ferry me to the top of the biggest cataract of them all, the Garganta del Diablo, the Devil's Throat.

Despite the early hour, the train was full. Sitting opposite me was a Japanese couple. She wore a sun hat and white cotton gloves. He wore a black T-shirt across which was emblazoned in silver capitals: "IT'S BETTER TO BURN OUT THAN TO FADE AWAY."

This man appeared to take his hyperactive logo seriously. He hopped up and down with his Handycam, leaning precariously out of the train as he filmed his wife, who sat stoic and expressionless, ignoring him entirely. I rather suspected that she was hoping her husband and his Handycam might fall out of the train and together meet their demise in a single labor-saving moment.

Several minutes of footage later, we reached the end of the line and all ambled at the speed of the shortest-legged shuffler down the narrow wooden walkways leading to the viewing platform that looked down on the upper lip of the cataracts.

Iguazú means "big waters" in the Guaraní language (the Guaraní are the tribe indigenous to this area). Their legend has it that the falls were created by the rage of a river god:

The god had been promised the sacrifice of a girl, Naipi. Naipi, however, fell in love with a local tribesman, Caroba, and the couple attempted to elope so as to avoid Naipi's horrible fate. The river god was livid. In a fit of jealousy, he collapsed the riverbed along which the lovers were escaping. Naipi tumbled over the edge and became a rock at the foot of the falls while Caroba was transformed into a tree at its head.

I wondered which tree, and which rock, were meant to represent the lovers. There seemed to be a lot to choose from.

Whichever they were, they certainly seemed to have incensed the river god, if the temper of the cascades was anything to judge by. The water pranced in furious currents down the river toward the two-tiered precipice. As it tumbled down the first step, it became angry, turbulent, and frothy. By the time the choppy whiteness rocketed over the final cliff edge and plunged sixty-five feet to the pool below, it had been transformed into a frenzied, bubbling, ear-splitting storm. As it smashed into the water beneath, huge clouds of spray ricocheted back up into the air, obscuring the view, so that the cascade appeared to plummet into a bottomless pit.

The water roared and crashed; it seethed and churned. It hammered, buffeted, pummelled, and trounced. These falls are bigger than Niagara's. On average, the water flows here at a deafening 1.8 million liters (or about 500,000 gallons) per second. An ordinary bathroom shower runs at about 0.1 liters per second—which meant that the water careering off these cliffs in front of me was equivalent to *eighteen million* people taking a shower all at once. That's roughly the same as the entire population of Australia taking a shower, all together, on this very precipice. (It's better, I find, not to imagine them naked, nor indeed to contemplate the terrible consequences of dropping the soap.) And that's just on an average day. When these cataracts are really chucking it down, the water cascades at nearly four times those levels.

I left the viewing platform and walked from the summit of the Garganta del Diablo down to the Circuito Superior. The rough pathway was far removed from the bustling train and the crowded wooden walkways. During the whole of my half-hour stroll, I saw only a handful of people.

Fat, lazy lizards dragged their copious bellies across the hot, red dirt. Butterflies with wings like saucers swooped dizzily about my head. Some were yellow with striking black stripes, others were tiny white-and-brown creatures that circled in swarms. The birds in the trees cackled and chattered like a gathering of football rattles. Insects hummed. Ants as long as my thumb scuttled through the soil, sleek and bulbous like strings of shiny black baubles.

I arrived at the Circuito Superior, the upper circuit— another arrangement of boardwalks that gave views of the falls from a different perspective—and then walked around the lower circuit. This last was the best route by far. Steep steps weaved down the hillside and, from below, the sight was more sensational still. The Garganta del Diablo lay to the left now, and as the cascading water hit the pool below it created great frothing waves above which hung many yards of fine eddying mist. And above that, the most awe-inspiring vision of all—an explosive mass of somersaulting, cartwheeling white.

Parts of the film *The Mission* were made here at the Iguazú falls. In the opening scene, a Jesuit tied to a cross is sent plummeting to his death over the drop. The director of the film, Roland Joffé, originally wanted to use genuine

Guaraní tribespeople as actors on his set. He traveled to this part of Argentina in an attempt to search out the remaining Guaraní, but found the tribe decimated and its culture largely lost. He therefore ended up filming with the Colombian Waunana people, who still live largely according to their old customs. Interestingly, when he first suggested to the Waunana that they might work with him to make his movie, he and his colleagues had to explain to some members of the tribe the very concept of make-believe. The Waunana had no theater in their tribal tradition and, though they sometimes watched television, they considered most of what they saw to be true. Would any of them be killed during the filming process? they asked with great concern. Only when they had been reassured that the blood would be shed by a bottle did they consent to take part.

But there were no special effects in force at Iguazú today. This pounding hydropower was quite staggeringly real. I stood and stared at it for a long, long time. And then, just to make sure I had seen these falls from every possible angle, I took a ride in a jet boat into the tumbling waters themselves. It was very fast, very wet, and an awful lot of fun.

The National Park in which the cataracts thunder is famous not only for its waterfalls but also for its range of wildlife and vegetation, so, after lunch, I headed out on its nature trail. I had high hopes of seeing monkeys swinging between the trees and perhaps a brightly colored toucan or two.

I asked for directions at a kiosk and was handed a safety leaflet.

"*Señor Visitante,*" Mr. Visitor, the leaflet began, "In the

Iguazú National Park there reside some species of animal
that are potentially dangerous to humans."

Slightly alarmed, I read on.

"For your security, we ask that you:

—never let children wander more than a few yards
from you

—avoid walking alone."

(Oh dear. I had broken a rule already, then.)

"—don't feed the wild animals

—don't come to the park with your pet."

The leaflet went on with a recommendation not to stick
one's hands down holes where snakes might be hanging out,
and instructions on how to react to a meeting with a puma
or a jaguar.

"If the animal is aggressive:

—do all you can to appear larger than it is

—do not squat down or pretend to be dead

—if the animal attacks, push it firmly backward."

Push it firmly backward? At which point of the attack, exactly, should you start to push? Before or after the hungry
feline has sunk its pointy teeth into your sweet, soft flesh?
And then, the final straw:

"IMPORTANT: In all cases, inform the park ranger
where you saw the cat, and tell him how your encounter
went."

To be honest, this leaflet rather spoiled my walk. I am
generally a law-abiding person and I was upset to have broken the "do not walk alone" rule so early in proceedings. The
path was deserted—all those people on the Garganta del
Diablo boardwalk clearly hadn't scheduled a jungle stroll
into their itineraries—and no sooner was I out of screaming
distance of civilization than my nerves began to play tricks
on me. That crunch in the undergrowth—was it a foraging

coati, or a jaguar preparing to pounce? That crackle of twigs—had a toucan lost its footing, or was a snake sidling down to ensnare me? While one part of me longed to peer through the foliage to see which exotic creature stumbled about within, there was another part of me that just wanted to run out of there as fast as my sneakers would carry me.

In the end, I didn't spy any very interesting wildlife on my jungle walk. I saw several fat black lizards with speckled white backs. One of them was so surprised to see me that it almost leaped out of its skin when I came mooching along. But in general, it seemed, the jungle creatures were either asleep or in hiding that afternoon, so after an hour or so—at which point I became rather hot and keen for a snooze myself—I turned back and headed for town.

I ate in a delightful restaurant that evening. I really loved the Argentine way of eating, I decided as I was served approximately half a cow with fries and a small bottle of Malbec. I wasn't eating beef every day, but when I did it was unfailingly spectacular—and this meal would cost me the same as I'd pay for take-out fish and chips at home. In the background, '80s tunes crooned out of the stereo—Survivor singing "Eye of the Tiger" (but would they have survived the teeth of a jaguar, that's what I wanted to know), Queen, Supertramp, and Men at Work. I finished about half of my steak, drank my wine, then sat back contentedly with a chamomile tea and worried about the fact that I knew all the lyrics.

13

The Missionary Position

"**Hello, may I help you?**" asked the very friendly English-language welcome screen of the cash machine in Posadas. "Please dip your card in and then take it out so we can begin."

I'd taken the six-hour bus ride along the straight, well-surfaced road that cut through the vibrant green jungle to Posadas from Puerto Iguazú. The bus's conductor, that day, had gone for a curious selection of onboard film: We were accompanied for the last section of the journey by a screening of Mel Gibson's controversial *The Passion of the Christ*. Even if we chose not to look (and a quick survey of the passengers revealed that almost all of them had averted their wincing eyes), we couldn't help but hear the whistling whips cracking against flesh and the martyred moans of Jesus that seemed to echo round the bus for hours.

Maybe the idea was to get us all into a good Christian

frame of mind, for Posadas is the nearest big town to San Ignacio Miní and Santa Ana, two of the principal mission ruins, and it was to visit these remains that I had come here. Still, I wasn't sure that all this flagellation was really in the spirit of things, for the Jesuit missions are generally reckoned to have been veritable havens for their Guaraní converts during a period of aggressive slave-hunting by the priests' fellow Europeans.

I spent the night in Posadas, a pleasant but dull town on the banks of the river Paraná, which forms the border between Argentina and Paraguay.

"I used to work for the bus company in the 1960s and '70s," the taxi driver who ferried me from the bus station to my hotel revealed. "Back then, the road to Iguazú was dirt all the way. The journey used to take twelve hours—and that was when we were running to schedule. When the weather was wet, though, the road just turned to swamps of red mud and then it took us forever to get through. One time, it took us twenty-four hours to get there."

I wondered what it must have been like for the Jesuits who settled here in the seventeenth century. Then there would have been no road at all, just thick, impenetrable jungle. The only real thoroughfare would have been the river.

I checked into my hotel, then went to drink a beer at a waterside bar. This part of town seemed to have been newly renovated; concrete walkways were planted with palm trees at regular intervals. As evening fell, the sky turned from its earlier royal blue to a paler hue, then became electric in intensity before darkening to a deep navy. The river rippled with the reflections of lights that twinkled on the Paraguayan bank. It was hard to imagine Guaraní and Jesuits negotiating this waterway by raft and boat.

The following morning I left my luggage at the Posadas bus station—I'd decided to spend more time here in the northeast than I'd initially planned but had been unable to change the date of my return flight to BA, so I'd abandoned my air ticket and settled instead for the overnight bus. That wouldn't leave until seven-thirty in the evening, so in the meantime I had the whole day in which to investigate the mission ruins.

My first port of call would be San Ignacio Miní—to get there I needed to find transport to the village of San Ignacio. The terminal was a maze of ramps and staircases, with corridors branching out over two stories.

"Just go into that office there." A taxi driver gestured when I asked him if he knew which companies served my destination.

I did as he suggested. "What time does the next bus leave for San Ignacio?" I asked the woman behind the counter. It was then just before ten o'clock.

She stared at me with an expression that implied I had asked for the next rocket to Mars, then slowly shook her head.

"We don't go *there,*" she said.

I tried another office across the way. The woman behind this second desk was considerably more chipper.

"We have a bus going to San Ignacio at ten-thirty," she chirruped, "but you need to buy your ticket at the office up-stairs."

I trudged upstairs. I peered to the left and to the right, but I couldn't find an office that fitted her description. Weary now, I asked at another of the kiosks.

"The bus is right there!" bellowed the man in the kiosk. *"Look!"* He rushed out from behind his desk and jabbed his finger excitedly at the bus bays below. *"Run!"* he yelped. *"Run quickly, and you'll catch it!"*

I ran. I galloped frantically down the ramps, tore down the staircases, and careered along the concrete corridors until, finally, I arrived breathless at the bus bay.

"Oh no," said the bus driver. "This bus doesn't go to San Ignacio. We're going in the opposite direction—to Resistencia."

I dragged myself back upstairs and, this time, managed to locate the ticket office. The ten-thirty bus didn't exist, said the sage behind the counter, so I'd have to wait till eleven. The ten o'clock bus, on the other hand, had been sitting in its bay all along but due to my ludicrous running around I'd missed it.

When the bus finally rolled up at eleven, I found I had been allocated a seat next to an outrageously smelly man. His face was drawn and pallid. He appeared to be traveling, too—he had long, raggedy hair and filthy ripped jeans, and looked as though he had washed neither body nor clothes in at least a year. What's more, he was a fidgeter, and his every action—putting on his sweater, getting out his map, preparing his maté—seemed to involve wafting his pestilent armpit in my face.

I was happy, therefore, when the bus finally arrived in San Ignacio even though the village turned out to be a run-down, two-street little place. Dusty, doleful children asked for coins. A few optimistic souls sat on the concrete step outside the church where the buses stopped, and waited for transport out of there. Other than that, there was nobody about. It was as though the town had been evacuated and these few unfortunates were the final stragglers waiting for the last bus to spirit them to a more fruitful land.

I made my way to the ruins of San Ignacio Miní. Outside the mission's walls a row of forlorn-looking stallholders displayed faded postcards and tatty souvenirs. There were very few tourists; nobody seemed much interested in their wares. And then I went through the gateway to the mission settlement, and my spirits soared.

Nearly two hundred and fifty years have passed since the Jesuits were expelled from what is now Argentina (the country didn't exist with its present borders until the nineteenth century), and after they left, their heritage fell into ruin. But still, so many years later, this land on which the priests and Guaraní worked and prayed radiated a strange serenity. The contrast between the world inside the mission walls and the ramshackle, depressing village outside was astonishing. The modern-day settlement ought to have been the livelier by far—after all, it was inhabited by real flesh-and-blood folk—but, bizarrely, the village seemed to be the place that had died while the mission grounds sang with a silent vitality.

The red sandstone buildings had crumbled long ago (most of what little stood was a reconstruction) but the large central lawn was well tended. Over one side of the grassy expanse towered the ruins of a huge, terra-cotta-colored church. Its tumbledown facade was impressively ornate. An intricately winged angel presided over columns topped by an elaborate cornicing of curling leaves. Below, a smooth stone plaque had been inserted on which, beneath a crown and between two unfurling feathers, were intertwined the letters A and M.

The spacious interior of this church would once have

resonated with Ave Marias; now, the sweet chirping of birds took the place of human song. But curiously, despite the fact that the place was in ruins, the graceful atmosphere of the church and its surrounding rooms—the library, the priests' quarters—suggested that those men of the cloth had only temporarily stepped out. The remains of the Jesuits who had died at the mission lay entombed in stone sepulchres at the head of the church, but their ghosts seemed still to roam free in this small haven from the world, and to infuse it with their spirit.

Historical accounts relate that the Jesuit missions were harmonious, humane places. Even those who disapprove of the missionary concept would have to concede that these religious establishments offered the Guaraní a sanctuary from an evil more odious by far. Portuguese slave hunters, or *bandeirantes,* were active in this area; indeed, the *bandeirantes* of São Paulo raided the original Jesuit settlements in the 1630s, carrying off most of their inhabitants, and the Jesuits and remaining Guaraní were forced to escape by raft down the perilous Paraná river to rebuild their missions farther west.

These missions, while disciplined, threatened with none of the horrors of life outside their walls. The Guaraní, therefore, arrived of their own volition—and they came in their thousands. At its peak in the 1730s San Ignacio Miní had a population of a little under four thousand; all the missions in this area combined—there were thirty of them—are reckoned to have housed nearly sixty thousand people.

The Jesuits and the Guaraní lived communally. Their principal income came from agriculture: the dominant crop was *yerba mate,* but they grew cotton and tobacco, too, and raised livestock. According to the historian David Rock in his book *Argentina 1516–1982,* the San Ignacio Miní mission possessed in 1768 three thousand sheep, seventeen thousand cattle, eight hundred oxen, seven *yerba mate* plantations, and around eighty thousand cotton plants. This strong farming base, and the system of organized labor instigated by the Jesuits, meant that not everyone had to till the land. Some women worked in textiles and handicrafts; men could train as masons, scribes, and musicians.

"A few days ago, musicians from the nearby Yapeyú settlement performed for us . . . They sang vespers, the mass, and litanies as well as some canticles, all in such a way and with such art and grace that, if you had not seen them, you would believe that these musicians had come from India or from one of the best cities in Europe," wrote Father Strobel, a priest recently arrived in South America, to a fellow priest in Austria in June 1729. Presumably Father Strobel was partisan in his views but, nonetheless, his descriptions of the Indians' devotion to the Jesuits are striking:

"The honesty and extreme piety of the Christian Indians can hardly be exaggerated . . . Their innocence, their fear of God, and their sanctity so light up their faces that just looking at them lifts our spirits and fills us with abounding joy."

The surplus of labor meant that the missions were also able to create sizeable militias. Following the raids of the early 1600s, the Jesuits established fighting units to protect their settlements from further attacks and it was, in part, the existence of these armies that spelled the missions' downfall.

The Jesuit armies were the strongest military force in the region; their enemies were able to add military threat to the long list of complaints they had against the order. Foremost among these gripes was the resentment that many of the Spanish and Portuguese colonialists harbored over Jesuit wealth and influence. They were frustrated that the

missions sheltered so many Guaraní, and therefore prevented the *comuneros* from exploiting their labor to the full.
(Their anger was such that they attacked the missions again
in 1732, kidnapped as many Guaraní as they could carry off,
and caused a dearth of labor in the settlements that led to
famine.)

There were other factors, too. Argentine historian Félix
Luna points to Masonic elements in the Spanish and Portuguese governments, as well as the negative impact of
Jesuit corruption in France. Political movements in Europe
at that time resulted in the expulsion of the Jesuits from
Portugal and Brazil in 1758, and from France in 1764. In
1767, Carlos III of Spain followed suit and expelled the order from Spain and its South American territories. The
priests were rounded up and deported to Italy; the missions
fell into disrepair.

I stood on the flagstone terrace that flanked the priests'
quarters. It was bordered by a balustrade whose curved
hourglass pillars were carved from that same red stone.
Beyond, a green lawn stretched, and then there was jungle.
A palm tree stood higher than the rest, its spiky branches
bursting haphazardly from its tip. All around, foliage in jade
and emerald shot, untamed, from the soil.

I walked around the grounds, through grassy alley-
ways between long straight rows of moss-covered, tumbledown walls. Three hundred years ago, these Guaraní
dwellings would have been orderly, industrious places. Each
family would have tended its own vegetable garden as well
as working on communal projects. Some of the houses, the
ones near the church, had been reconstructed so that the
doorways and window openings could be seen. Others,
farther away, had just been left to crumble beneath the
vegetation—thick coats of algae and entwining tendrils of

trees—that had slowly, over the centuries, taken over from Jesuit rule. By one decaying wall, a tree had grown around a stone pillar, its trunk entirely encasing it. They called it the tree with a heart of stone.

I came out of the mission grounds and had some lunch in a deserted restaurant where I was the only customer. A few yards away, workmen hung strings of tiny lights across the restaurant garden in a bid to make this godforsaken spot a little more welcoming. I wandered back down the desiccated, dun-colored street and sat with three or four others on the wall outside the church, waiting for a bus out of there. I was heading back toward Posadas, but on the way I was going to stop off at the nearby Santa Ana mission.

The bus arrived and we set off once more along the road—that same highway between Iguazú and Posadas that I had traveled along yesterday, and again in the opposite direction this morning. I was beginning to feel that I knew this stretch of tarmac rather too well. We reached an intersection; the bus driver shouted to me that this was Santa Ana.

I had thought San Ignacio unprepossessing, but Santa Ana was dowdier by far. There was almost nothing here at all. A gas station whose forecourt was cluttered with dust-encrusted trucks stood to the left. A couple of run-down buildings slumped along the main road. An old man hobbled off into the distance along a secondary road that ran perpendicular to the asphalt. I half wondered if I should hobble after him; there seemed nowhere else to go.

"Can you tell me the way to the mission ruins?" I asked the girl at the gas station counter. She looked bemused, as if she had never heard of such a concept. Then, after a few moments' deep thought, her frown disappeared and she smiled.

"Oh yes, just walk down there"—she waved toward the

main road in the direction in which my bus had disappeared some minutes earlier—"and turn left before the *yerba mate* factory."

I headed off in the direction she indicated, and walked for quite some time. I was all alone: There was nobody else foolish enough to be trekking along the verge of this road howling with lumbering trucks and buses. It was hot under the broiling sun. I soon began to wonder why I had come all the way out here, to the middle of nowhere, to see a patch of grass and a pile of derelict old bricks. Every few minutes I'd spot a building in the distance. "That *must* be the factory!" I hurrahed to myself with delusional desperation. But each time I drew close I found the construction on which I'd pinned my hopes to be just another featureless hovel in which one could have fabricated little more than a cup of tea.

Finally, after a time that seemed interminable but was probably only fifteen or twenty minutes, a monolithic gray metal building reared up before me like a mirage. High security gates encircled it. Inside, forklift trucks glided along tarmac roads and lifted things. Just before the factory, a tiny earthen path ran up an incline to the left—but there was no sign to indicate that this was the way to the ruins of a once-prosperous mission.

I began to climb the hill. Some minutes passed; there was still no sign of the ruins, and what little optimism I had left began to evaporate into the hot, subtropical air.

I came across a road-building gang toiling in the red dirt.

"Is this the way to the mission ruins?" I asked one of the hard-hatted characters.

"Ah yes." He grinned. "Not far to go now. Just keep going up here."

There was a caretaker at the mission but, otherwise, the

place seemed to have been altogether abandoned by the human race.

The buildings were in an even worse state of repair than those at San Ignacio Miní. Odd bits of scaffolding supported those few fragments of the church that still stood upright. Other stone blocks had tumbled down and lay littered, greenish gray, across the grass. Upon the dilapidated walls, cacti and trees had sprouted, their roots winding down into the gaps between the stones. Fat weeds with luscious leaves and tall swaying grasses clawed their way upward through the weather-beaten brickwork, which was dappled with silvery green circles of algae. Yet, as at San Ignacio Miní, there was a remarkable sense of calm and beauty. It was odd that here among so much ruin, amid the plainly visible ravages of time, a profound sense of order and stillness prevailed. It was almost as though the joyfully disciplined spirit of the Jesuits and their wards continued to permeate the place; as though here, in this remote backwater behind a shabby, no-hope town, their spirits had chosen to live on.

14

It Takes Two to Tango

Buenos Aires's Retiro station was a bustling, jumbling hive of a hullabaloo at eight o'clock the following morning. I battled my way through the crowds to the taxi booth. It seemed almost unbelievable, I considered as I traveled up the Avenida del Libertador toward my lodgings in leafy Palermo, that I'd been in Argentina for five weeks already. I now had a couple of days to enjoy the city high life; then I'd be heading out into the pampas before flying south to explore the wilderness of Patagonia—but I only had another four weeks in which to see it all. I was beginning to wonder whether I should have allowed more time to rove this enormous, wonderfully varied country.

My bed-and-breakfast was a delightful little place with a bright pink-painted exterior, just a few minutes' walk from the grassy expanses of Palermo's famous parks. During my first few days in Buenos Aires I'd been staying downtown, but now I had decided to move on from the suits of the business district and kick back, instead, in one of the city's most sought-after residential areas.

Palermo may be a fashionable neighborhood today but when the governor of Buenos Aires, General de Rosas, built himself a mansion here in the early nineteenth century—complete with a staff of three hundred—it was several miles out of the city center. It was only just becoming respectable when, in 1901, the Borges family moved with their infant son Jorge Luis into their house on the corner of Serrano and Guatemala streets, a block from where I was staying.

Jorge Luis Borges was one of the most influential writers Argentina has ever produced. He came from a middle-class family: His mother, Leonor, was steeped in her family's past glories—her grandfather had been a military hero—and regaled her young son with horrible tales of the tyranny of General Rosas, under whose rule her family had lost its estates.

Borges stayed firmly under his mother's thumb for most of his life; his relationship with her was partly to blame for his failure to build lasting attachments to other women until his twilight years. When, in his mid-fifties, his ailing eyesight declined and he was no longer able to read and write, he became entirely dependent on his elderly parent, who supported him unremittingly.

One of Borges's principal concerns was the issue of Argentine identity. Having spent most of his teenage years and early twenties in Switzerland and Spain, and influenced by his Europhile family, Borges had a multifaceted view of the Argentine: He believed that a person was shaped by influences from many places. Viewing his countrymen as individuals rather than citizens, he disliked the concept of a "State." He loathed the Peróns with intensity—he detested their form of inward-looking nationalism and spoke out against them time and again. The Peronist authorities didn't like Borges much either. In 1946, a couple of months after Perón had been elected president, Borges found that he had lost his job in a Buenos Aires library and had been redeployed as the Inspector of Poultry and Rabbits in the public markets.

I checked into my bed-and-breakfast, then walked down those streets that Borges would once have known so well. In the cool early morning, women hosed the pavements outside their homes to render them fresh and clean for the coming day. Suited office workers sat in corner cafés and gulped enlivening espressos. The scene probably hadn't changed much since Borges's day, I reflected: Back then there would have been rather fewer motorcars and rather more fedora hats, but the buildings, the pavements, and the suited figures in the coffee shops—all these would have imbued the Palermo streets with a bustling personality similar to today's when the writer stepped out to meet his literary friends.

I stopped for a coffee among them, then strolled across the Avenida Santa Fe and past the city's zoo, outside which bright red, pug-faced buses marked "Escolares" disgorged rows of white-coated schoolchildren. I joined the dogwalkers and their charges striding down the Avenida Sarmiento toward the city's parks. In these grassy retreats the dogs, released from their leads, frolicked among the fallen jacaranda petals while their guardians slouched on cool, shady benches.

Farther down in the Rosedal there were no dogs, just impeccably edged beds bursting with roses and long straight pathways interrupted by fountains that shot sparkling jets into the clear blue sky. I turned right, out of the parks, and continued my tour down the Avenida Figueroa Alcorta, where the Museo de Arte Latinoamericano sat stark and modern. Inside, curvaceous paintings surrounded spiky installations. Some of these works of art were frankly disturbing: In the middle of one room, a papier-mâché crocodile guzzled a pink plastic woman in its wide-open jaws. I wondered what kind of comment this was meant to make about contemporary Argentina.

I continued my walk southeast, dropped in briefly to the Patio Bullrich shopping center, and then carried on weaving my way through the streets until I reached the Plaza Libertador General San Martín. I strolled through the leafy park, past yet more dogs, and then down the steps toward the far end of the park that gives onto the Malvinas (Falklands) memorial.

Two very young naval enlisted men dressed in pristine white bell-bottoms, white shirts with blue knotted scarves, and flat sailors' hats stood to attention with their rifles before the long list of names of those who had fallen in the 1982 conflict. Above the marble plaques, torches were lit. It was a moving tribute, but a frustrating one: The flames of remembrance burned eternally for the dead, but the Argentine government had responded to the needs of those soldiers still living with a chilling amnesia.

I'd talked about the conflict with Luciana when I had been at Estancia Los Potreros.

"It was terrible, because our government lied to us," she'd said. "They told us we were winning. Everybody gave what they could to the war effort—women even donated their wedding rings to raise money for the soldiers. But later we found out that the soldiers had nothing. They were just boys, still teenagers. They didn't have enough proper clothing or equipment, and they were fighting against a professional army. And then, when they came back, the people were ashamed. Nobody helped them. Now those boys have grown up, but they have nothing. Some of them are begging in the train station. We are all taught from when we are very small *Las Malvinas son Argentinas,* and the Argentine people really believe that the islands should be ours. But our government was very stupid."

That evening, I delved into a more distant world of poverty and despair: I went to watch a tango performance. The dance first kicked off in Buenos Aires in the second half of the nineteenth century. Argentina was rich and immigrants eager for work streamed off the boats that docked in the city's port. From Italy, Spain, Russia, France, Portugal, and the Ottoman Empire they arrived in their droves: In the ten years from 1880 to 1890, the population of Buenos Aires almost doubled. But when these men arrived they found that all was not glitter and gold. They were far from home and family, their lives were hard, and women were few. Popular legend has it that these newcomers, desperate for company and comfort, frequented the city's brothels, and that it was within those consoling walls that they struck the first chords of the music for which the city would soon become famous—for the tango is the dance of sorrow. It sings of loneliness, disenfranchisement, and unrequited love, and these were sentiments that the immigrants knew too well.

It wasn't until the early twentieth century that the tango cast off its seedy reputation and became *de moda* in upper-class salons. Argentina was booming. The poor may have been crooning about hardship in their pungent tenement blocks, but the rich were stinkingly so. Young men from good families set sail on grand tours to see the world. These men were great aficionados of tango (though, doubtless, their mothers would have disapproved of the establishments in which they must have learned the steps) and by 1912, tango was all the rage in Paris. In London, "Tango Teas" kicked off in the Waldorf Hotel in 1913; that same year a Tango Ball was held at Selfridges.

Newly infused with glamour, the tango lunged and thrust its way back to the upper-crust ballrooms of its homeland. By the 1940s, everybody was dancing tango in BA. Juan Perón was a fan and used the popularity of the dance as a political tool.

Then, in 1955, the military overthrew the Peronist government. Perón went into exile and everything that he had encouraged—Argentine nationalism and, in turn, the tango—was actively discouraged. The tango itself was not banned (though certain songs were) but other regulations were brought in to suppress its popularity. Curfews made dancing clubs difficult to maintain. Rules forbidding more than three people to meet made dancing impossible. Between 1955 and the collapse of the military dictatorship in 1983, hardly anybody in Argentina learned to dance the tango.

It's all changed now, though. When the military regime fell following its catastrophic handling of the Falklands issue, the Argentines were seized with a collective sense of vigor. They rushed to classes to learn just about anything—and the tango took off once more.

I made my way to the historic dance hall of the Confitería Ideal. This building would have seen most of the leaps and slides of the tango's popularity over the years: *Porteños* had been dancing here since the early twentieth century. The show was due to start at ten, but at nine-forty-five still only seven or eight tables—square, with white-and-red cloths flanked by wooden curved-backed chairs—were occupied in the ballroom.

Regularly spaced between the furniture, marble pillars stood immutable, unchanged by time. From the elaborately corniced ceiling hung curving brass chandeliers that twisted toward bulbs cocooned in globes of frosted glass. Some of the bulbs were missing, though—or had simply come to the end of their natural lives, their filaments extinguished. Above the mahogany-paneled walls, interspersed with arched, age-speckled mirrors, the streaked white paint bubbled and peeled. It was as if those 1950s dancers, harangued by the military dictatorship, had fled from the stage in a hurry, and nobody had been back since.

But then, slowly, the hall started to fill up, and at a little after ten o'clock eight dancers took to the stage. Instantly, they lit the dim room with electrifying vitality.

With poker-straight faces, but oozing a sexuality that verged on the wanton, the men firmly grasped their partners—for tango is a supremely macho sport—and hurtled into a display of sensational dexterity. The dancers spun and twirled, kicked high and sank low, and entwined their perfectly toned limbs around each other until the audience swooned.

On the other side of the hall I noticed a solitary man dressed in a pink shirt with rolled-up sleeves and a tie. He sat with his chin resting on his hand in front of a half-empty bottle of beer. He wasn't old—perhaps in his thirties. I wondered what brought him here, alone, in his suit that evening. Was he an itinerant worker in town for a few nights and seeking entertainment, just as those early *tangueros* had done? Maybe he wondered the same about me.

Onstage, the dancers continued to plunge and lunge. In between sets, the women changed their dresses with a lightning speed matched only by their footwork. They emerged in rich red velvet, then tight black dresses adorned with beads whose hems were so short that, in the more provocative poses, the audience could see every inch of their fantastically muscular legs. They appeared in whirling chiffon and flowing emerald green. Sometimes they danced in pairs, sometimes in foursomes; sometimes all eight members of the troupe performed together. In between acts, an old man, stooped and almost bald, played the accordion; another came out and sang solo numbers.

The show was truly captivating. It was hypnotic and seductive. I could well see how it might have distracted those impoverished immigrants from the tedious business of being hungry. Having seen such a virtuoso performance, I was eager to give it a try myself and so, the following night, I decided to attend my first tango class.

I went this time to La Viruta in the Palermo district, just a street away from where I was staying. It was a Friday night; on weekend evenings, classes ran till midnight, then the *milonga,* the open dance session, began. The room was usually packed with around seven hundred *porteños*.

The venue was nothing special—a large, plain basement hall whose chairs and tables had been pushed to one side. Groups of people dressed in jeans and T-shirts shuffled around, some looking more nervous than others. There were all types—the young and the old, the fat and the whippet-thin, the bald and the hairy, the macho and the meek. I wondered whether my fellow students came here often. I felt certain that some of those short, overweight, sweaty types, who looked such unlikely contenders for this outrageously sexy dance, would soon prove themselves to be maestros.

Personally, I was feeling anxious. While last night's professional display had been slick, sexy, and inspiring, it was only now that I remembered that I, myself, was unlikely ever to achieve such death-defying routines and leg kicks, even if I practiced every day for the rest of my life. Over the last twenty-four hours I had somehow managed to overlook a painful reality—I am terrible at dancing. As a teenager, the whole process was agonizing. In my twenties, I figured out that the consumption of ludicrous quantities of alcohol inspired a kind of fluidity and devil-may-care attitude that took the pain out of the endeavor, temporarily at least. Now, I simply refuse to dance at all. So what on earth was I doing here? All these Argentines probably assimilated tango moves in the womb. They breathed them with the Buenos Aires air; they sucked them in through their pores.

And then, just as my neuroses reached stomach-churning heights and I was about to bolt for the door and freedom, a bellowing man gathered us all around. The beginners, he hollered, would go to the far end of the room. Those who had attended more than two classes would take the middle section. And the advanced would dance at the other end. There was no way out.

The beginners' class took to the floor under the tutelage of a man in a billowing red silk shirt, and a willowy woman with long blond hair and bronze satin combat pants. With supreme patience, they taught us an initial sequence of seven steps—and then told us to find a partner and practice. My first victim was twenty-year-old Guillermo.

"I have come here with my girlfriend," he announced emphatically as we clasped one another gingerly and stumbled through our paces.

But a series of partners later—Andrés (dark, debonair, and dominant), then Eduardo (diminutive and clammily nervous)—and the steps became more fluid. Until, that is, it was my turn to dance with the teacher.

"Stop," he cried out, horrified, after my first two steps. He fixed me with a stern and steely gaze, and rasped, "In tango, it is the man who leads."

15

How to Spend a Fortune

In 1847 **Don Fermín Cuestas,** the proprietor of the Dos Talas estancia near Dolores, struck a deal. His ranch was in the middle of the flat, featureless pampas. No trees grew here naturally—other than the *ombú,* whose spongy wood was useless—so if landowners wanted timber and firewood they had to plant them.

Cuestas told Don Pedro Luro, a French Basque immigrant who owned a store in Dolores, that he would pay him a flat fee for every tree he planted on his estate. Then Cuestas went to Europe for five years. When he returned, he found that Luro had planted so many trees that he owed him more money than the estancia was worth. He had no choice but to write over his seventeen-thousand-acre property to the Basque.

Luro was a worker. He had been penniless when he'd first come to Argentina at the age of seventeen. He had toiled as a laborer in a meat preservation plant in Buenos

Aires before managing to gather enough money to buy a boat to ferry passengers across the Riachuelo River. Carefully saving all he could from his customers' fares, he put enough aside to upgrade his venture to hired carriages; then he acquired his store in Dolores.

Even now that he found himself an *estanciero,* Luro wasn't going to rest. He continued to work hard and to acquire property, spending long months away from home, camping out and braving the floods and Indian raids that were common in those days. By the time he died in 1890, at the age of seventy, he owned nearly ten thousand acres of land as well as hotels, factories, salting houses for preserving meat, and various *graserías*—gruesome-sounding establishments where sheep were boiled down for their fat. And in between all that, he managed to see his wife sufficiently often to father fourteen children.

It was in the very bed where Don Pedro must have done all that fathering that I slept when I stayed at Dos Talas.

"This is the founder's bed," said Sara, whose husband Luis de Elizalde is a direct descendant of Pedro Luro, as she showed me to my room. It was an attractive piece of furniture, although, compared to today's king- and queen-sized frames, it seemed a little narrow for two. Indeed, it might even have been rather tight: Luro's wife Juana was an ample woman, if the portrait that presided over the dining table downstairs could be trusted. (Luro himself was thinner, and gazed steely-eyed from the opposite wall.) I would have thought that Juana might easily have filled the entire bed with her own comely bulk—which could explain why Pedro chose to sleep so often beneath the stars.

Neither Pedro nor Juana would have slept in this room, though. They lived in the house immediately behind this one, now owned by Luis's sister. This house was built in

1893 for Agustina, Pedro's daughter, when she married. (Her husband, Francisco Sansinena, also put his mark on Argentine history—he was responsible for the first refrigerated ship that transported Argentine meat to Europe.)

"Pedro, the founder, was a terrific worker," Sara explained to me as we ate an *asado* lunch under the trees in front of the house. "He was always traveling to look after his business interests. Often he would sleep outdoors just like his *peones*. But his children, they just spent it all. They spent a fortune!"

Sara's family was the first to have lived full-time at Dos Talas since Pedro Luro's days. Generations in between had used it as a summer retreat from the city, and the place had fallen slowly into disrepair. For twenty years now, she and Luis had been restoring the house and working on the land.

Around us lay immaculate lawns and painstaking paths designed by the French landscape architect Charles Thays, who also created many of the glorious green spaces of Buenos Aires and other cities. Pedro's daughter Agustina commissioned him to build a park with tree-lined avenues, a rose garden, a lake, a maze, and a model orchard with every conceivable kind of fruit tree.

"Agustina and Francisco kept houses in Buenos Aires and Paris," Sara continued, "and here at Dos Talas they employed sixteen people just to look after the house and garden."

In none of their projects had any expense been spared: Even the tiles of the pigeon house had been imported from France. Sara pointed across the lawn to where a cherubic stone figurine stood.

"I went to Paris once, and I was astonished to find the original statue at the Louvre! I had no idea it was there. It was beautiful, carved from marble. Of course, everyone tells me, 'Oh no, the one in your garden is the original. The one at the Louvre must be a copy!'"

But the most extravagant enterprise of the estate lay some distance from the house, down a tree-lined avenue. Its construction was inspired by tragedy: In 1914, Julieta, the eldest daughter of Agustina and Francisco, was killed in a car accident in France. Her parents were devastated, and they dealt with their grief by doing what they did best. They spent a truly extraordinary sum of money.

In Julieta's memory, Agustina and Francisco built a chapel. Never ones for abstemiousness, they decided it was to be a replica (on a slightly smaller scale) of the French cathedral Notre Dame de Passy, where their daughter's embalmed body lay until it could be transported to the Recoleta Cemetery in Buenos Aires.

Agustina and Francisco hired the services of an architect named Villalonga, and he sourced materials from the most elegant corners of Europe. The altar was made from Carrara marble. The majolica came from Venice. The statue of Christ was carved in Spain, the harmonium constructed in Germany. Then there were the marble flagstones, the stained-glass windows, the retable, and the Byzantine cross, many of which were sourced from the rubble of desecrated Italian churches when the First World War drew to a close.

"They spent so much money, it's almost unbelievable." Sara shook her head. "They thought they could have anything they liked without doing any work for themselves. That's the problem with the whole of Argentina—we live in a country rich with resources, but the people don't want to work. Argentine people are so lazy! They think they have a right to wealth and riches—but they don't work to make the most of what we have."

I took a walk to the chapel after lunch. It had become unused and overgrown over the decades until Luis had decided to renovate it: He'd had to use his own two hands, as family funds no longer stretched to a workforce employed from across the globe.

It was now a delightful place. The small, white-rendered building was encircled by carefully tended grass. The surrounding trees cast strongly defined shadows onto the paint that dazzled bright white in that afternoon's brilliant sun, but showed the specked effects of age in the shade. Four shallow stone steps led up to an elegantly arched door. Above this four cambered windows rose, two on either side of the entrance, their line echoing the incline of the door's awning, and, in the middle of these, an elegant flower-shaped window blossomed.

From inside, the stained glass still shone brilliant blue, green, yellow, and red. On the left-hand wall an ornate gilt cross framed a painting of a skeletally thin Jesus Christ. Above the crucifix, an arched mural depicted a clothed and upright Christ flanked by two bowed and sorry disciples against a background of gleaming gold paint.

The chapel's glory days may have faded now, but the artifacts within still murmured of a muted brilliance. Yet, although the adornments that furnished the tiny nave must still have been worth considerable sums, there was nothing brash about them. The impression was not one of opulence, but of a dignified austerity. The atmosphere was quiet, calm, and cool, and I was happy to sit alone on a wooden pew, to contemplate the windows, the retable, and the murals, and to consider the huge fortune and momentous ill luck which had blown over the family that brought them here.

When the heat of the day had subsided I took a ride in the family carriage with three fellow houseguests from New

Zealand and the family's *peón,* Abel. Abel had dressed for the occasion in his best black woolen beret, a white shirt with a red neck scarf, a waistcoat, and bombachas.

This horse-drawn carriage would have been the principal form of transport for the family before the days of motor-cars. Again, it was a narrow contraption, and I wondered how the fleshy Juana would have fared. On the other hand, perhaps her padding had been to her advantage: The vehicle was fitted with large, hard wheels and no suspension, and the family's journeys in those days would have taken them over roads far rockier than the immaculate swoop of the drive down which we were to ride.

Abel tapped the horse to start and we set off on our tour of the Dos Talas estate. We rolled down an avenue of naked, silver-trunked trees that glimmered in the sunlight as though they'd been polished. We coasted down leafy prom-enades, past run-down houses that had not been lived in for years, and other buildings which stood jam-packed with furniture that the family had accumulated over the genera-tions. I could have rummaged in those rooms for weeks. We drove through a grove of green bamboos that shot bolt up-right toward the sky, and through smatterings of white and violet lupins. As we turned one last bend the sun dipped low in the sky, tingeing with a startling whitish pink the upper tips of the clouds that had gathered as though returning home to settle for the night.

We drank our aperitifs that evening in the library, where three thousand books in Spanish, French, and English lined the walls. Here lay the legacy of another eminent ancestor, Elena (Bebé) Sansinena de Elizalde. Bebé was the president of the

Asociación Amigos del Arte (Association of Friends of the Arts) for twenty years. Here, in this very library, she entertained as her guests the literary and intellectual luminaries of the day such as Federico García Lorca and José Ortega y Gasset.

Bebé was also a great friend of Ricardo Güiraldes, a famous Argentine writer and the author of *Don Segundo Sombra,* which is still considered to be one of the most important works on gaucho life ever written. The novel presents an idealized portrait of the traditional gaucho: The narrator is a young boy who latches onto a famous and respected wanderer, Don Segundo Sombra, and from him learns to live as a noble free spirit. Güiraldes wrote some pages of his work right here at Dos Talas when he and his wife came to stay with Bebé in 1921. One day, he rode out from the estancia to the *cangrejales,* the mudflats that teem with crabs surrounding the Ajó estuary. When he returned, he wrote the chapter of *Don Segundo Sombra* in which the narrator rides with his mentor across similar terrain and comments on the black mud that looks as though it has been scourged by smallpox with its thousands of tiny holes, and the crabs that scurry as if from danger.

The gaucho was the epitome of freedom. A good gaucho was stoic, silent, and a sensational horseman. He ate only meat and drank only water; we today can only recoil in horror at the thought of his colon.

"This was the first night which I passed under the open sky, with the gear of the *recado* [the flat gaucho saddle] for my bed. There is high enjoyment in the independence of the gaucho life—to be able at any moment to pull up your horse, and say, 'Here we will pass the night.' The deathlike stillness of the plain, the dogs keeping watch, the gypsy group of gauchos making their beds round the fire, have left in my mind a strongly marked picture of this first night, which will never be forgotten," Charles Darwin wrote in *The Voyage of the Beagle*.

Darwin had arrived on Argentina's shores aboard the *Beagle* in 1833. On August 11 of that year, he set out on horseback from Río Negro with an Englishman resident in the area, a guide, and five gauchos. They were heading north toward Bahía Blanca; Darwin would then travel overland across the pampas to Buenos Aires.

But, while the freedom of the gauchos was romanticized by visitors such as Darwin who saw them as men of simple needs and easy contentment, these wandering souls were just as frequently demonized as lazy and belligerent in a country keen to assert itself as "civilized." Gauchos were wary of matrimony; unmarried mothers were common in the early Argentine countryside. Gauchos had no fixed job and no permanent lodgings. Their lifestyle was attended by cruelty and criminality. Even W. H. Hudson, who saw his childhood on the pampas through rhapsodic eyes, took issue with Darwin's idyllic perception:

"Darwin . . . says that if a gaucho cuts your throat he does it like a gentleman: Even as a small boy I knew better—that he did his business rather like a hellish creature reveling in his cruelty."

The gauchos' nomadic life ended when great stretches of the green pampas came under private ownership. As the estancias became better established and laid claim to the cattle of the plains, the gauchos could no longer wander at will and slaughter a cow whenever they felt hungry. (Apparently they used to kill an animal just for its tongue, which they would eat, then leave the rest of the animal to rot.) In addition to this, the estancieros were short of labor and so were eager to enlist the gauchos and their skills, just as they were eager to protect their property from the rampages of vagabonds and idlers. Their influence ensured the introduction of labor laws that made the gaucho lifestyle impossible: Any man without formal employment would be classified as a vagrant, arrested, and drafted into the army. And so, as the nineteenth century progressed, these nomadic spirits were increasingly forced into regular farmwork; today's "gauchos" are more accurately *peones*—farm laborers.

The political activities of the landowners were not universally endorsed, however. For fifty years following Argentina's independence in 1810, a bitter battle was waged between the rural Federalists, who advocated provincial autonomy, and the cosmopolitan Unitarians, who tended to look toward Europe for ideas and insisted that Buenos Aires should be the seat of government. Even today there is a division in Argentina between Buenos Aires and the provinces that has its roots in this early dispute between the two factions.

The most colorful character among these combatants was Juan Manuel de Rosas—he whom Borges's mother so hated and who, as governor of Buenos Aires, built his mansion in Palermo. Rosas was a red-blooded pampas man who came from tough landowning stock. His mother gave birth to twenty children. Only ten survived, but over these Doña Agustina ruled like a tyrant, whipping her sons even when they were teenagers. Perhaps it was her influence that shaped Rosas's later management style. When as governor he was presented with lists of prisoners, he was said to run his eye cursorily down the page and scribble prescribed punishments—"flog him" or "shoot him"—beside the names.

Rosas was virulently anti-Unitarian (though his enthusiasm for authority meant that he, paradoxically, concentrated power in Buenos Aires as his opponents desired).

When he was governor of Buenos Aires he went so far as to dictate that citizens' clothes be red, the color of the Federalists, and never blue, the color of the Unitarians. In his biography of Rosas, *Argentine Caudillo,* John Lynch quotes the British minister in Buenos Aires as having written to Lord Palmerston in 1848:

"Every citizen of the Argentine Confederation in Buenos Ayres is obliged to wear a species of uniform, which is the distinctive mark of federalism. His waistcoat must be red, he must wear a red ribbon around his hat, and at his button hole another red ribbon bearing an inscription of 'Life to the Argentine Confederation' and 'Death to the Savage Unitarians.' The women are likewise bound to wear a knot of red ribbon in their hair."

Rosas was not highly educated—he spent only a brief period in school—but he was tremendously well versed in the wild ways of the pampas. With his wide-set eyes, patrician nose, and pronounced sideburns that hung like the hides of freshly butchered beasts, he was an accomplished horseman and adroit in the gaucho arts. His absolute rule started on his estancia. To prevent knife fights among his men when they'd been drinking, he forbade them to carry knives on Sundays. If they were caught breaking this rule, the punishment was two hours in the stocks. If they were found going to work without a lasso, they received fifty lashes. The unusual characteristic of Rosas was that he insisted that he himself was subject to the same disciplinary system and, if he broke the rules, he obliged his servant to mete out the designated punishment.

His power circle soon expanded beyond his farm. Rosas became governor of Buenos Aires from 1829 to 1832 (Argentina was not at this time politically united). When the House of Representatives refused to grant him absolute power in 1832, he left government and embarked instead on his Desert Campaign to eliminate those indigenous peoples who were unfriendly to landowners. Rosas's forces were originally staffed by his own dependants—the men who worked for him on his land. They had no choice but to follow him into his militia. But his forces also included local natives who were affiliated to him in some way, as well as villains and outlaws who sought refuge on his land and, in return, fought for the caudillo.

When Darwin rode through this part of the world in 1833, he came upon Rosas and his men. He was impressed by Rosas himself. "He is a man of extraordinary character," he wrote, "and has a most predominant influence in the country, which it seems probable he will use to its prosperity and advancement."

He was rather less taken with the general's men, however.

"The soldiers were all cavalry; and I should think such a villainous, banditti-like army was never before collected together," he observed. Darwin was particularly taken aback by the soldiers' custom of slaughtering all indigenous women over twenty years old. "When I exclaimed that this appeared rather inhuman, [a soldier] answered, 'Why, what can be done? They breed so!'"

Rosas returned to government in 1835: A prominent caudillo, Facundo Quiroga, had been assassinated and, desperate to rid the country of anarchy, the House of Representatives agreed to accord Rosas absolute power.

What followed was seen as a bloody dictatorship by some; others considered Rosas's rule to be a successful bid to bring a violent and intractable country to order.

W. H. Hudson, for example, remembers that his family had a great respect for Rosas, as did many of the Anglo-Argentine families of that time. The Anglos were a minority and the Unitarians of Buenos Aires would never safeguard their interests. They therefore supported Rosas, who, at least, protected the investments of landowners.

A portrait of Rosas took pride of place in the Hudson family drawing room, flanked by portraits of the dictator's deceased wife, Captain-General Urquiza (Rosas's right-hand man), and two other military figures.

"The central portrait inspired us with a kind of awe and reverential feeling, since even as small children we were made to know that he was the greatest man in the republic, that he had unlimited power over all men's lives and fortunes and was terrible in his anger against evildoers, especially those who rebelled against his authority," Hudson wrote in his memoir *Far Away and Long Ago*. "Quite naturally I followed my father and came to believe that all the bloodshed during a quarter of a century, all the crimes and cruelties practiced by Rosas, were not like the crimes committed by a private person, but were all for the good of the country."

Others didn't agree. "Don Juan Manuel Rosas . . . applied the knife of the gaucho to the culture of Buenos Ayres, and destroyed the work of centuries—of civilization, law, and liberty," wrote Domingo Sarmiento in his essay *Life in the Argentine Republic in the Days of the Tyrants*. (Sarmiento didn't like Facundo Quiroga much either, and presumably wasn't too sorry about his violent demise. "His rage was that of a wild beast," he wrote. "The locks of his crisp black hair, which fell in meshes over his brow and eyes, resembled the snakes of Medusa's head. Anger made his voice hoarse, and turned his glances into dragons. In a fit of passion, he kicked out the brains of a man with whom he had quarreled at play. He tore off both the ears of a woman he had lived with.")

But whatever one's political position, one thing was for sure: The reign of Rosas was sanguinary. The Argentine penal system had always been harsh but Rosas took the blood-letting to new levels. There was no judge or jury—Rosas alone could, and regularly did, send a citizen to his or her death. His political death squad, the *mazorca,* rode around Buenos Aires forcefully ensuring loyalty to their leader by means of torture and assassination.

Rosas was ousted in the end, of course. He was defeated in battle by one of his staunchest supporters, Justo José de Urquiza, who had joined forces with the Brazilians and turned against him. Eventually Sarmiento would lead the country into a new era of education and Europhilia. In the meantime, Rosas disguised himself as a humble soldier, took refuge in the house of the British chargé d'affaires, and escaped to England. He lived the last twenty-five years of his life, rather quietly, just outside Southampton.

Still, despite the success of politicians and landowners in eradicating the true gaucho, his myth lives on—and the morning after my carriage ride I made a small, ineffectual attempt at mimicking those free spirits of days gone by. I went out riding on the pampas.

Abel, our driver from yesterday, was enlisted to saddle up some horses for the Kiwi guests and me. And then we rode out, away from Charles Thays's park and into the big green sea.

In the days before trees and fences, the pasture stretched flat toward the horizon with no landmarks whatsoever. They say that when the wind blew, the moving blades of grass gave an effect like waves. Now there were copses and partitions, but still the pampas seemed to extend forever. We trotted on and on, across the endless expanses of turf shorn short by the cattle. Occasionally a thistle or a smattering of tiny yellow dandelions would break the rhythm of this smooth, verdant carpet; far away on the distant horizon there rose an occasional thicket of trees, diminished to tiny shrubs by the perspective. Every now and then we came across a herd of cattle.

Upon a shallow lagoon, roseate spoonbills with pale pink plumage paddled. Under the strong sunlight, their pastel feathers blushed back a brighter hue from the water's reflective surface. Whistling herons dived deep with their long beaks. They seemed to stand in pairs: Some fed while others loitered, facing each other like nattering old couples.

Where the water was deeper, black-necked swans swam. Kestrels swooped across the clear blue skies. Vermilion flycatchers with their shameless red crests flitted overhead amid yellow-headed goldfinches, hummingbirds, swallows, and scissor birds.

The sun beat down, scorchingly hot. The shadows were short and intensely dark. Abel was still wearing his knitted beret, but today he wore no waistcoat and the sleeves of his striped cotton shirt were rolled up.

The gauchos of old would have ridden for weeks, cantering through this land, stopping just for food and rest. The pampas tribesmen would have charged across these very meadows as they conducted raids on the despised white settlers: In 1821 they unleashed a devastating attack on nearby Dolores, razing it to the ground. A few years later, Pedro Luro would have set out across this same green pasture as he embarked on his lengthy business trips accumulating wealth.

And us? We padded about gently for a couple of hours and then returned to the shade of the trees on the lawn outside the house, where a bottle of chilled white wine awaited us and a rack of ribs was being expertly grilled over the open fire.

16

And Then There Was Snow

I was astonished when I hauled myself out of bed at five-fifteen the following morning to find two staff members up and in the kitchen, preparing my breakfast of melon, warm croissants, and coffee. Sara had even gotten up just to say good-bye. So it was with the warm glow of outstanding hospitality that I left at six o'clock in a taxi that would ferry me back to Buenos Aires and the airport.

The light over the pampas was milky soft as dawn broke. Horses and livestock grazed silently in that wide-open space. But I was leaving all this now. My time in Argentina's northern half was up. I'd traveled through the arid deserts of the northwest, the wine lands of Mendoza, the riotous jungles of Iguazú, and the missions, the city, and the pampas, but now I was heading south. The last three weeks of my trip would be dedicated to Patagonia.

"Where are you from?" the taxi driver asked.

I said I was from England.

"Oh," he said sadly. "They hate us there, don't they? Because of the war."

I said that I didn't think the majority of British people were greatly worried by the issue of the Falkland Islands anymore. The conflict was years ago, and the islands were thousands of miles away . . .

"Yes, you're right," said the taxi driver, more animated now. "The people are all right, but the politicians—they create havoc. It's always the politicians that make trouble." He slapped his hand on the steering wheel with frustration.

While the British may not spend much time thinking about a kelp-covered archipelago far away in the southern Atlantic Ocean, for the Argentines the sovereignty of the Falkland Islands—or the Islas Malvinas—is still a highly emotive issue. Many Argentines are deeply offended by the very words "Falkland Islands" and insist on using the name "Malvinas" even when speaking English.

The history is as boggy as the land but, briefly, it runs like this: the first ship to land was the English *Welfare;* it docked on West Falkland in 1690 and John Strong, the *Welfare's* captain, named the body of water between the two main islands "Falkland Sound" after Viscount Falkland, who had helped to finance his voyage. There was evidence that the indigenous peoples had once hunted on the islands—a kind of fox was discovered that must have been left by them—but when Strong and his crew anchored the islands were uninhabited.

Strong duly sailed on his way and over the decades that followed the islands were visited by ships of various nationalities. In the 1760s, a French colony briefly set up home there until the Spanish forced it to disband—it was the French who named the islands the Isles Malouines from which "Malvinas" derives. The British, meanwhile, returned to a different part of the islands in 1766 and claimed them for the British Crown.

Obviously the Spanish weren't pleased. They considered the islands to be theirs under the ancient Treaty of Tordesillas, a territorial agreement which had been drawn up between Spain and Portugal in 1494 and which the English had always refused to recognize. Various disputes ensued, and settlements were peopled by both sides. In 1820, the newly independent Argentine government asserted its own authority over the archipelago and granted the administration of East Falkland to a Frenchman named Vernet, who was also given permission to found a colony. There followed numerous squabbles and skirmishes. Most notably, in 1829, Vernet seized three renegade American sealing ships; two years later an American naval officer razed his settlement, Port Louis, in retaliation. At this point, Vernet lost interest in his cold little colony with its rain-drenched sheep and cows, and fled back to the bosom of civilized Buenos Aires, leaving just a few Argentine troops to keep an eye on the place. When the British reappeared on the scene in the early 1830s, they overthrew these scant Argentine units with ease, and in 1833 they took definitive control.

The argument has persisted—sometimes raging, sometimes simmering—ever since. In the 1960s the Argentines took the issue before the United Nations, who decreed that the two countries should enter into talks to end the long-running dispute. These discussions continued, sporadically, over the years that followed. In 1980 the British Conservative government proposed a system of "lease-back": the colony would be ceded to Argentina, but the British government would lease back administration of the islands for a certain number of years until the date of a final handover. The islanders themselves objected, however. Argentina was at the time governed by a military regime with the blood of its own people fresh on its hands and the islanders had no wish to be handed over, with leasebacks or otherwise. Increasingly, Argentina's premier, General Galtieri, lost patience with the slow speed of negotiations and, on April 2, 1982, the first Argentine troops—those unfortunate, ill-equipped conscripts—landed at Stanley. If there's one thing that both British and Argentines now agree on, it's that his decision was a foolish one.

My taxi drove on through the pampas toward the domestic airport to the north of the city—where another Anglo-Argentine incident was looming.

"You have no reservation for this flight," said the man at the check-in counter.

"No reservation?" I was horrified. "But you're holding my ticket in your hand!"

"Yes, but there is no reservation." He scanned the computer screen. "You didn't show up for a flight . . . let me see . . ."

"From Iguazú to Buenos Aires," I concurred. He was right; I hadn't taken that flight. I'd needed to change the date, but all the alternative flights had been full and I'd taken the overnight bus instead.

"Well, because you didn't take that flight, all your subsequent flights have been canceled," he said, "including your return flight to England."

What? I was astonished. I'd never heard of this happening before. I was prepared to accept that it was irritating for an airline if a passenger didn't show—but wasn't that why they sold standby tickets? Surely, if I'd paid for a seat on a plane, it was up to me whether or not I sat in it.

"I can put you on standby, but the flight is full. You will

have to take another flight later in the day. And you'll need to go to the sales desk to try to get your other tickets reinstated."

Feeling spectacularly grumpy, I stomped over to the sales desk and explained my predicament.

"Well, it's all your own fault," the bald-headed man said with a supercilious shrug. I very nearly thumped him. "And now all those other flights are full. I don't know what I can do for you."

I glared at him with an expression I usually reserve for overzealous traffic wardens and strode off to the departures lounge. There I spent an unhappy couple of hours on line for standby, being bumped off the list, sprinting with a band of fellow desperadoes to the next desk, and being bumped off again, until finally, somewhat battered, I made it onto a plane to Bariloche.

Patagonia is vast. The Argentine side alone is bigger than France. It's not just the region that is large, though. The native Tehuelche who used to roam through this part of the world—before the Europeans either slaughtered or "civilized" them—were reputed to be huge.

"One day (without anyone expecting it) we saw a giant who was on the shore, quite naked, and who danced, leaped, and sang, and while he sang he threw sand and dust on his head . . . He was so tall that the tallest of us only came up to his waist," wrote Antonio Pigafetta, Ferdinand Magellan's chronicler, of the first of these tribesmen he saw when Magellan's armada stopped in Patagonia.

Magellan was a Portuguese explorer who had defected to the Spanish side during those two nations' cutthroat race for the lucrative spices of the East. He and his crews were the first Europeans to set foot in Patagonia—they spent the winter of 1520 on its shores waiting for the weather to improve before they continued their perilous voyage south—and it is Magellan who is generally credited with the naming of the region. He is said to have referred to these "giants" as *pathagoni,* from the Spanish *patacones,* or dogs with big feet.

Magellan's remit was to find an oceanic route to the Moluccas (also known as the Spice Islands and now a part of Indonesia). Spices were sensationally valuable in the sixteenth century—the sale of a single bag of nutmeg provided enough profit to enable a man to live comfortably for the rest of his life. Magellan hoped to prove that the Spice Islands lay in Spanish territory, as dictated by the Treaty of Tordesillas, and therefore to claim their riches for Spain. In doing so, he would delight the young Castilian king, Carlos I, as well as reaping considerable material reward for himself.

The Treaty was a curious piece of paperwork by modern-day standards. It had been drawn up twenty-six years earlier by Pope Alexander VI, who had been forced to intervene to settle disputes between the Spanish and the Portuguese in their contest for spices. With this treaty—and with a mesmerizing sense of his own authority over the unexplored corners of the earth—the Pope had quite literally divided the world in half: The western part he had bestowed on Spain, the east he had given to Portugal. The exact location of the dividing line became an issue of some contention (this was before the days of precise mapping, or, indeed, the discovery of longitude) but it was generally agreed that it ran from North to South Pole, cutting through the middle of what is now Greenland, through the Atlantic Ocean, and through a part of South America.

Magellan came up with a revolutionary proposal: He

would arrive in the East by sailing through Spain's territories to the west. But in truth, when he set out from Seville in 1519, he had no idea what he was taking on. Nobody had yet navigated a route around the world; nobody even knew if it was possible to do so. This was an era in which people still believed that the ocean boiled at the equator, and that supernatural beasts ruled the waves. Magellan's assertions of what he would achieve were, for the most part, the swagger and braggadocio of a man desperate for glory—for, while he was a highly skilled seaman, there were a few vital facts of which Magellan was ignorant.

To start with, Magellan had no idea that the Pacific Ocean existed. No European had crossed it before; maps of the day simply didn't show it was there. Magellan thought that, once he had successfully traversed the South American strait that would subsequently be named after him, he would reach the Spice Islands in a matter of days. But he didn't even have any real idea about the existence or location of the strait: Previous forays indicated that it might exist, but no European ship had yet succeeded in sailing through it—and reports suggested that it lay much farther north than it really did.

The outcome of Magellan's brave but blind posturing was an extraordinary journey, an expedition awash with swashbuckling heroism, dastardly mutinies, egotism, violence, cruelty, and death. Only one ship of the original five eventually succeeded in sailing around the globe. When she finally docked in Seville after her three-year voyage, just 18 of the original 237 men had survived to tell their tale, and the majority of them were so sick they could neither walk nor speak. Magellan himself never made it back to Spain: He was butchered by Filipino tribesmen after a foolish attempt to show off his fleet's military prowess backfired.

When Magellan's armada wintered on the shores of Patagonia, though, its crews knew nothing of the horrors that would later befall them. They were kept busy instead trying to survive the foul weather—instead of boiling oceans, they had found icy Patagonian tempests—and the murderous rage of their captain, for it was here that Magellan's underlings mutinied. He meted out heinous punishments including the drawing and quartering of the leaders, the display of their heads on spikes, and the abandonment of two high-ranking Spaniards on these hostile shores.

Pigafetta, meanwhile, spent these landlocked months attempting to learn the Tehuelche language, and recording their customs:

"When these giants have a pain in the stomach, instead of taking medicine, they put down their throat an arrow two feet or thereabout in length, then they vomit of a green color mingled with blood. And the reason why they bring up this green matter is that they often eat thistles. And when they have a headache, they make a cut across their forehead, and the same on the arms and legs, to draw blood from several parts of their body."

Tehuelche medicine was still terrifying Europeans more than three hundred years later. In the 1840s an American named Benjamin Franklin Bourne undertook a voyage from New Bedford, Massachusetts, to California; he was hoping to make his fortune on the Californian gold fields. His route—down the entire eastern coast of the Americas and up the other side—seems tortuous; it's incredible to think that, even in the first half of the nineteenth century, North America was so little charted he couldn't have traveled overland more quickly. In the event the journey took Bourne even longer than he had anticipated, for he suffered an inconvenient delay: Off the coast of Patagonia he went ashore to barter for food with the Tehuelches and they took him prisoner, then subjected him to their primitive nomadic life and constant death threats for ninety-seven days.

During his reluctant sojourn with the Tehuelches, Bourne suffered from a severely infected cuticle. He later described the treatment to which he was subjected in his account of his experiences, *The Captive in Patagonia.* "The chief... looked as calm as beseemed a surgical examiner, and in a good-natured guttural exchanged a few words with his assistant, who placed himself by my side, and fixing his eyes steadily on me, began swinging his hands and howling like a wild beast. The comparison was not far out of the way, for he gave a sudden spring, fastening his teeth on my neck, and commenced sucking the blood, growling all the while like a tiger!"

Bourne concurred with Antonio Pigafetta on the issue of the Tehuelches' size (although anthropologists today assert that the Tehuelches were probably only about six feet tall and that their gargantuan appearance was due to the enormous moccasins they wore on their feet and the animal skins they draped over their bodies).

"In person they are large; on first sight they are absolutely gigantic. They are taller than any other race I have seen," Bourne wrote. "They exhibit enormous strength, whenever they are sufficiently aroused to shake off their constitutional laziness and exert it... Feet and hands are large, but not disproportionate to their total bulk. They have deep, heavy voices, and speak in guttural tones,—the worst guttural I ever heard,—with a muttering, indistinct articulation as if their mouths were filled with hot pudding... They are excessively filthy in their personal habits. Hydrophobia, so to speak, is a prevailing distemper; they never wash themselves."

Bourne clearly wasn't a fan, but given the torments to which he was subjected, that's hardly surprising. The tribal lifestyle—constant wet and cold; continual moving of camp; a meager diet of almost-raw meat—was naturally difficult for a man accustomed to the comforts of nineteenth-century Massachusetts. More disturbing still for Bourne was the fact that—according to him—certain factions of the tribe were distressingly eager for a little variety in their meals, and wanted to kill their prisoner and eat him. (With the comfort of hindsight, it seems unlikely the Tehuelches would actually have chopped Bourne up and gnawed on his bones, as there is no evidence that the Patagonians were cannibals—but still, poor old Bourne didn't know that and, in any case, the prospect of merely being murdered was presumably distressing enough.) Twice during the period Bourne was held captive, the tribesmen staged "fatal rings" or powwows during which the death of a person was usually agreed on. It was only through wildly exaggerated promises of the goods that would be paid over for his ransom, and highly imaginative descriptions of the punishments his people would mete out as vengeance for his death, that Bourne managed to convince the Tehuelches to let him live.

In twenty-first-century Bariloche, however, there wasn't a thistle-munching, cuticle-curing giant to be seen.

"Weren't you supposed to come tomorrow, on Thursday?" asked the landlady of my bed-and-breakfast. She was a small, gray-haired lady who didn't look capable of butchering a mosquito. She also appeared to be somewhat confused.

"No," I said, smiling rigidly and trying to sound upbeat. "I booked for Wednesday, Thursday, and Friday nights."

"But I thought you said the first?" She frowned anxiously.

I took a deep breath. "Today *is* the first, señora," I told her slowly. "It's Wednesday, the first of December."

The señora looked much relieved. "Oh!" she said, a lot more brightly now. "Well, that's excellent then. You'd better come in."

I deposited my bags in my room and, before any further calendaring conundrums could present themselves, slipped out to investigate the town. There was a kind of *Sound of Music* wholesomeness to the place. (I sincerely hope the dissatisfied Austrian gentleman from El Molino didn't come here—I'm afraid he wouldn't have liked it at all.) The air was clean and fresh; while the skies were blue and the temperatures felt mild, it was noticeably cooler here than it had been farther north. The main street and square were lined by timber-and-stone chalets—the Alpine style of the town had been influenced by the Swiss and Germans who had been among the first to settle here in the 1890s and early 1900s. Restaurants served fondue, wild boar, and trout fresh from Lake Nahuel Huapi on whose southern bank the town sat. Every third shop seemed to be a chocolatier. Outdoor-clothing stores sold tents, climbing equipment, and every conceivable item made from fleece.

Most of the customers of those shops and restaurants wouldn't have been resident in Bariloche, though; they would have been vacationers passing through. In winter, this area was one of Argentina's prime skiing lands, and in summer it was a haven for hiking and outdoor activities. The setting was stunningly pretty in a picture-postcard way: deep blue skies hovered above snowcapped mountains, lakes shimmered the color of a summer twilight sky, and intensely green pine trees made a break for the heavens.

As if all that wasn't romantic enough, it actually *snowed*

the first night I stayed here, a phenomenon that seemed truly fantastic after the blinding heat of the pampas just a day earlier.

"Where are you going today?" asked my landlord as I munched through my breakfast *magdelena* and gazed at the fast-diminishing sugary sprinkling on the pavement outside. He was a doddery but kindly man who looked as though he was in his seventies.

I hadn't actually made my mind up yet; I'd thought I'd wander into the town and see what delights presented themselves.

"Well, you wait here, and I'll show you," he said. He tottered off. I waited. He pottered about some more. He appeared to have forgotten about me altogether and I was just about to get up and make a run for it when he stared at me quizzically, and then said, "Ah yes, the map." A short while later, he returned and spread the map on the table.

"Okay," he said. "This is what you must do. You must take the bus number twenty from here"—he drew a circle in pen around the junction of Morales and Rolando streets—"and get off here." He jabbed his finger at a point marked Cerro Campanario. "From there you can take a chairlift to the top of the hill. The view is incredible, but you must go in the morning, señorita, because the light is better. Then you must get back on the bus and go to here"—he jabbed his finger at the famous Llao Llao Hotel—"and you can have a coffee and look at the magnificent view. You are going to have a very nice day, señorita, a very nice day indeed."

And with that, he hobbled off.

I went down to the bus stop as directed and soon discovered that the old man had omitted to tell me something: The view from the bus window, too, was astounding. Bushes of broom flashed from the roadside, brilliantly, blaringly yellow. Following last night's smattering of snow, the sky had cleared and was now a proud peacock blue, smeared lightly with lines of cloud that streaked across the canvas like white wedding streamers. Beyond the almost indecent efflorescence of broom, the lake lay blue, and the mountains lined up behind like a serene procession of nuns in stony gray habits and pristine white wimples.

I arrived at the Cerro Campanario and clambered aboard the chairlift. Its whirring and clanking conveyed me back to skiing holidays of years gone by. But beneath the cables and swinging seats, a thick carpet of pink and purple lupins grew in the place of snow. On either side of the clearing under the lift, the mature dark green branches of pine trees sprouted with sappy young tips. Fresh, pert, and pale, they sang with the new life of spring. I felt a profound sense of calm and well-being. The world out here was silent other than for the gentle creaking of the cables. The air was cold and crisp. I sensed my shoulders drop as my lungs filled with the sweet, pine-scented air.

The view from the top looked onto a section of the lake decorated by coiling promontories and small green mounds of islands. In places, the land had curled around to join up with itself, creating smaller, subsidiary bodies of blue. Toward the shore, the water shifted from the darker hue of the deeper water into a pale turquoise in the shallows, while on the banks emerald-green grass gave way to forests of perfectly toned, tapering conifers. On the other side of the lake, the white-capped Andes encircled this Eden as though protecting it from the pernicious influences of the uglier world beyond.

The whole of this area was donated to the Argentine state in 1903 by Francisco Moreno, also known as Perito

Moreno. (Perito means "expert.") The land had been given to Moreno by the government in recognition of his life-long work exploring and surveying the land of northern Patagonia; when he endowed it back to the state, he stipulated that it must be preserved as a national park for the enjoyment of the Argentine people.

Moreno was the first non-native Argentine to set eyes on Lake Nahuel Huapi: He was galloping about the Patagonian "desert"—whose indigenous tribes posed considerable dangers to white men—from the time he was in his early twenties.

The Indian chief Shaihueque originally denied Moreno permission to visit the lake, but he managed to enlist the support of another chief, Quinchahuala.

"Quinchahuala took a liking to me since I accepted a plate of food from him consisting of cornmeal with blood and raw tripe, and I ate it without a visible display of revulsion," Moreno later wrote. As a result of Quinchahuala's intervention Shaihueque allowed Moreno a week's absence from his camp, and the young adventurer set out with his team.

"Serenely beautiful vistas awaited us near an Argentine lake even more impressive than Geneva's Lake of Leman. When I finally got to the lake, I flew the Argentine flag. For the first time, our national colors, sky blue and white, were reflected in its fresh, crystal clear waters," he recorded.

As well as exploring the land, Moreno gathered exhibits for his Natural Science Museum that still stands in La Plata today. Specimens included a collection of human skulls: "I am still holding on to the head (Catriel's). I just looked in on it and it still exudes a foul odor even though I cleaned it up a bit. I will take it with me to Tandil. I do not want to part with this gem, which is the envy of many," Moreno wrote to his father on April 5, 1875. There were animal exhibits too. "Let me know how my museum is doing and if you have picked up the condor bones and the lion from the embalmer," he instructed his long-suffering parent on October 13 that same year.

I wondered whether Perito Moreno would have approved of the creaking cable car as it carried me back down the hillside: Certainly it fulfilled the explorer's goal of making the land accessible for the people, but I couldn't help wondering what he'd have made of the less than serenely beautiful scaffold and cables that hauled them to that viewpoint.

Back on lower ground, I completed my circuit as instructed, continuing my bus journey to the Llao Llao, one of Argentina's most historic hotels. It was designed by the architect Alejandro Bustillo, and first opened its doors in 1938. I drank coffee and ate apple tart in the hotel's plush café with its conservatory-style glass front that looked over the tips of the pine trees to the lake and the mountains beyond. And then I climbed back on the bus and returned to town.

I was detained the following morning by a series of dull administrative tasks, which meant that I was forced to disobey that morning's breakfast-time commandment: to take a full-day hike into the hills behind Bariloche. Instead, I clandestinely booked myself on an afternoon kayaking expedition on Lake Moreno, which lies west of Bariloche, just before the Llao Llao Peninsula.

It was windy on the lake that afternoon, and it felt tremendous to paddle at full force into the wind as the waves crashed over the kayak's bow. Also in our group was a Canadian woman with her three-year-old son, Griffin, who stood in the front of their boat dressed up like a water-proofed Teletubby and roared with laughter as the waves broke in his face, and an Equadorian couple who hadn't quite mastered the art of kayaking and spent most of the time spinning around in circles. We stopped for a break on an island, drank coffee, and ate *alfajores*—Argentine biscuits filled with the ubiquitous caramel *dulce de leche*—and then paddled for home.

I went back to town, and strolled around those outdoor-clothing stores and chocolate shops for a couple of hours more. Two days ago, they had seemed fun and exciting, hunkering beneath their Alpine chalet timbers, but now the attraction of so many outlets selling exactly the same goods was beginning to pall. But no matter: It was time for me to move on. I was heading in the morning to Estancia Huechahue for a week's riding that was going to present more challenges than any of my equine adventures so far.

17

Cowgirls and Indians

Estancia Huechahue is huge: At nearly twenty-five square miles, it's slightly larger than New York's Manhattan Island—though it's home to considerably fewer people. While more than one and a half million people live in Manhattan, Huechahue's resident population reaches a peak of fifteen in the busy months of summer; in the winter, just three people live there.

Still, it wasn't the extent of the farm that really concerned me when I arrived that Saturday morning. I was more worried by far by the size of the bottle of ibuprofen that was sitting by the bathroom basin: It was a bumper container of five hundred tablets. I was used to finding shampoo and conditioner in guest rooms—but I didn't think I'd ever been given enormous quantities of complimentary painkillers before.

"We ride hard here. People find they need them," explained Jane Williams, the owner of the estancia, when I tentatively inquired as to whether every room was supplied with quite such a large bottle of drugs or whether, perhaps, it was all a mistake and some previous headache-prone vacationer, careless in their packing, had left them behind.

Jane paused and drew hard on her cigarette. She was an attractive, dark-haired woman whose suntanned face was now weathered by many years of Patagonian elements. She wore black bombachas and a black T-shirt over her lean, muscular frame; within seconds of meeting her, one could see that she was a woman who didn't just ride hard, but approached all other aspects of life in an energetic, no-nonsense way as well.

Originally Jane was from London, but twenty-odd years ago she married an Anglo-Argentine and moved to his family's Patagonian estancia. When, some years later, her husband was killed in a farming accident, leaving her in sole charge of both the ranch and her two small children, the locals expected her to sell up and move back to England. But Jane wasn't the packing-up kind. She stayed on and, on top of running the business, she also undertook to educate her sons at home until they were old enough to go to boarding school in England. Clearly there was nothing halfhearted about Jane—and, I feared, she didn't look as though she'd tolerate feebleness in others.

My burgeoning nervousness wasn't eased by the other guests. Jane's visitors generally arrived and left by plane from the nearby town of San Martín de los Andes, but I had come on the bus from Bariloche. I'd arrived a couple of hours before the minibus would depart with the previous week's contingent; when they had been dropped off, the newcomers would be picked up at the airport and would appear at the estancia mid-afternoon.

"Ah, so you're one of next week's group," commented

one jodhpur-clad man, limping in after the last ride of his holiday. He looked at me in much the same way one might regard a gladiator shortly to be invited to joust with the lions. "Well, I really hope you know how to ride!"

He disappeared to take a shower while I sat on the terrace and shared a jug of coffee with Alice. She and her husband Marcus were here for two weeks' holiday from their city jobs in London; they were now halfway through their fortnight's break. Alice had taken the morning off.

"My back hurts," she explained. "Most of the people here are pretty experienced riders and we've been putting in some long hours with lots of hard canters. So," she smiled brightly, "how's your riding?"

How was my riding? Totally rubbish, of course! Heinously, humiliatingly under par. Nowhere near good enough; many, many leagues from anything approaching competent. For heaven's sake, I'd clambered into the saddle for the first time just a few weeks ago. I'd been gambolling about the place having picnics and tea breaks and looking at the pretty view. Yes, I'd cantered a little and found it rather fun—but I'd done nothing that had inspired the consumption of five ibuprofen, let alone five hundred.

Suddenly, I was deeply frightened. I even briefly considered retreating to my room, downing the whole bottle of pills, and putting myself out of my misery once and for all. But on the other hand, I reflected, it might cause less grief among my close family members if I stayed sitting here on the terrace with a joyful smile fixed to my face, pretended everything was absolutely fine—and awaited the arrival of Caroline.

Caroline is a friend of mine who was flying out from England to spend that week with me at Huechahue. She was arriving on the afternoon flight to San Martín and would be

at the estancia in a couple of hours. Her riding, we reckoned, would be about the same standard as mine. Perhaps,
then, we could wade through the ibuprofen-induced haze
together.

Caroline and I had survived some difficult situations in
the past. We met when we were eighteen—we were both
employed as waitresses in the same Swiss ski resort. We
worked in different restaurants but both endured similar
levels of madness. Caroline's boss used to lose his temper on
a regular basis.

"Je vais casser le restaurant!" I am going to smash up the
restaurant! he would scream before grabbing pats of garlic
butter, lovingly prepared by the Romanian kitchen assistant,
and hurling them at the wall, where they would stick, briefly,
before sliding slowly and greasily down to form a gooey yellow mess on the floor.

My establishment was no calmer. We serving staff—
cheap seasonal labor with no experience and limited language skills—were howled at almost continuously even
when no misdemeanor was apparent. But the low point in
my waitressing career came when there was a "big breasts
competition" in the disco that took up the lower floor of the
building in which our restaurant was located. The *patron* and
the two Portuguese kitchen boys were most intrigued by
the forthcoming display, and talked of little else for several
days. Their principal point of interest was whether any of
the English waitresses (there were three of us) were sufficiently well endowed to enter the contest. One day, their
curiosity could stand no more. They grabbed me and dragged
me into the kitchen toward the meat weighing scales.
Happily I escaped before any measurements could be taken,
and as I was too young and naïve to know that one could
take issue with one's employer for inappropriate horseplay

with one's breasts, that was the end of the whole unfortunate episode.

Caroline and I used to meet in our hours off to consume enormous multicolored ice creams and to regale each other with the doleful tales of our respective workplaces. When we left Switzerland we went traveling around Europe by train with so little money that we were forced to eat bread with tinned sardines for every meal. We camped in temperatures so cold we had to wear the entire contents of our backpacks just to get to sleep. We had endured a lot. But nothing had ever been so bad that we'd swallowed five hundred ibuprofen.

The minibus departed with last week's guests; we waved them off and I thought back to my own bus journey that morning. The surroundings had seemed sparse and desolate after the vibrant blues and greens of Bariloche. For mile after mile, the bus had coasted through arid expanses of sandy scrub. Very occasionally, a turning or a gateway had indicated the presence of an estancia somewhere in the wilderness beyond. Perito Moreno would have been pleased: One of his fondest dreams had been to turn the barren expanses of northern Patagonian into productive farmland. "I reveled in the natural beauty of this land of promise. What a positive transformation it would undergo once festivals exulting labor replaced the orgies with which the Indians celebrated the unrestrained flow of liquor," he wrote in March 1916, when he was an old man looking back on the achievements of his life.

The road I'd traveled along would have cut across exactly the same area that Moreno had struggled through in much more difficult circumstances a hundred and twenty-five years earlier. In early 1880, Perito Moreno was once more in the Nahuel Huapi area when he was captured by

Chief Shaihueque of the Manzaneros tribe. The Manzaneros were determined to kill him, so Moreno executed an intrepid escape plan: He crept out of the camp in the dead of night and with his two native companions he floated on a raft down the Collón Curá and Limay rivers toward Neuquén. For a full week the three fugitives traveled with little food to sustain them.

"The seventeenth was a gloomy day. We were extremely tired and hungry and had nothing to eat except for some roots," Moreno subsequently wrote. They had fled from the encampment six nights earlier on February 11. "Although there was no shortage of water, our thirst was unquenchable because we had come down with a devastating case of fever."

On the morning of February 18, Moreno and his companions had to abandon their raft because their arms no longer had the strength to steer it. They continued by foot along a trail.

"It was a pitiful sight. Three starving men walking, falling, and desperately quenching their thirst with water that was not fit for drinking. Drink we did, though, every time we stumbled upon a puddle. In one of those water holes, I lost consciousness and lay amid the reeds for a long time."

Finally, the following day, the bedraggled trio reached salvation in the form of a military fort.

I thought again of the ibuprofen, then looked around the comfortable estancia with its well-stocked kitchen and cellar and considered that, relatively speaking, things really weren't so bad.

The minibus arrived bearing Caroline and three others: Suzanne from Iowa was fifty-something though perfectly preserved, presumably with surgical enhancements. She later confessed to having brought with her six pairs of designer sunglasses. Ron was from New York, where he worked as a cardiologist. He was suave and faultlessly gleaming. I later discovered that even after galloping through a dust storm he stayed immaculate, something like the human equivalent of a self-cleaning oven. Anthony was younger—in his thirties—and an IT controller from Harrogate. Later in the day, the last two of our group joined us: Angela and Bill. Angela had just retired from her career as a psychiatrist and Bill was an anesthesiologist; they came from Glasgow. At least we had a good supply of doctors to hand should anything befall us that the painkillers couldn't handle.

We had tea and panettone, and Yvonne, Jane's business partner, appeared. Yvonne was Anglo-Argentine. She was born in Argentina and had lived here all her life—she no longer had a British passport. As a small child she had learned to speak Spanish and English simultaneously so that now she didn't know which to call her mother tongue. She was a gentle woman with a relaxed demeanor, long blond hair, and easy-smiling, blue eyes.

"So, how much riding experience do you have?" she asked Caroline and me. We were due to go for our introductory ride in about an hour's time; there seemed little point in casting too bright a sheen on the lamentable situation. We confessed our feelings of inadequacy.

"Ah, don't worry." Yvonne smiled. "They're good horses here. But you've got to ride them properly. We've had guests before who've ridden their horses into trees—but it was their own stupid fault. They just were sitting there, doing nothing. You've really got to ride the horse."

Caroline and I exchanged secret glances of terror. Then we packed in one last fortifying hunk of panettone and went to meet the horses of Huechahue.

Both Jane and Yvonne rode with us that evening, with Jane taking the lead. I was riding a gray called Nevado. He had an amiable character and a pleasing tendency to avoid contact with the passing shrubbery.

We walked and trotted out into the open hills.

"Is everyone happy to canter?" Jane called from in front, and with that we hurtled off into the wild expanses of sparse, spiky grass, slaloming along a narrow serpentine track that coiled first to the left and then to the right.

We slowed to climb a tiny path by a lake. As the sun sank low, the evening rays struck the dry heath and illuminated it a rich, coppery gold. We turned for home, cantering along a wide earthen track into the setting sun. The horses' hooves kicked up swirling clouds of dust, and those last shafts of low light caught each dancing mote so that we seemed to career through a multitude of spinning, glinting flecks. Faster and faster we flew, blinded by the light and the dust that somersaulted around us, unable to see any obstacles that might be lying in our paths and hoping, fervently, that the horses had some idea of where they were putting their hooves. It was an adrenaline-surging first ride but, deep down, I rather enjoyed it.

If that was the gentle introductory outing, though, what would a whole day's hard riding feel like? I wondered as I ate my breakfast the next morning. We had a full-day excursion on the estancia scheduled.

I was riding a different horse today.

"This is Tony the Pony," Yvonne introduced us. "He's a good horse. He's responsive and forward-going. He used to cartwheel a bit but I don't think he's done it for a while."

"Cartwheel?" I asked, astonished.

"It means he used to move off while the rider was getting on."

We rode out and picked our way through a remarkable basalt canyon whose ornate black cliffs rose up around us like smoke-smeared Gothic spires. Ibis soared and plovers screeched. We climbed a little to reach a vast flat meadow—and then we took off again. Tony was cantering hard, following the others. Then the rhythm of his hooves changed as they pounded into the grassy plain. Now, instead of bounding along in a canter, he moved faster still. His hooves seemed to skim over the abundant green meadow with the grace of a flying fish that flits over the surface of the ocean. This, at last, must be the gallop! I realized with breathless delight as we surged on and on across this wide-open space. The sense of speed was fiercely exhilarating. I'd traveled fast before—two years previously I'd enjoyed some intoxicating moments as I became acquainted with the throttle on the motorbike I'd ridden around New Zealand, and the year before that, when I'd cycled around Spain, the speed of some of my descents down the mountains of the Pyrenees had quite simply terrified me. But this was different. Because the horse itself was a vital, living creature with a robust personality, and because he seemed to be enjoying scorching over this green open meadow through the crisp, fresh air as much as I was, there was an extra intensity to this trip. The power, athleticism, and sheer energy of the horse beneath me was invigorating; the knowledge that a fall from his back

at this speed could be very nasty indeed added an extra fris-
son. It was a potently exciting ride.

"Watch out for the dark green patches—that's where
the land is boggy," Yvonne warned us as we reached the
other side of the meadow blessedly unscathed. For the first
time, it occurred to me: A hard hat, which I'd previously de-
nounced as prissy and English, might not be such a bad idea.
I could do myself some serious damage if I came off a horse
at these speeds without one, I reflected out loud.

"You'd do yourself some serious damage if you came off
at that speed *with* a hard hat," Bill said, shrugging.

We stopped for lunch. We unsaddled the horses; delighted, Tony rolled in the dust, which rose about him in
clouds and turned his white coat a muddy brown. A couple
of the gauchos had driven out here in a jeep. They'd arrived
before us and built a fire; now they roasted pork chops and
served us salad and cold beers. We sat on tree stumps and
feasted. Then we each found a shady tree, rested our heads
on the sheepskins from our saddles, and settled into a soft
and cozy siesta.

We took a different route home, climbing high. The land
turned greener now. Smooth, rounded clumps of vegetation
lay interspersed with fine, flowing grasses and craggy rocks.
It was a spacious, expansive world out here. The contours of
the hills rose and fell, the valleys turning to shaded ruts,
then mere crinkles as they stretched ever farther toward the
distant horizon where the ridges of snowcapped mountains
formed a final jagged line against the sky.

The sun was low once more by the time we arrived back
at the house. As we crossed a final meadow, its rays cast our
forms into swooping shadows. Tony the Pony's body loomed
long on the golden grass, his legs stretched like a giraffe's,
his torso blown up to monstrous proportions. Astride his

back, higher up and less distorted by the low angle of the sun's beam, I took my place in this work of shadow puppetry as a diminutive mannequin.

Castration is not ordinarily an acceptable topic of conversation over breakfast, but for us it held a special relevance. We were to spend the morning herding cattle. Once we had assembled our four-legged quarry into the corral, we would separate the cows from their calves—and then watch as one of the gauchos castrated the males. Finally, as the icing on the cake, the pot of gold at the end of the rainbow, we would barbecue the testicles and eat them for lunch.

The men in our group were behaving in a disappointingly squeamish manner. Ron, who as a medical man surely ought to have been made of sterner stuff, was declaring outright that he would neither watch the castration nor eat the little delicacies afterward. Marcus, Anthony, and Bill, meanwhile, were playing rather halfheartedly with the bacon on their plates and trying to avoid committing themselves one way or another.

"What's the matter with you?" Caroline and I wanted to know. Knowing what pleasures today's schedule held, we had discussed their reticence in our bedroom the night before. "It's not as if anybody is asking you to have *your* testicles chopped off, then watch as a bunch of hungry bipeds eats them for lunch. Why do you empathize so strongly with the cow? You eat its legs, you eat its back, you eat its rump. Why are you so picky when it comes to the tiny matter of its very small balls?"

But the men in our group were unwilling to answer. And then breakfast was over and it was time to ride.

I was on Tony again today. We saddled up and clambered aboard, then took a lesson in the art of rounding up cows.

"This is called a *rebenque*," said Francis. Francis was eighteen years old and the son of a friend of Jane's from England. He and Jane's elder son, Simon, were both spending their gap years before college working out here on the farm. Francis held up a short leather whip with a stout handle and a wide, palette-shaped thong.

"You hold it like this," he went on, slipping a couple of fingers through the leather loop attached to the handle. "And then, when you ride into the cattle, you swing it round like this." He rotated the whip from his fingers so that it spun around fast like a single blade of a large electric fan.

"The cattle don't like the movement, and they don't like noise, so you have to make lots of noise, and swing the *rebenque* at the same time. That way, you'll get them to move."

Wonderful. We were going to make cowboy noises. Should that be a wild and high-pitched whooping, or more of a macho "yee-ha"? Eagerly, we tried out our new sounds as we trotted off to the paddocks.

We divided into two groups; in the spirit of competition, we split into the boys versus the girls. The boys were to ride with one of the gauchos off to the left. The girls went with Jane to the right. Each group would ride around its patch starting at the outside and working inward, herding the cattle as we found them, until we all met in the middle. We would then funnel the animals into the corral. It sounded really quite simple.

And to start with, it was. Indeed, for the first ten minutes or so, we found no cattle at all, so we just trotted along our prescribed route without so much as a yee-ha between us.

Then we spied some. With a wild ululation Suzanne bounded into the fray and in an instant had the bovines under her designer-clad control. Gradually, we gathered more. They mooed and mewled and cooed and caterwauled; we yodelled and yowled and bawled and barked. For just a few minutes, it all seemed to be going rather well in a stentorian kind of way.

To increase our efficiency, we split into smaller groups. Suzanne set off up a steep, rocky incline in search of stragglers. I followed her, not so much to help as to pretend I was doing something. I didn't hold out high hopes for my skills as a cattle herder. Suzanne, on the other hand, was both an accomplished rider and a highly confident cowgirl (maybe she'd been practicing back home in Iowa), and I was working on the premise that, when you have no idea what you're doing, it's usually a good idea to ally yourself to someone who has. So Suzanne galloped up and down rounding up cows while I climbed half the hill and then stood around doing nothing because I'd driven Tony into such a steep rocky patch that, for a time, I couldn't persuade him to slither back down.

Finally, Tony and I stumbled gracelessly to the bottom of the hill and met up with Caroline. We rode around for a while shouting "whoah-whoah-whoah-whoah" and "yeeeee-ha" and waving our whips. After about half an hour of concerted cowboy noises, we felt very pleased with ourselves: We had managed to herd a large group of cattle from one field, through a gate, and into another field.

And then somebody came along and told us that they should have been in the first field all along, so we had to herd them back out again.

By now, quite frankly, I was ready for a handful of ibuprofen—or at the very least a bottle of cold beer. Finally we arrived back at the corral. There were certainly more cows in it now than there had been when we'd started—but the hills, sadly, were still full of escapees.

"Shall we go and round them up?" Jane asked cheerfully. She cantered off energetically, clad as ever in black bombachas and T-shirt, a red *faja,* and dark sunglasses beneath her black beret. Ron set off in hot pursuit, and, still anxious not to show myself up as the good-for-nothing gauchette I really was, I gave Tony a kick and belted out behind them.

We tore up the hillside, through lines of trees intent on decapitating us, down terraced fields, and then back up again. By now I was just holding on for dear life. As we charged through one last field on our way back to the corral, Tony gave a snort. We pulled up and he turned around to glare at me.

"Enough now," he very clearly said.

Tony had his way; he was allowed to rest under a tree. We human participants had not yet finished our morning's work, though: We were now required to charge around the corral on foot, trying to separate the cows from their calves.

It was an exhausting business. Through judicious *rebenque*-waving and a few carefully timed "yee-ha's" we were supposed to encourage the herd to trot toward a gate in the fence that separated one enclosure from another. At the gateway stood one of the gauchos and Jane's son Simon. They were supposed to filter the animals going through the gate, allowing only the fully grown cows to pass through while keeping the calves on the other side. Of course, the cows followed their calves where they could. They would charge back up the corral, where we were to run at them in turn, frightening them back toward the gate. I'm afraid I wasn't much help. Each time a large, horny cow came at me, I hopped nimbly out of the way.

But we were running behind schedule. It was past lunchtime already—and the male calves were still intact. And so, after all our concerns and excitement, there would be no testicles on the menu. Instead, we sat around the fire, drank refreshingly cold beer, and tucked into traditional gaucho fare—bread with hunks of meat sliced from great strips of cow that were threaded onto stakes and driven into the earth beneath the fire.

After lunch the testicle-cutting man appeared on the scene and, having made such a noise over breakfast, I felt obliged to go and watch. The calves were herded through a narrow wooden corridor. The first couple of animals at the front of the line were females; they were let go. Then came a male. He was channeled into an almost-cylindrical wooden contraption which was fastened around his body like a barrel. Then a handle was turned, spinning the barrel—and the calf inside—onto its side. A trapdoor level with the calf's hindquarters was opened and his upper leg brought out and tethered tightly to a post so that he could not kick. And then, the chopping-man plunged his knife-wielding hand into the hole.

He was a swarthy man, with a thick crop of hair that once would have been lustrous black but was now flecked with gray. He wore the traditional gaucho's red neckerchief over his pale blue shirt and brown chunky-knit sleeveless cardigan. Jane stood by his side, recording the goings-on in a green notebook.

The knife man sawed and sawed. He seemed to be taking an awfully long time. Angela, Bill, Caroline, and I stood and watched, wincing, and commented that he could do with a sharper knife. (I was later told that a blunt knife does the job better because, for some reason, the calf loses less blood and the wound heals more quickly.) Surprisingly, the

calf made no noise, though it attempted to thrash about
with its tethered leg. The worst, though, was when this little
steer emerged. The dreadful deed done, his leg was untied
and reinserted through the trapdoor. The barrel was turned
and its catches released, and the calf was sent out into the
corral to find his mother. He was totally silent; not a whim-
pering note crossed the lips of this horrified castrato. His
eyes were wide and glistening. He staggered for a few steps,
then minced across the enclosure squeezing his back legs together, his tuft of a tail wedged between them.

Despite all my brave talk, I now began to feel distinctly
queasy myself. Strange, high-pitched ringing noises echoed
in my ears; I began to sweat, and my vision went gray and
starry. Unwittingly mimicking the castrated calf, I hobbled
back to the fire and sat weakly on a tree stump. Ron, who
had determinedly stayed there all along, could scarcely con-
tain his mirth.

On the Tuesday morning, we visited some Indian burial
caves. It was incredible that this one estancia spanned such
an astonishing variety of land. There were the black basalt
canyons, and the intensely green meadows over which we'd
galloped that first day; there were the sparse brown cattle
paddocks; and now we were to explore these caves set into
a hillside before wide-reaching green plains that stretched
to far-distant white-capped mountains.

We tethered our horses to a fence, then climbed up the
rock face. At first, it seemed that there was little to see beyond a shallow, cramped chamber, but then Jane pointed
into a narrow crevasse that cut between some jagged rocks.
We were to lie on our tummies and slither down that hole,

crawl along on our hands and knees for a couple of yards, and then we'd be able to stand.

Nervously, with torches in hand, we squeezed ourselves down the narrow hole and then, each in turn, exclaimed in wonder at the unexpected space that opened up before us. We were in a huge room now, a dark, damp, cavernous hall. Jane had brought candles which she placed on the rocky shelves so that this wide, cool space flickered in the weak yellow light. On the walls, red and yellow geometric patterns were daubed—the pictographs of the indigenous tribe.

The tribe that used to inhabit this part of Argentina was called the Manzaneros—the Apple Country People—after the fruit that grew in their valleys. (The first apple trees were believed to have been brought over the Andes by Jesuit missionaries intent on sowing the seeds of Christianity among the Indian tribes. The apples did rather better than the priests, who soon perished.) In 1870—a few years before Perito Moreno reached these parts—the Englishman George Musters visited a Manzaneros tribe not far from here. Musters was traveling through Patagonia in the company of a number of Tehuelches; the Tehuelches and Manzaneros had previously been hostile to one another but at the time of Musters's visit relations were thawing. With his native guides, Musters crossed the river Limay; they met the Manzaneros at the point where the Río Caleufú meets the Collón Curá just to the south of Estancia Huechahue. In his book *At Home with the Patagonians,* Musters wrote of the snow-clad mountains that lay in the distance—presumably the same ones we admired that day as we visited the burial caves.

The explorer had a high regard for the Manzaneros— "Their personal habits were excessively neat and cleanly, the morning bath never being omitted by men, women, and children, who all regularly trooped down to the water just before dawn; and their dress was much more carefully attended to than that of the Patagonians"—and he admired their production of wheat and organized harvesting of apples.

But most fascinating of all is Musters's description of the tense yet colorful scene in which the two tribes greeted each other a hundred and thirty-five years ago, in a valley not far from here.

"On arriving in sight of Cheoeque's [the Manzaneros chief whom Moreno referred to as Shaihueque] ancestral halls, we observed the Araucanians or Manzaneros form-ing into line and maneuvering about half a mile distant . . . Thus we remained for about half an hour watching the Manzaneros, who presented a fine appearance, dressed in bright-colored ponchos and armed with their long lances; they maneuvered into four squadrons, each with a leader— from whose lance fluttered a small pennon—moving with disciplined precision, and forming line, wheeling, and keep-ing their distance in a way that would not have discredited regular cavalry."

The tension ended when hostages were ritually ex-changed and the welcome ceremony began: The Tehuelches charged toward the Manzaneros with terrific excitement, and each was greeted by the chief who was dressed in a blue poncho, a hat, and leather boots. "When he arrived at my number I felt rather ashamed of my dress, a simple mantle not in a very good state of repair. He, on his side, having asked who I was, appeared rather astonished at hearing I was an Englishman," Musters wrote.

Shaihueque laid on a banquet for the Tehuelches and their peculiarly clad British companion. He served beef, mutton, and horsemeat from great cauldrons that bubbled over the fires in his well-appointed tent.

"The guests sat down as they could, while Cheoeque sat, as the Spaniards say, 'on horseback' on a chair in the middle of the toldo [tent], dressed in a magnificent cat-skin mantle, and holding a 'revengue' or hide whip in his hand, with which he ever and anon chastised an intrusive dog, or even one of his numerous sons if they came too near, or made too much noise."

I wondered whether Shaihueque had ever donned his magnificent cat-skin outfit and ridden over the plain that stretched out before us now. This land would have fallen well within his territory, before the government packaged it up and parceled it off to industrious estancieros. Those same men with whom Musters dined, with their lances and bright-colored ponchos, must have known this place well. Maybe some of them had even been buried in these caves whose deep caverns we explored.

Shaihueque's skeleton was certainly not here, though. From 1879, General Roca decimated the Indian population of northern Patagonia with his "Conquest of the Desert": the cold storage plant had been invented and the whites wanted more land for lucrative beef production. Shaihueque was the last to surrender—he was captured with thousands of his tribesmen in 1885. Moreno went to visit him in the Buenos Aires barracks where he was imprisoned.

"When I visited Shaihueque at Retiro I was struck by the vivid memories etched in my mind of my terrible experiences at Caleufú and Quem-quem-treu, where I suffered hunger and looked death in the face," he wrote in an article for the newspaper *El Diario*. "Nevertheless, when I entered the small room containing what was left of the tribe whose company I had once shared, all I felt was sadness . . . The tanned, naked chests, the disheveled hair, did not belong in Buenos Aires."

I wondered if any of those last Manzaneros had taken refuge here as Roca and his soldiers had hacked their way through the indigenous world. Strategically, these caves' location must have been brilliant: They were imperceptible from the outside, yet from their entrance one could see for miles across the plains. But, whatever may have happened here, these chambers were now deserted. Of the tribe that once roamed these lands, just pictographs remained.

Our evening ride later that day took us to the cliffs where the condors nested. We climbed on horseback into the setting sun, through more golden grasses and scrubby green shrubs. At the cliff's foot, we dismounted and left the horses in Simon's care, then scrambled up the precipitous rock face. At the top, we found ourselves on a wide, flat plateau. Below us, and stretching far into the distance, round brown hummocks undulated smoothly; one hill was entirely flat at its top, as though its summit had been sliced off by some vengeful deity bearing a superhuman scythe. A river meandered through the valley. We crossed the green, rock-littered mesa until we reached the cliff edge on the other side.

There, perhaps twenty or thirty mighty condors performed their evening acrobatics. They soared and dived, swooped and spun. They were so close to us that we were able to observe every detail: their rounded hooked beaks, their feet hanging weightlessly from their bodies with their curving claws and vicious talons. From here, each fabulous feather stood out. The light caught on the birds' wings, turning those jet black plumes a glistening silver as they glided, serene and effortless, before the snow-smattered mountains. As the sun dipped lower the sky turned from a cobalt blue to an inky indigo. The clouds began to close in, their luminescent white contours streaked with purple smudges and smears.

Yvonne had brought a bottle of wine and some glasses; we drank and watched the condors, and listened to Suzanne, who regaled us with a mind-blowing tale from her wide repertoire of doom:

"Did you ever hear about that man in Alaska who got eaten by a bear?" she asked, her voice heavy with horror.

A pair of condors spiraled through the evening sky showing off to their peers with daredevil moves.

"He was quite well known—he'd been observing the bears for years. Then, one night, when he and his girlfriend were in their tent in the woods, they heard a rustling sound outside. The man went out—and the bear attacked him!"

There were several of them now, these astonishing birds of prey, all trying to outdo each other as they flapped their powerful wings, then twirled through an astonishing gymnastic set right before our eyes.

"The terrible thing was," Suzanne continued to recount in low, dramatic tones, "he hadn't turned off the microphone on his video recorder. So later, when they found his remains, they replayed the tape and they could hear the screams of this man as he was eaten alive. They could hear his girlfriend shouting to him from the tent. And then the bear ate her too."

The sun was low now. We had finished the wine,

Suzanne's bloodthirsty tale had reached its grisly conclusion, and we had to head back to our horses. We wouldn't have wanted to negotiate our descent down that cliff in the dark or, who knows, one of us might have slipped, met our own unfortunate demise, and ended our days as carrion to those glorious, majestic creatures who reigned in the overhead skies.

18

Tony's Revenge

According to the Mapuche tribe, no man—or woman—should dare to climb Mount Lanín. Legend relates that a group of young tribesmen was once out hunting. They were hotly pursuing a huemul, an Andean deer, which took off up the slopes of the mountain. In their eagerness to bag the deer, the hunters ran up the hillside after it—but in doing so they enraged Pillán, the god who lived at the summit. Pillán unleashed his fury and the volcano started to steam. Ash rained from the sky and the boiling ground shook. Only one woman could placate Pillán and save the tribe—and that was the chief's daughter, the beautiful Huilefún. In order to deliver her people from Pillán's wrath, she had to offer herself to him as a sacrifice.

Huilefún climbed the mountain. A condor flew overhead, then swooped low and clasped her in its claws. The giant bird carried her to the crater of the flaming volcano and dropped her into the blazing abyss. Then the air grew cold, and snow fell for many days. The volcano was extinguished—and to this day Lanín has been covered in a shroud of white.

It was a little worrying then when, on our first morning in the Lanín National Park, we started to climb steeply upward. We were going to be spending the next three days riding through the park; at night we'd be camping beneath the stars. It seemed a touch foolhardy, when we were so subject to the whims of the elements, to be starting out quite so brazenly—but, on the other hand, Lanín has not thrown a lava-spewing temper tantrum for many, many years, so maybe we were safe.

Yvonne was going to be our guide for the next few days, and so Jane had driven us all to the park that morning in the minibus. We'd hurtled along the road, fast and furious.

"Jane drives the same way she rides," I'd laughed, safely out of earshot in the backseat.

We'd come to a police checkpoint.

"I just want to see what Jane tells them," Yvonne had whispered, squashed onto the bench beside me. "I never know what to say."

Jane had hit the accelerator and roared straight through.

But now, amid the serenity of the natural world, our pace was slower. We picked our way along the upward slope. The weather was warm—we were comfortable wearing T-shirts—and the horses' flanks heaved and poured sweat as they hauled us up the steep, winding incline. I was riding Tony again. He was a strong horse, and every now and then he broke into a trot to aid his momentum—or perhaps he just wanted to get it over with. Up and up we went, then up and up some more.

Finally, we arrived at a plateau stippled with blades of grass and specked with jagged little rocks where we stopped to rest and to tighten our girths. We were just about level with the snow line now. Occasional tiny white flowers sprouted through the scrub, echoing in miniature form the brilliant swaths of icy crystals which spread before us and then grew ever denser and deeper as the mountain rose to its peak.

Below us, the park rolled out in spectacular beauty. The stony gray hills descended to a valley and a brilliant blue lake. Then we turned around and made our way back down.

I wondered what Tony made of all this. He was a straightforward, forthright kind of a horse and I wasn't completely sure he would understand the worth of his having trawled all the way up that precipitously steep hill just so that the idle good-for-nothing sitting on his back could admire a pretty view. I could only imagine the thoughts that must now be going through his head.

"Good lord," he was probably thinking. "I've climbed all the way up that bloody hill, and now she wants me to carry her back down again. Aaaah—nasty-looking drop there. Just thinking about going down's giving me vertigo. Oooh, my knees . . ."

Or something like that.

We rode through forests of southern beeches. On the higher slopes, lanky-limbed lengas reigned, then we came to stockier *ñires* trees with many-branching trunks, and tremendous coihues. Slender yet statuesque, they towered, timeless, over us.

Brilliant scarlet notros flowers blazed in prodigious, prolific bushes, their stamens and fine, narrow petals reaching out to the forest like thousands of beckoning fingers. Tiny wild strawberries sprouted around the horses' hooves.

Coming out of the woods, we left the soft earthen paths and picked our way over harsh black lava beds upon whose surface the horses' hooves clipped and tapped. The small, round boulders were pitted and dimpled like a gathering of sooty, cellulite-plagued bottoms.

We stopped by a stream where the grass was lush and green. When the horses had drunk from the clear, fast-flowing water, and we had tethered them to bushes to graze, we laid out our picnic lunch in the shade of the trees—quiche and salad and a few glasses of wine. The gauchos built a fire and brewed coffee and we kicked back for an hour or two.

We rode on through dense groves of coligue canes. The coligue is a plant of the bamboo family; it lives in colonies. From amid one multitude, a capacious black and white cow loomed. With its dark eyes peering out from its blotchy face, it resembled a very lost panda.

The coligue flowers just once in its life and then, after this single brief blossoming, it dies. Immense tracts of these cane forests had passed their bloom. The arid stalks stuck out spikily from the ground: they were no longer green but the color of bleached sand. Their days of sappy flexibility were long past; these canes were stiff and arthritically rigid, and the fine tendrils that sprayed from their swollen knots were gray and dry with age.

We rode through them, walking, trotting, and cantering. Sometimes, riding at speed, we turned a bend into a section that leaned lopsided toward the center of the path, forming a low tunnel of treacherous dry sticks, and we had to duck down over our horses' withers to avoid being whipped around the face and neck. On other occasions we just had time to raise a hand to ward off an overhanging cane. As the sun crept lower, its dying light penetrated these groves in shafts and lit the long-dead plants a pale, whitish gold.

After one last breathless slaloming canter through the tight bends of the forest, we arrived at the shore of a lake,

perfectly still other than for the almost imperceptible movement of a solitary grebe. From its far shore, the brilliant,
glittering Mount Lanín frowned majestically down on us.

We walked around the lake's sandy bank until we found
to our overwhelming joy a grassy meadow on which had already been erected a series of two-man tents. The gauchos
and Francis had come on ahead: The fire was roaring and the
steaks were ready to sizzle. Our luggage with its fresh
changes of clothes lay in a neat pile. We bathed in the lake,
wrapped up in warm fleeces, and gathered around the fire
to eat.

Now that we were out in the wilds, away from the delights of en-suite bathrooms and well-lit mirrors, the sartorial superiority of our American contingent was becoming
dazzlingly apparent. Suzanne's saddlebags didn't appear to
bulge more than anyone else's—yet every time a change of
clothes was required she reappeared from her tiny tent resplendent in a different pair of glisteningly clean jodhpurs,
with T-shirts and sweaters that blended in tone. (On one
particularly exciting occasion, she even surfaced in a little
black number with a leopard-print stripe.) She always had a
pair of sunglasses to match. Ron was much the same. He'd
spent some time riding with the cowboys on the dude
ranches of North America, and wore full-length leather
chaps over his jeans to prove it. Whenever a change was
called for, he appeared in a new, perfectly pressed shirt.
How his linen stayed so sharp after a day in a saddlebag, I
had no idea.

We British, by comparison, tended to emerge from our
tents looking murky and clunky and generally ill-matched. I
was wearing an assortment of old sports tops and fleeces
over my bombachas; one of them was a rather misshapen
garment that zipped into the waterproof jacket I'd picked

up for ten pounds in a Chinese street market. I felt I was failing horribly as far as appearances were concerned—but perhaps effortless style was something these Americans had drummed into them at an early age along with perfectly pearly teeth and immaculate fingernails.

Our mattresses that evening were constructed from the horse blankets and sheepskins we'd ridden on during the day, but once Caroline and I had accustomed ourselves to the fact that our tent stank of animal sweat, we slept well. The next morning, though, Tony seemed a little slow.

"Come on, Tony," I yelled at him time and again as I booted him hard in the flanks. But Tony didn't seem interested. It was strange. Usually he was a lively animal who loved to canter, but that day we were getting left behind. Everyone else loped off into the distance while I, for all my attempts at spurring, could scarcely persuade Tony to trot.

"I think there's something the matter with Tony," I pronounced to Yvonne. "He just won't go. What do you think it could be?"

Yvonne shrugged. "I think he's probably hungry," she said. "I don't think that spot we left them in last night was terribly good. I don't think he's had enough to eat."

I was overcome by remorse. There I had been whacking and kicking and shouting at the poor horse, and he'd had no breakfast! While I myself had been merrily stuffing my face with meat and veg last night, and cereal and fruit this morning, I hadn't given a thought to poor Tony, who must have been standing, forlorn, with not enough grass to fill his rumbling tummy.

When I finally caught up with them, I told the others of Yvonne's diagnosis.

"*Hungry?*" Ron laughed and laughed. "You didn't fall for that, did you? He's a *horse!*"

"Well, um, well, maybe poor Tony *is* hungry," I said. "I tied him to a very nasty bush last night; maybe he's feeling a bit deprived. Maybe that's why he's going so slowly."

Bill turned around and grinned, and raised a cynical Scottish eyebrow.

We stopped for lunch in a particularly plenteous field of grass and plump yellow buttercups where, I hoped, Tony would be able to eat his fill. The fat, juicy blades were scattered with shoots of wild mint whose sweet scent hung in the air.

While the horses gorged themselves on grass, we passengers feasted on chicken barbecued over the fire, potato salad, beetroot, and fresh pineapple, and washed it all down with a few cold beers.

There was an old rusting railway engine in the clearing where we had our picnic. I had no idea how it could have found its way into this verdant meadow in the middle of a national park. There was no track in sight, so it seemed unlikely that it had come under its own steam: Somebody must have dumped it here.

There was once an ambitious strategy for the building of railways in Argentina: Profit-minded British entrepreneurs pumped money into the construction of tracks in the nineteenth century, but they never made it to the southern territories. In the early twentieth century, the Argentine government decided to make tracks of its own. It stamped its approval on the construction of three lines in Patagonia, but the work was slow: The line from San Antonio Oeste on the Atlantic coast to Bariloche was started in 1909 but, what with the economic effects of the First World War and the departure of those initial enthusiasts from government, the line wasn't completed until 1934. Even then, these lines weren't a great success. The idea behind the Patagonian railways was to open up the uninhabited south rather than to serve existing settlements. They never attracted sufficient passengers—travel by road was faster—and the few lines that were built were never linked up as originally proposed.

During the second half of the twentieth century, funding fizzled out further and the rust set in on the Argentine railways. Today, there are very few passenger lines still running. (One exception is La Trochita, renamed by Paul Theroux as the Old Patagonian Express, which still trundles under the power of its original 1922 steam engines over a part of its original route.) And so the lines sit and crumble, much like the locomotive in our lunchtime meadow.

It wasn't until after lunch that we found out why Tony, too, had been a little rusty. We had roused ourselves from our siestas and had gone to saddle our horses.

"That's not Tony!" Yvonne shouted as I untied a horse—exactly the same horse I was certain I had tethered to a tree earlier. "That one's Tony!" She pointed to another white horse, strikingly similar in appearance, that Angela was leading down the hill. But Angela's horse had a red leading rein. I could have sworn that I'd tied Tony up with a blue one.

"Did you have a red rope or a blue one?" I asked Angela suspiciously.

"A red one," she said. "And I'm certain the knot I've just untied was one of mine—it was the knot I tied earlier."

Tony's morning malady was suddenly abundantly clear. Tony had not been hungry. He hadn't been suffering from a rumbly tummy. Tony, quite simply, had not been himself.

Reluctantly, Angela relinquished Tony and we rode on through this natural wonderland. Magellanic fuchsias flaunted their capricious pink and coquettish purple garb through the undergrowth amid smatterings of tiny, timid, pure white orchids. We picked berries from the michay bushes and ate them: They say that if you swallow this tiny blue fruit you're sure to return to Patagonia. Palosanto bushes, translated as "holy sticks," sprouted their crucifix-shaped foliage. Evergreen maniu trees tapered to their high crowns and perfumed the forest air. We passed yet more brazen red notros.

We arrived on a different shore of the lake. The ground was soft and sandy here, the sky was clear, and the water shimmered so that Mount Lanín's reflection echoed back perfectly from its surface. We cantered along the beach, then climbed high along a ridge to a waterfall whose banks gave onto yet another remarkable vista of the volcano. Back at the lakeside, the shore was littered with silvery driftwood. The blue sky reflected off the water's surface, casting it a deep azure. We cut through the shallows, lifting our legs high around the horses' necks as they waded through the cool, clear water up to their haunches. As Tony and I strode through, I heard a tremendous splashing behind us: Suzanne was charging by at a canter.

We made our way through a capacious forest of monkey puzzle trees whose spiky branches curved and twisted, confident and dramatic, high into the cloudless sky. Finally, we climbed one last hill, and arrived in a meadow that looked out over the lake and glorious, white-shrouded Lanín once more. We'd seen the mountain many times now from various vantage points but it still had the power to evoke total wonder, even at the end of several days' hard riding. Now the snow glistened on its peak with a radiance seen usually only in dramatic reenactments of divine interventions, or in spangling dental advertisements. A cluster of resplendent monkey puzzles soared and swooped; a bright red notros bush bloomed ravishing red against the cool green of the grass.

Toward the back of this exquisite meadow, in front of an old wooden hut draped with drying animal skins, an ancient white-bearded man sat on a rickety chair. He was the owner of this land; we would be camping that night with his permission at the lakeside. His beard and mustache were neatly trimmed but the sneakers on his feet were ragged and unlaced. They looked as though they had seen many years' service. His belt cinched in the waist of his too-big bombachas so that they fell in thick folds about his hips. Yvonne stood and chatted to him for a while; I couldn't fathom the meaning of a single sound that rolled from his tongue. It was incredible to think: This was the first person we'd met in the last two days in the forest. All that time we'd been walking and cantering about, over all that distance we'd covered, we'd not met another soul. We had been entirely alone with the fresh air, the flowers, and the astonishingly scenic views.

As we stood and waited while Yvonne made small talk, Tony finally decided he'd had enough. It was time to get rid of this lumbering woman and that cumbersome saddle and bags, he clearly thought. He bent his forelegs, and dropped to his knees.

For a fraction of a second, I wondered what he was up to. Then I realized: He was preparing to roll. Terrible visions of an agonized death by squashing flashed before my eyes; with a lightning speed inspired only by the fear of imminent flattening, I leaped off his back.

We bathed with breathtaking brevity in the crushingly cold lake and gathered once more around the fire. After a day of clear blue skies, the clouds had started to gather and the temperature had dropped. We wrapped up in warm clothes, jackets, and hats, and finished off our fetching outfits with long woolen ponchos.

The hottest topic of conversation that evening was the matter of who was going to marry the astonishingly old man. Yvonne reckoned he was about ninety years old. He owned this patch of land, which was among the most beautiful any of us had seen anywhere, but he wasn't married and he had no children. When he died, the land would revert to the National Park—unless he could be seduced into matrimony before he expired, in which case this sensational inheritance would pass to his wife.

Would it be worth it? Caroline and I wondered. What services, exactly, would one have to perform for this superannuated creature? Very few, we suspected. He would be well entrenched in his own ways. A little cooking, perhaps. Maybe one might run an occasional feather duster around the decrepit old hut. But surely he couldn't live for long?

That night, after dinner, we were treated to music and dancing. One of the men strummed a guitar. Another tried to sing a traditional gaucho song, but became overwhelmed by nerves and dissolved into debilitating giggles after the first two lines. We washed our stew down with whisky, and then Domingo, one of the gauchos, asked me to dance. Caroline was taken by another of the men, and Suzanne by a third. I was at least a head taller than Domingo and I was dressed in such a bulky assortment of clothes, with a poncho on top, that my movements—which would never have been elegant—were limited to an elephantine stomp. We would have seemed a curious sight had, perhaps, the old man creaked down the hill to take a look at us. Again and again we danced beneath the monkey puzzle trees, shuffling around ineptly to the chords of the guitar until, finally, we managed to execute our escape and retired to our tents.

Tony was feeling frisky the next morning, so it was a bad time for me to break one of the cardinal rules of riding. We'd packed away the camp and were ready to start out on the final day of our journey. I'd put my left foot in the stirrup and had just swung my leg over when he decided to go for an impromptu bolt.

The big problem was, I wasn't holding the reins at the time. You should always hold the reins when mounting a horse. I'd been told this time and again. But I'd been riding Tony for several days now and he'd never tried any of his cartwheeling tricks. Deviously, he'd lulled me into a false sense of security.

Off we hurtled up the hill. Tony was running flat out, though the incline prevented him from managing a fully fledged gallop. I had one foot in its stirrup, the other foot hanging loose, no reins, and, to cap a difficult situation, my leather cowboy hat had fallen down over my eyes so I couldn't see a thing.

Was a bolting horse possessed of sufficient sense not to crash into a tree? I wondered from the black world of the inside of my hat. I think about ten seconds passed before finally I managed to reach down and grope for the reins, and to pull Tony up to a stop.

We stood for a moment, Tony throwing his head and skipping slightly while I grimly gripped the reins in a short stranglehold. Caroline trotted up beside me.

"Did you do that on purpose?" she asked.

Firmly back in control, we continued our ride up and down earthen tracks and over one precariously broken bridge. Alongside the path grew tiny violet plants. They looked like diminutive bluebells that had received a nasty shock and turned pale with fright.

My back was starting to ache now. We'd spent long stretches trotting and cantering in the last few days and my riding technique was still rudimentary. I winced as Tony broke into a jolting trot once more. Ron must have noticed—as we slowed down again he pulled out of his pocket a handful of white tablets.

"Here, take a couple of these," he said. So that was why he'd been looking so relaxed and comfortable: He'd had his hand in the ibuprofen bottle.

We stopped for lunch in a meadow where wild sweet peas grew among the grass. We settled down on the soft ground and then, just as we were well and truly comfortable, Tony staged his final act of rebellion.

"No!" Yvonne suddenly shrieked at the top of her voice as she leaped to her feet and took off across the grass. Tony had decided to take another roll—but this time he was tethered to the low branch of a tree. Fortunately, Yvonne managed to stop him before he did himself any damage—which was more than could be said for the camera I had foolishly left in my saddlebags.

We indulged in a few final canters through the trees. Bill

was whipped in the face by one overhanging branch—it caught him on the mouth, giving him a bloody smear down the side of his face. He looked like a gluttonous vampire after a particularly rich feast. And then, finally, we arrived at a river. There was a road on the other side; Francis would soon be there at the wheel of the minibus, ready to drive us back to hot baths and soft beds.

We unsaddled the horses, then crossed the river in a tiny wooden boat. Behind us, the gauchos drove the horses into the glistening, crystal-clear water. As a small herd, they waded up to their knees, then to their haunches, and then they started, gracefully, to swim. For a few minutes only their heads were visible above the surface; then they found their footing on the sandy bed of the opposite bank and, with their wet coats glinting sleekly in the sunshine, they emerged once more into the crisp Patagonian air.

19

On Ice

There was a mighty roar, then a crashing sound that suggested the world had come to an end. From my bench in the sun, I peered out at the glacier face: A tiny white speck crumbled from the immense wall of ice and tumbled into the turquoise lake below; the waters churned and surged as they welcomed their newest iceberg. What looked to me like a minute chip trickling from this gargantuan mass of ice must, in fact, have been a thunderous hunk. The noise was phenomenal, almost apocalyptic. What was more, the time delay between sound and sight implied that this staggering magnitude of frozen vertexes, cliffs, and crags was much farther away—and much larger—than it looked. And it looked truly enormous.

I was now at the Perito Moreno Glacier. I'd left Estancia Huechahue the morning following our return from the Lanín National Park. I'd bidden farewell to Jane, Yvonne, Caroline, Tony, and the others and flown down to El Calafate in the far south (my canceled flights had now, mercifully, been rebooked). From there I'd taken a day trip out to the Perito Moreno ice field. This glacier is just one of many attractions in an area rich in natural wonders (there are 365 glaciers in the Parque Nacional los Glaciares—one for each day of the year—and that's before you've started on the mountains, lakes, forests, and wildlife) but, horribly, I was running out of time. I wouldn't be able to see them all, on this trip at least, as I only had ten days left before I was due to fly home to London. I was still eager to visit the remote islands of Tierra del Fuego and the Welsh settlements on the Atlantic coast—and that left just one day in which to sate my appetite for all things icy.

Had I been full of verve, spirit, and derring-do, of course, I'd have strapped on my crampons and hiked out across the ice—but I wasn't. I was exhausted after all that cantering, galloping, herding, and bolting. I had no great inclination that day to exert myself at all. And so I didn't. I took a minibus out to the glacier, I took a little boat trip up to the cliff face, and I went for a very gentle stroll around some boardwalks. And then, for a couple of hours, I sat on a bench in the sun and just stared at this titanic expanse of ice.

The glacier was mesmerizing. It wasn't just its size, although that in itself was magnificent: The glacier front rises to the height of a twenty-story building and stretches more than three miles across. What really struck me about this glacier, though, was its incredible, indisputable beauty. It was more radiant by far than any glacier I'd seen in the past. I'd come to think of these rivers of ice as rather overrated attractions—geologically staggering, I'm sure, but I'm not a geologist and I'd always thought them disappointingly muddy and brown, streaked as they tend to be with moraine. The Perito Moreno Glacier, though, was sensational. The white ice glistened. It towered into amazingly sculpted pinnacles, and then carved itself into astonishing glowing blue crevasses.

The depth of color was dazzling. Glacier ice is very dense—if you were to put a block of glacier ice in your gin and tonic, it would melt more slowly than a cube from the freezer tray. This is because glacier ice is compressed over thousands of years as it is pulled infinitesimally slowly downhill by gravity; it's compacted further still by the weight of fresh snow falling on its surface. And it's because of this density that glaciers and icebergs (which are bits of glaciers that have broken off) appear to be blue. The ice is so compact that not all the colors of the spectrum can pass through it. Weaker red light is quickly absorbed. Some of the hardier blue light, however, is able to penetrate this thick, difficult mass, and when what is left of the light reemerges from the glacial depths, we see it as blue.

I'd seen photographs of blue icebergs before, of course, but I'd always thought that extraordinary hue was due to some kind of photographer's trick. Now I realized that the opposite was true. The photographs I'd seen hadn't enhanced the color: This ice exuded a blueness that no image I had ever seen had been able to capture.

The ice quite literally shone. From its crevasses, a thousand electric-blue lightbulbs seemed to beam. It was as though the ice itself was possessed of a tremendous energy. In the deeper chasms, the ice appeared the color of a lurid snow cone that lightened to shimmering turquoise as each face climbed to a peak.

In places, the elements had carved these freezing mountains into seductive curves, then whipped their summits into sharply tapering spires. Other sections fell away in sheer smooth drops, like a lustrous sorbet sliced by a knife.

And then, as the glacier rose on and up into the distance, and the peaks and gullies grew ever farther from the eye, the surface of this great expanse of ice took on the appearance of millions of sugary rosettes, the finely piped icing of a cake baked for an army of Patagonian giants.

I sat and stared, and gazed, and marveled. Every now and then, a chunk of the glacier wall would tumble and roar. It was a sunny day, an incredible sight, and I was happy for once not to move at all but just to sit still and look on in wonder. And then I climbed back on the minibus and returned to El Calafate, ready to travel the following morning to the very end of the inhabited earth.

20

The End of the World

"*Lomo,*" **said the menu** under the meat section. And then the English translation: "Tender lion."

I wondered what a tender lion did when it was out in the wild, or wherever it lived, and not sitting in slabs in a restaurant kitchen waiting to be served to hungry diners. Did it purr beatifically and lovingly stroke its prey? However it displayed its tenderness it would seem unkind to eat it, I thought, so I ordered the sea bass instead. In any case, I was now in Ushuaia, at Argentina's austral tip, where the fish was served fresh from the freezing waters of the Atlantic and reputed to be fantastic.

I had arrived in Ushuaia mid-afternoon and was sitting ready for dinner in the Bar Ideal, a green-and-cream-painted establishment built from corrugated iron, and one of the settlement's oldest hostelries. Ushuaia is the main town of Argentine Tierra del Fuego. It's the southernmost town on earth—the next stop's Antarctica. "*Bienvenidos al*

Fin del Mundo!" cackled a calamitous signboard. Welcome to the End of the World.

Presumably, the town's earliest inhabitants found the place apocalyptic enough, for Ushuaia was founded as a penal colony. Following the apparent success of the English model in Australia and the French enclaves in New Caledonia and Algeria, the Argentine authorities decided to establish a convicts' settlement in their own desolate southern territory and thereby solve two pressing problems. First, the penitentiary in Buenos Aires was overcrowded, and the authorities wanted somewhere nasty to dispose of hardened repeat offenders. Second, the Argentine government had in 1881 signed the Boundaries Treaty with Chile and it was anxious to inhabit this barren outpost in order to protect Argentine sovereignty.

The ticket to Tierra del Fuego was received by exiles-to-be with dread and trembling—and for good reason. The journey to these hostile, unpredictable islands would for almost all of them be a one-way affair, and the voyage was a grisly punishment in itself. It took about a month to sail to Ushuaia from Buenos Aires. Convicts were transported in shackles; each was given a large chamber pot, then confined to the hold for the duration of the voyage. By the time they docked at their destination, prisoners would be enshrouded in the fine coal dust that had penetrated their dungeons. And then they had nothing to look forward to: sentences here were long, and conditions arduous.

The first convict boat arrived in 1884 and the town of Ushuaia was officially founded. (There was, before this, a British missionary settlement in Ushuaia but no Argentine authorities oversaw the region.) To start with, though, the prisoners weren't held in the town itself but were detained on an outlying island, the Isla de los Estados. The first convicts were military malefactors, but it didn't take long for a civilian penal settlement to be founded alongside: The first civilian offenders—both men and women—arrived in 1896.

"Prisoners that have been sent to me are already settled down, working, and on the road to regeneration. Of the women prisoners, six have married, three to other prisoners, and another three to residents already settled in the territory," wrote Godoy, the governor of Tierra del Fuego, to the Argentine Minister of Justice in August that year.

It wasn't until 1902 that the prison was moved to Ushuaia itself, and a few years later still that the military and civilian prisons were merged. The penal colony never took off but still, until 1947 when a decree from Juan Perón closed the place, Ushuaia's prison housed some of Argentina's most notorious criminals.

On my first morning there, Argentina's "Siberia" was overcast. Powerful jets of rain shot down from the leaden skies. The foreboding mountains that ringed the town were enveloped in a thick mist. And so I decided that, rather than trying to see the natural sights of this saturated place, I'd pay a visit to the old prison—it had now been refurbished as a museum. I dressed in thermals, hat and gloves, and full-length raincoat, and made my way there.

The prison roof was leaking. Seeping water formed pools in strategically placed buckets. There were, however, generously roaring heaters that took most of the chill out of this former jail. But this was midsummer. What would it have been like to have been incarcerated here on a bleak winter's day seventy or eighty years ago? According to the information boards that related the history of the prison, the inmates always preferred to work than to sit immobile—indeed, it was the prisoners who built the town of Ushuaia and its infrastructure. Little wonder they wanted to keep moving, I thought to myself as I attempted to dry out in front of one of the blazing furnaces. If they had sat still in here for long, they would surely have congealed.

In the cells, frigid replicas of former inmates posed. Most interesting, I thought, was Cayetano Santos Godino, who was incarcerated here after a killing spree in which he slaughtered a series of small children. Godino was a short man with large, sticking-out ears. The doctors of the day believed that the source of his evil lay in his outsized ears and so, on November 4, 1927, prison surgeons executed a crude form of plastic surgery to reduce their dimensions and thus, they hoped, to lessen Godino's propensity for murdering babies.

Feasibly, I suppose, it might have worked. I can see that after the operation Godino could well have spent so much time clutching his head and moaning, "Ow, my ears hurt," that all homicidal thoughts might have deserted him. But, seemingly, they didn't. Rumor had it that his grotesque appendages subsequently grew back and, with no available children to slay, he one day threw a cat in the fire instead. His fellow prisoners were enraged by his cruelty and, in a tremendous display of their own benignity, beat him so severely that he died.

Also locked up here, and now sitting in his cell in papier-mâché glory wearing a blue-and-yellow-striped prison suit and cap, was Simon Radovitsky. Radovitsky was a young Russian anarchist who was convicted of the murder of a Buenos Aires chief of police and his secretary in 1909: He threw a bomb at the police officer's car as he was leaving the funeral of a friend at the Recoleta Cemetery. Radovitsky's indefinite sentence included the stipulation that he should be confined to his cell for twenty days each year to mark the anniversary of the murder. Radovitsky was imprisoned for nineteen years here in Ushuaia and he spent half his sentence in solitary confinement. Presumably he got used to the cold.

The weather cleared a little in the evening and I took a stroll through the streets. As the clouds began to rise, the light became pale and watery. Slowly, the glacial peaks that encircled the town were unsheathed; they dwarfed the huddle of colorful corrugated-metal buildings at their feet, leaving them looking tiny and vulnerable. Above the roofs, old wooden churches stretched their spires toward their rather misty heaven. Chink by chink the sun filtered through and the people who walked in the streets began to drag long, skinny shadows behind them. Their silhouettes appeared to have been elongated like tightly stretched elastic.

Down at the port, huge passenger cruisers paused before departing for the icebergs of Antarctica. Smaller sailing vessels lay at anchor, rocking back and forth with the ebb and flow, their masts reflected in the perfectly still, clear water.

As I stood on the waterfront and gazed at the boats, a little boy stopped beside me on his bicycle.

"*Tienes novio?*" Do you have a boyfriend? he asked me.

"Not right now," I said. "Do you have a girlfriend?"

"No," he said. He paused a moment, then asked, "Where are you from?"

"England."

"Oh . . . can you speak English?"

"Yes."

"Can you speak it well?"

"Yes," I said, "I can speak it very well."

"Oh," said the little boy. "Say something in English then."

"What do you want me to say?"

"Um . . . *perro*."

"Dog."

"Oh . . . I'm from here."

"It's a nice place. You're lucky."

The little boy grinned and pedaled off.

And then, the next morning, the skies were brilliant blue. Taking advantage of the improved weather I walked for three hours in the Tierra del Fuego National Park.

The first part of my walk took me along a path that followed the coastline of the Beagle Channel. The temperature had risen noticeably since the day before so that, as I walked, I had to strip off layers of clothing. Sandy coves and stony promontories dipped in and out of the icy, navy blue water. Along the beach, mussel shells lay strewn, gleaming purple-black among the pebbles. The sharply hewn rocks at the ocean's edge glinted like polished platinum in the sun. In one grassy nook, amid a cluster of white dandelion heads whose seeds had yet to float away, a gray-and-white upland goose tended her gosling. A short distance across the narrow channel, that same stretch of water along which Darwin, FitzRoy, and the crew of the *Beagle* had sailed in 1832, the snow-smattered mountains still stood enthroned. This was just one more infinitesimal day in their eternal, stony reign.

The path turned away from the shore and meandered through woodland. The ground underfoot was soft and spongy now. Trees reached out with their long, low branches that stretched and swooped just above the ground like greedy tentacles. The sun's rays seared through the foliage and threw intense shadows upon branches and trunks draped with pale green webs of lichen. Clusters of orange honeycombed globes the size of golf balls clung to the bark; when the sun shone on them, they lit up like glowing spheres of light. These were a type of fungus—the Argentines call it *pan de indios,* Indian bread, because the Ona and Yámana, the people indigenous to these parts, used to eat it.

The Yámana were a tribe of canoeists. Astonishingly, even in this freezing climate, they wore no clothes or animal skins. Instead, they always kept a fire burning, even inside their canoes. It's thought that these fires gave the region its name: Tierra del Fuego means Fireland. In the early days of European exploration, when the Yámana saw a sail on the horizon, they would pile green branches onto their camp-fires so that those out fishing would see the smoke and take heed. When the first European ships came to these parts, their crews' first impression would have been of endless coils of rising smoke.

If the Europeans' first impressions were unsettling, their second impressions were generally less favorable still.

"These were the most abject and miserable creatures I anywhere beheld," wrote Charles Darwin from the *Beagle* in 1832. "On the east coast the natives, as we have seen, have guanaco cloaks, and on the west, they possess sealskins . . . But these Fuegians in the canoe were quite naked, and even one full-grown woman was absolutely so. It was raining heavily, and the fresh water, together with the spray, trickled down her body. In another harbor not far distant, a woman, who was suckling a recently born child, came one day along-side the vessel and remained there out of mere curiosity, whilst the sleet fell and thawed on her naked bosom, and on the skin of her naked baby! These poor wretches were stunted in their growth, their hideous faces bedaubed with white paint, their skins filthy and greasy, their hair entangled, their voices discordant, and their gestures violent. Viewing such men, one can hardly make oneself believe that they are fellow-creatures, and inhabitants of the same world."

When Captain FitzRoy had first visited these parts during his initial voyage in the *Beagle* from 1826 to 1830 (Charles Darwin sailed only on the second voyage), he had captured four Yámana tribespeople and taken them with him to England. One of these hostages had soon died of smallpox. The remaining three—Jemmy Button, York Minster, and Fuegia Basket—had become veritable celebrities among fashionable society of the day. They had been educated in the English language and the gospel, and had even been presented to King William IV and Queen Adelaide at St. James's Palace.

Now on his return journey, FitzRoy brought his Fuegian protégés back to their native land. He also brought a young catechist named Richard Matthews—the idea was that Matthews would stay ashore with the three Fuegians and introduce their delighted friends and families to the joys of Christianity.

Matthews didn't last long. About a week after they'd bade the missionary and his three converts farewell, FitzRoy and his entourage returned to the place where they had left them. They found Matthews distraught. He had been robbed and harangued by the Yámana, who, armed with stones and stakes, had besieged his encampment day and night.

"Another party showed by signs that they wished to strip him naked and pluck all the hairs out of his face and body. I think we arrived just in time to save his life," wrote an alarmed Darwin.

With abject eagerness, Matthews leaped back aboard the

Beagle, leaving Jemmy Button, Fuegia Basket, and York Minster to fend for themselves among their tribe.

"Our three Fuegians, though they had been only three years with civilized men, would, I am sure, have been glad to have retained their new habits; but this was obviously impossible. I fear it is more than doubtful, whether their visit will have been of any use to them," Darwin wrote. Indeed, when the *Beagle* returned to this part of the coast a little over a year later, its crew found Jemmy "a thin haggard savage, with long disordered hair, and naked, except for a bit of blanket round his waist." So ended the first European attempt to enlighten the people of Tierra del Fuego.

A second bid to convert Fuegian souls was launched eighteen years later, in 1850. Captain Allen Gardiner, one of the founding members of the Patagonian Missionary Society, put ashore in Tierra del Fuego with a catechist, a carpenter, and three Cornish fishermen. The Fuegians robbed and tormented the missionaries so perniciously that the Christians had to withdraw to their boats; the canoeists then followed them onto the water and pelted them with rocks. Forced to flee, Gardiner and his cohorts finally found a cove secluded enough to hide them from those whom they had hoped so fervently to save—and there, one by one, they starved to death.

Allen Gardiner was the last to die: He finally perished about six months after his party's initial landing. During the course of his immensely slow expiration, he had plenty of time to think. He formulated a plan, which he wrote down and left to be found by his countrymen when they came looking for him. His idea was that a mission settlement should be established first on the Falkland Islands. From there missionaries could begin, little by little, to interact with the Yámana, to gain their trust and to learn their language. Only when these aims had been accomplished would it be safe to try again to establish a mission among them.

Five years later, in 1856, the man arrived who would change definitively the relationship between the whites and the indigenous tribes of the end of the world—or, more accurately, the boy, for Thomas Bridges was only thirteen years old at the time. His family's story is told by his son, Lucas Bridges, in his memoir *Uttermost Part of the Earth*. It's an awe-inspiring tale of extraordinary courage and indomitable pioneering fortitude, blended with a humanity and deep affection for the indigenous population that was unusual among European settlers in those days.

Thomas Bridges was an orphan who had been adopted by a Bristol clergyman, the Reverend George Pakenham Despard. Following the dismal fate of Captain Allen Gardiner and his disciples, Despard volunteered to carry out Gardiner's final plan—to set up a missionary community on the Falkland Islands—and so, in 1856, he left with his family for the far-flung south.

As Gardiner had proposed, Despard befriended some of the Yámana people and brought them to live on Keppel Island in the Falklands. The Yámana learned some English; the English learned some Yámana. After some years, when relations were considered to be sufficiently amicable, a small party of missionaries set out for Tierra del Fuego in their schooner, named the *Allen Gardiner* after their unfortunate predecessor. For five months, the folk on Keppel Island heard nothing. Eventually, fearing the worst, Despard went to investigate. He found the *Allen Gardiner* entirely dismantled and her crew all dead except for one, the ship's cook, who was half mad with distress, virtually naked, and covered in boils.

The cook related the dreadful tale: The crew had toiled to build their church despite constant harassment from the locals. After a week, the construction had been sufficiently advanced for them to hold their first religious service. All except for the cook had attended; he had stayed on board the schooner and had watched in horror as, halfway through the first hymn, the Yámana had stormed the church with clubs and stones and had brutally murdered the missionaries.

It might have been safe to presume after all this bloodshed that the Yámana people didn't much want to be converted to Christianity. Any normal mortal might have decided by now that the Yámana should be allowed to get on with their own lives in their own land in the way that pleased them—and Despard concluded exactly that. Deeply grieved by the failure of his mission, he gave up hope of establishing a settlement in Tierra del Fuego and returned home to England. Only one white man remained on Keppel. He was Thomas Bridges, Despard's adopted son, who was now eighteen years old.

For a year, Bridges lived with only the Yámana for company. By the time the next superintendent, the Reverend Whait H. Stirling, arrived from England, Bridges was fluent in the Yámana language and had begun to compile a dictionary.

When Bridges subsequently visited Tierra del Fuego with Stirling he was able to talk easily with the Yámana people and to allay their fears. Finally, in January 1869—almost ten years after the massacre in the half-built church, and a full fifteen years before a representative of the Argentine government would officially found the town—the first mission building was set up in Ushuaia, and Stirling, together with a friendly Yámana couple, moved in. Thankfully, he lived to tell the tale.

At the same time as Stirling was settling into Ushuaia, Bridges was recalled to England: The Missionary Society had decided that, in order for him to continue his work, he should be ordained. It was during this trip that he met his wife, Mary Varder, who came from a little village called Harberton in Devon. They were married five weeks after their first meeting and two days after the ceremony they left together for the Falkland Islands.

Mary Bridges must have been blessed with tremendous grit and an unassailable spirit of adventure—but still, it is almost impossible to imagine what thoughts must have passed through her mind in the weeks that followed her marriage. It's extraordinary to contemplate her sudden change in fortune: One day, she must have been sitting comfortably, wistfully single perhaps, in a cozy Devon cottage making lace and eating clotted cream with her friends and family around her; six weeks later she was throwing up ship's biscuits—for she was terribly seasick—as she voyaged with a man she scarcely knew to the most inhospitable ends of the earth, with the intention of setting up home in a place where previous white visitors had been attacked, robbed, and even bludgeoned to death by the natives. Goodness only knows what possessed her to go.

The Bridgeses stayed for two years on Keppel Island before eventually making Ushuaia their home. Their final passage from the Falklands was a dreadful one. On arriving at last in Tierra del Fuego, now with an infant daughter in her arms, Mary turned to her husband and said, "Dearest, you have brought me to this country, and here I must remain, for I can never, never face that ocean voyage again."

And there she did remain—for more than forty years.

Harberton was never forgotten, though, and it was after his wife's native Devon village that Thomas Bridges named his estancia when he finally left the mission in 1886. Harberton lies fifty-three miles to the east of Ushuaia and is still managed today by descendants of the Bridgeses. And so, I decided to take a trip out there and see something of this exceptional family's history for myself.

The weather had once more taken a turn for the worse and the slate skies gushed with rain. I was traveling in a minibus with four or five others. The windows steamed up in the cold, damp atmosphere so that we perpetually had to wipe them to see anything at all—but even then, visibility was minimal. We were engulfed in a thick black spouting cloud.

The tarmac road turned to *ripio* and still we thundered on through the downpour. We drove through a gateway—the entrance to Harberton—then progressed through a forest where trees ripped from their roots lay amid the damp vegetation and slowly rotted. They were draped in pale green old-man's beard that in these conditions resembled dripping, mold-bedecked cobwebs. In the lagoon, pots were strung to catch shellfish. A beaver swam.

We reached an exposed hilltop where trees stood so whipped by the wind that their branches extended sideways like masses of matted hair blown by a gale—but these boughs were solid. So ferocious were the elements in this wild, exposed spot that they had grown that way. The locals called them *arboles banderas,* flag trees. I wondered what desperate thoughts must have filled Mary Bridges' mind when she first tried to make her home in this desolate place. It was a long, long way from Devon.

We arrived in the warmth of the house. All the materials

for the homestead's construction had been transported by
ship from England. The timbers had been sawn in Mary's father's workshop in Devon, although, during the family's
first, desperately harsh winter here, Bridges was forced to
use some of that imported wood to build a shelter for their
perishable goods and to hew new boards for their house
from native materials. The current owner, Tommy Goodall,
had now turned one room into a little café where we gratefully drank tea and ate orange cake. Tommy himself stood
behind the café's counter. He was a rotund, beaming, white-
bearded man dressed in blue denim dungarees.

"Sorry about the weather," he said in a cheerful voice
that suggested he wasn't very sorry at all, "but there's not a
lot we can do about it."

Tommy was the grandson of Lucas Bridges' younger
brother, Will. Tommy's own granddaughter, Amalia—the
great-great-great-granddaughter of Thomas and Mary
Bridges—took us out in the family's boat to Martillo Island,
just across the water, where penguins nested. She was seventeen years old and would, after her long summer break,
complete her final year of school in Ushuaia. In the meantime she was spending her holidays working at Harberton.

We made our way out over the channel, which was
silkily calm even on a day like this. A short distance from the
boat, a group of perhaps forty black-browed albatrosses
bobbed upon the water's surface. As we approached, they
flapped their wings and flew away with an effortless ele-
gance.

On the pebble beach of the island, hundreds of
Magellanic and gentoo penguins congregated.

"These goslings are black and have feathers over their
whole body of the same size and fashion, and they do not fly,
and they live on fish. And they were so fat that we did not

pluck them but skinned them, and they have a beak like a crow's," wrote Pigafetta of the penguins Magellan's crews hunted for food. It seems curious, even given the lack of National Geographic Channel in the early sixteenth century, that anyone might confuse a Magellanic penguin for a goose, but clearly Pigafetta was stuck for comparisons.

I was happy that, having consumed a good-sized hunk of orange cake in the Harberton tea shop, I wouldn't need to eat a penguin myself, for they were winsome creatures. They came to about knee height and, entirely unconcerned by the rain and cold, they clamored vociferously and flapped their flightless wings. Some waddled with a comical, high-speed gait into the water. As the lapping waves hit their torsos they thrust forward and, suddenly, their movements were no longer awkward; instead, they dived and twirled through the icy water with a smooth, artistic grace.

We climbed up a hummock where among long grasses yet more penguins nested in pairs. Some lay deep within their dark earthen burrows so that, if I peered closely, I could just make out a shiny, beady eye within. Many stood in the open, dwarfed by the tall, green blades. A few birds cared for their chicks but mostly they posed as contented couples, preening each other every now and then. They stared at us unstintingly and rotated their heads through remarkable contortions as though some sense might be made of these strange visitors if they looked at us upside down.

The noise up here was deafening: The penguins warbled to one another, pointing their beaks high toward the sky, opening them wide, and screeching for all they were worth. What they were telling their friends, I don't know.

As I stood among the penguins, sometimes cheerful, sometimes coy, but always delightfully engaging, I realized: The rain didn't bother me anymore. Instead, I was seized by the transfixing serenity of this wild corner of the earth. Yes, the weather was lousy, but somehow here at the end of the world it felt right that way. The sky and water shifted between shades of gray; the penguins' costumes were monochrome; the pebbles on the beach lay black. Even the grass was muted, as though the chlorophyll had been leached from its blades. But there was an incredible beauty and calm in this desolate spot. Mounds of land, uninhabited by humans, rose and fell through the mist. The air was perfectly fresh and resonated with a profound sense of peace. I felt that I had arrived in a very damp paradise. I suspected that Mary Bridges might have felt the same.

Far too soon, we had to climb aboard the boat and make our return journey to Harberton. A cormorant stood on the tip of a craggy rock that jutted into the sea. Its jet black feathers, long craning neck, and angular, pointed beak created a perfect silhouette against the still, gray heavens above.

Back at the house, most of our group retreated to the tearoom once more, but I joined a couple of weather-resistant diehards in a tour of the farm. We saw the old shearing shed, and a steam-powered engine that had been brought out from Britain to drive the shearing tools. The garden still had a very English feel to it. Unlike the violent and unpredictable world beyond its white picket fence, this was an ordered place with a neat lawn, a blossoming fuchsia bush, poppies, roses, violets, and lupins. Behind the house and up a hill a tiny graveyard with white wooden crosses and small headstones paid testament to those who had ended their days in this very last stronghold of Englishness.

Sadly, the Yámana, whom the Bridges family had tried so hard to protect, all perished in the end as well. They learned to tend crops and to cultivate the land, but their immune

systems didn't adapt as quickly as their minds. As white people increasingly settled in the south, the native population
was ravaged by diseases such as measles and influenza that
their bodies had no way of withstanding. By 1910, there
were just a hundred of them left. Today there are none.

It was late by the time we started back for Ushuaia. Just
above the line of the road, the hills were covered with a fine
sprinkling of virgin snow. As we drove, the clouds, at last,
began to disperse. The soft, languorous light penetrated the
rising cloud with a golden coral-colored glow. The gray
canopy lifted and the weak yellow sun engaged in one last
dance with the dying day.

I spent the next afternoon chugging up and down the
Beagle Channel in another little boat. I was to visit an uninhabited island rich in wildlife that had been named for its
shape by the Bridges family—it was called Isla H.

Flightless steamer ducks flapped comically along the
water's surface while South American terns dipped and
dived gloatingly overhead. I disembarked with a small group
of fellow visitors, and we walked on the island. By the water's edge, lurid green algae lay in a thick, slippery carpet.
We climbed upward amid sprouting wild celery, bushes of
calafate with tiny purple berries, and clumps of yellow-
flowering senecio. It was a remarkably beautiful habitat—
and delightfully different both from the land I'd seen around
Harberton yesterday and from the National Park I'd walked
in the day before.

A plump brown Chilean skua with a vicious curved
black beak perched upon an algae-encrusted rock and fixed
his predatory eye on a male upland goose who determinedly

guarded his goslings. The goose furiously flapped his wings; the skua abandoned his hope for a juicy lunch and flew away.

On the far side of the island, red-faced rock cormorants nested on a cliff face. They sat in pairs on their scruffy nests of straw, preened each other, and tended to their chicks. Some sat alone and called to their mates in a strange, glugging song that suggested malfunctioning drains.

We climbed back into the boat, and motored over to another island where scores of lardy southern sea lions lay beached and blubbery. The air here was thick with the pungent stench of stale fish. There was only one male that I could see; the many females constituted his harem. He was larger and darker than his women and wore fine, feline whiskers. Every now and then he would arduously haul himself toward one of his mates and make the roughest of romantic overtures. I considered what his breath must smell like, and felt happy that I was not required to be intimate with such a creature.

As we made our way back to land, raindrops once more began to fall. We hunkered down in the boat's cabin, drank instant coffee from plastic cups, and ate pale yellow cookies with hard pink icing.

21

Why I Wouldn't Want to Be
a Fuegian Sheep

In 1927, a dentist in Buenos Aires had just finished peering into yet another mouth when his patient, who happened to be an influential government man, delivered the nugget of information that would change his life. Way down south in Tierra del Fuego, the politician revealed, the government was parceling up land and selling it off. The dentist, whose name was Sebastián Luna, went home and mulled over this piece of news. He'd had enough of staring at other people's festering molars; he was tired of the city. And so he decided to throw in the towel (and the pink disinfectant mouth-swill) and move south.

Luna called his new home Estancia Rolito after his only son. He forced Rolito to qualify as a dentist, just as he had done, but Rolito was hooked on his wild new home. As soon as he'd gained his diploma he rushed back to the estancia and dedicated his life to farming. When Rolito died the estancia passed to his daughter, Annie, who runs the place today.

Annie sighed and looked out of the window. It had rained hard all morning but at last the weather seemed to be easing up. "Now we need two days of sun and wind to dry the sheep," she said.

I was sitting in her warm, cozy sitting room, having made the two-hour trip to the farm with a guide, María Silvia, that morning. Annie had been just twenty-five years old when her father, Rolito, passed away and she inherited the farm. She had already been married to Pepe, a Buenos Aires doctor, and had been living in the city with him and their two small children. But it had soon become clear that she couldn't manage the estancia from such a distance. The men who worked there were traditional in their ways. They had little respect for the instructions of a woman, and less still when the woman in question lived conveniently far away. They had cheated and robbed her until, in the end, she'd decided that she and her family should return here to live.

"In Buenos Aires, I am a respected person. But here— look at my hands! I have to be in the city for a whole week before I can get them properly clean!" Pepe exclaimed in mock horror as he sat comfortably by the fire in his corduroy bombachas and black Harley-Davidson boots. He was a cheerful, robust character. I had the impression that he was not concerned in the least about his dirty hands, nor about the many other hardships this southern land threw at him. On the contrary, he seemed to relish them.

The rain let up a little and I went for a short ride with Nunu, Annie and Pepe's daughter who lived here with them. My horse for the afternoon was a timid bay mare who rolled her eyes in horror when we were introduced. She didn't seem to want to be separated from her herd, to be saddled up and ridden by a strange-smelling foreigner.

Nunu, on the other hand, was warmly hospitable. She was in her late twenties or early thirties and was a thin, willowy, sympathetically smiling girl.

"I went to school, with my brother, in Buenos Aires from the age of five. We lived with my grandmother," Nunu told me as we rode through the wet green woodland, ducking beneath branches from which thick clumps of old-man's beard hung. Her grandmother had hated the countryside and had retreated back to the city as soon as her husband had died. But the rest of the family felt irresistibly lured to this persistently rainy, profoundly tranquil place. It was truly remote out here. The nearest neighbor lived six miles away; to visit the local town, the family had to drive for more than sixty miles—yet, even in the rain, there was something about the way the soft light filtered through the slowly lifting cloud, about the multitude of greens that enveloped us as we trotted through the trees, that inspired a deep sense of contentment.

We came out of the woods and rode across an open meadow. In the distance a herd of about fifteen guanacos loped across the grass. Guanacos still roamed in prolific numbers here as they had done for centuries. The Ona people, who inhabited this northeasterly part of Tierra del Fuego until white men and their diseases finally wiped them out, used to hunt guanaco to eat and wrap themselves in their skins (unlike the Yámana, who ate mostly fish and limpets, and went naked).

"A better broth cannot be concocted than that obtained from . . . a guanaco head," Lady Florence Dixie wrote in

Riding Across Patagonia, her account of the horseback journey she undertook in 1879 in order to escape the confines of Victorian society.

Lucas Bridges was less effusive. "At the very best, the guanaco is a disagreeable, ill-mannered brute. He chews the cud like a cow, mixing it with saliva, and has the unpleasant habit of spitting out great quantities of the nauseous blend, with unerring aim and in a most insolent manner, right in the face of his visitor," he wrote in *Uttermost Part of the Earth*.

Darwin also had a few words to say on the beast: "The guanacos have one singular habit, which is to me quite inexplicable; namely, that on successive days they drop their dung in the same defined heap. I saw one of these heaps which was eight feet in diameter, and was composed of a large quantity."

From well beyond spitting distance, they seemed to me to be elegant creatures, though. There were also about sixty wild horses in the grounds of this estancia, Pepe later told me, but we didn't see them that day.

We returned to the house for dinner, a delicious, home-made lamb stew. I asked about the sheepdog puppy that had been gamboling in the garden that afternoon and chasing the feet of everyone who walked by. He was a tiny fluffy thing about four weeks old.

"He'll start to work in about another month," Pepe explained. "He'll go out with the others and learn from them."

Annie and Pepe had about thirty working dogs on the farm. These animals were fit and fast; when they weren't working they were fed only two or three times a week to keep them lean. Their diet consisted of the meat of wild guanacos hunted by the *peones*.

When the men went out to herd the sheep, they would

use a team of about fifteen dogs to clear their quarry from the forest. Each dog was trained for a particular role: Some led, others penned the sheep from the sides to keep the pack tight, still others followed up the rear. It was vital that the dogs returned instantly to their handler when commanded to do so. But the really unforgivable sin in a sheepdog was to bite a sheep.

"If they bite a sheep, they are shot instantly," said Pepe grimly.

I wondered if the men formed a bond with the dogs and whether it caused them much emotional grief to have to shoot one.

"Oh yes," said Pepe. "There's always a bond. But at least we shoot them quickly. The Chileans are much more cruel. They hang any dog that bites a sheep by the neck with wire." Pepe grimaced. "They think that it serves as a warning to the others." He shook his head.

"Do they really do that? Or is that just what the Argentines say?" I asked.

"Oh no, they really do it. Most of our men here are Chilean. Our headman does that!"

There was a short, horrified silence before I ventured one last, gruesome question: "So—how long does it take a dog to die that way?"

"I don't know," said Pepe. "I've never liked to ask."

After dinner we retired once more to the armchairs by the fire. The living room was a homely place with an eclectic mixture of pictures and ornaments—an antique map of Brittany, a brightly colored tapestry of Ushuaia, two plaster sculptures of a man and a woman, and a collection of wooden animals on wheels that had belonged to Annie's grandmother. Through the windows, in the picket-fenced garden, a mountain ash bloomed white—it was a big, billowing tree that would have been imported from Europe many decades ago. It was still light outside, although the clock showed that the hour was late. At this time of year, darkness only fell for about four hours each night here.

We drank coffee and Annie and Pepe continued to talk about the farm. The men they employed were poor country people, Annie explained. Most of them couldn't read or write. They tended to blow their wages each month with two days of revelry in the village. Sometimes they'd come back to the farm with hangovers so debilitating they'd be unable to work and Annie would have to tend to them, taking them small cups of beer to wean them slowly off their poison.

"They say to me, 'You are my mother,'" said Annie. "I say to them, 'I'm not your mother. If I was your mother, I'd have killed you years ago!'"

A couple of months ago, Annie had employed a new cook to prepare meals for the *peones*. Annie had instructed her to ring the bell at twelve-thirty so that the men would know it was time to come in for lunch, and again at seven-thirty for the evening meal. All through the first morning, the bell had rung and rung.

"I thought it must be her children playing with it," Annie said. She still looked surprised by her own story, all these weeks after the events had occurred. "But it wasn't. So I asked her, 'Why do you keep on ringing the bell?' It turned out that she couldn't tell the time. In the end, we had to draw a picture of a clock face for her with the hands pointing to half past twelve. Now, when the real clock looks the same as the one in the picture, she knows it's time to ring the bell."

The following morning the weather had improved. Patches of pale blue sky split the clouds like scraps of stone-washed denim.

I took a tour of the farm with Nunu. We walked in a dramatic lenga wood whose trees were hundreds of years old. Many trunks had fallen; they lay rotting and moss-covered on the damp earth. We visited the shearing shed, a silvery corrugated-metal construction whose walls reflected the sun's fragile rays. Nunu pointed to a sparkling-new aluminum stepladder.

"I bought it last week," she said, and sighed. "The old one was the original, but it was broken and every time we tried to use it, the rungs just collapsed."

She seemed sad to have been forced to abandon the old set of steps. Privately, I thought that I myself might have succumbed to a trip to the ladder shop long ago. There are no stepladders dating from the 1920s in my home. But then, I considered, that might be because I am a soft urbanite. The people in this remote part of the world were made of sterner stuff. This may have been the twenty-first century, but down here they were still a-brim with pioneering spirit. They made do and they mended. They lived from the land—and they loved it.

María Silvia reappeared at lunchtime and we drove back to Ushuaia. As we traveled, a light covering of snow started to fall. Then there was hail. The Ona used to say that certain mountains in these parts lived once as human beings. If a person behaved rudely toward those particular hills, or pointed a finger at them, they became offended, enshrouded themselves in cloud, and besieged with bad weather those humans currently wandering at their feet. Somebody must have deeply upset a mountain that day.

I thought of Annie, Pepe, and Nunu and their damp livestock. There was no sun and wind to dry their wool this afternoon. There probably wouldn't be any tomorrow. It was a wonderful world out here but I, for one, was profoundly grateful that I was not a Fuegian sheep.

22

A Very Distant Relative

I was greatly relieved the next day that I hadn't been born a hundred years earlier, either, for then I might have been hauled across the oceans by loving parents intent on creating a new Welsh colony in Patagonia. After leaving Estancia Rolito, I'd flown up to Trelew, on Patagonia's Atlantic coast, then taken a taxi to Puerto Madryn. This was where, on July 28, 1865, the first hundred and fifty Welsh settlers disembarked from their ship, the *Mimosa*. There were five Evanses on board: Daniel and Mary, John, Elizabeth, and Thomas. (John was just four years old at the time. He later became famous as the sole survivor among a group of Welsh gold prospectors who were attacked by the native population—his horse saved his life by jumping a twelve-foot cliff.) I wondered just how distantly I was related to these people.

The Welsh settlers arrived in the dead of winter; they spent those first freezing months living in rough shelters within exposed cliffs on the sea front. Some while later they moved inland to the more amenable Lower Chubut Valley— but most of these hopeful pioneers weren't farmers and they had little idea how to till this arid land. George Musters, in his book *At Home with the Patagonians,* related that his Indian guides had seen the Welsh settlers reduced to eating grass. Fortunately for the Welsh, the Tehuelche loved their home-baked bread: Once the Welsh were able to mill flour, the Tehuelche would exchange half a freshly slaughtered guanaco for one loaf of bread, so much did they enjoy its flavor.

The Welsh contingent came to Patagonia in response to the Argentine government's offer to give land to European settlers who wished to establish a home here. These were the years leading up to Roca's "Conquest of the Desert"; the Buenos Aires authorities were keen to assert their control over the lawless, native-infested south by establishing settle-ments of industrious, land-tilling pioneers. The Welsh, for their part, wanted to found a pure Welsh colony at a time when Wales itself was suffocated by the cultural and reli-gious restrictions of the encroaching English. Not every-body thought their scheme a good idea. "Of all the wild mad schemes that have turned up of late, the wildest and mad-dest is the Patagonian scheme ... I hope that the Indians who will eat you all bodily a confounded indigestion," Aimé Tschiffely quoted a certain Mr. Jones as writing to his cousin, Mr. Williams, as the latter prepared to cross the Atlantic. Even George Musters, who could himself have been viewed as optimistic verging on unhinged as far as foolhardy adventuring was concerned, commented in *At Home with the Patagonians:* "The visionary scheme of a Welsh Utopia, in pursuit of which these unfortunate emigrants settled themselves, ought not to be encouraged, likely as it is to end in the starvation of the victims to it."

Still, there were many idealists who took no notice of this doom-mongering. Over the fifty years that followed the *Mimosa*'s arrival, about three thousand Welsh came to settle in this part of Patagonia and, for a while, they were successful in their attempt to re-create Welsh culture in this barren land thousands of miles from home. These days, migration, intermarriage, and schooling have meant that the Spanish language and Argentine culture dominate—but in a few small villages, the Welsh language can still be heard and the chapels continue to be active. I thought I'd pay a visit to one of the most traditional among them and see if I could dig out any distant relatives.

Maybe I'd arrived in Gaiman too early; at ten-fifteen on a Sunday morning the village was deathly quiet—though vivaciously pretty. Willows bowed; an apricot tree prospered in one garden. This was the Lower Chubut Valley where the river's water allowed plants and flowers to flourish in glorious contrast to the surrounding stark, flat desert.

I walked around the empty streets. Outside one brick house was affixed a blue metal plaque declaring that John Evans, the first pastor of Gaiman, had lived here. (He was a different John Evans from the one who arrived in Argentina at age four and survived the massacre; this one, according to the plaque, had been born in 1837.) His house was now a women's clothes shop. In the front window stood a mannequin dressed in a skimpy scarlet bikini. I trembled to think what the Reverend John would have made of such a creature taking up residence in his parlor.

A little farther down, there was a street called Juan Evans. I had no idea who he was, but presumably he must have been born later, after the Welsh began to integrate with the Spanish-speaking population.

I crossed the river on a rickety, swaying bridge and

wandered down a tiny lane. I was looking for the two Welsh chapels that were said still to thrive here, but as I wandered into increasingly minor residential streets I had to consider an ugly truth: I might not know a Welsh chapel if it leaped out of the bushes singing "Bread of Heaven." I asked for directions.

"Oh yes, just keep going down there," said the teenage girl who seemed to be on her way to spend this sunny Sunday with friends. She was dressed with a casual nonchalance that must have taken hours to perfect.

A few minutes later I came upon a spacious gravel courtyard. It was flanked by two simple, elegant buildings with immaculately maintained brickwork and tall, slender windows that peaked into arches. I tried to turn the handle of the white-painted wooden door of the larger chapel, but it was locked. Then, just as I was about to turn away, two people—a white-haired woman who bore an uncanny resemblance to Joan Hickman's Miss Marple, and a younger man—appeared.

"Is there any way of getting into the chapel?" I asked them.

"Oh, I'm afraid I don't have the key," said Miss Marple, looking concerned. Then she brightened. "But you can certainly take a look inside the other chapel, the *capilla vieja*. We're just on our way there ourselves. Why don't you come with us?"

I walked with Miss Marple and her escort across the yard toward the building on its far side. The old woman asked me about my journey. Was I just passing through?

I explained to her that I had Welsh ancestry; my surname, I said, was Evans.

"So's mine!" said the man.

"Yes, he's an Evans too!" said Miss Marple. I'd been here

about half an hour, and already I'd met a Spanish-speaking Patagonian Evans.

Given that our short walk across the courtyard was taken up entirely with exclamations about our shared surname, I didn't discover from my two new friends that a service was under way in the *capilla vieja* until we had already crossed the threshold. It seemed to be a children's service, or a Sunday school: As we crept in, the smaller inhabitants of Gaiman were bleating their way through a Spanish version of "Joy to the World" under the enthusiastic tutelage of a robust young woman who stood at the front and led with vigor. I felt suddenly conspicuous and seized with the desire to run—but it was too late. Miss Marple and Mr. Evans greeted friends and family. I scuttled to a back pew and sat there, slightly removed from the rest of the congregation, trying to look invisible. From the front of the hall, sepia photographs of austere pioneer preachers stared disapprovingly down. I wondered which of them was the Reverend John.

Really, I wasn't surprised to see these long-dead clergymen frowning. "Joy to the World" was written by a good, Nonconformist man, Isaac Watts—but the congregation was singing in *Spanish*. Those early settlers had been sticklers for their ancestral tongue: They saw the Welsh language as key to their colony's identity. The Argentine census of 1895 showed that more than 97 percent of the rural populations of the Lower Chubut Valley spoke Welsh. Schools were obliged to teach in Spanish from the end of the nineteenth century, but the pastors stuck fervently to their roots: It wasn't until the 1960s, a full hundred years after the Welsh had first arrived on Argentina's shores, that religious services were conducted in Spanish.

"Joy to the World" whimpered to a reedy conclusion, and the woman at the front started to talk.

"So," she pronounced perkily, "do we have any visitors here today?"

I was horrified. Everyone else was sitting in cozy little family groups. It was gut-wrenchingly clear that they'd all known each other since the day they'd burst into this slightly strange world—and that I was the only nonresident daft enough to find herself attending Patagonian Sunday school by mistake. Tentatively, I raised my hand a little, hoping that would be sufficient to satisfy the teacher.

"It's Señorita Evans!" trilled an old woman sitting at the front of the church. I'd only been in there a matter of minutes, but it seemed that Miss Marple had already managed to chatter to all her friends.

"*Señorita Evans!*" exclaimed the very eager lady at the front. She seemed truly delighted that I was participating in their weekly gathering. "Are you Welsh?"

I muttered something about my family a generation or two back, then conceded that I actually lived in London.

"Welcome!" said the very happy woman, still smiling despite my horrible confession. The children turned around and quite reasonably stared. And then, thank goodness, the piano clanged into action and the congregation struck forth with a Spanish translation of "Silent Night."

Miss Marple waved at me from across the aisle. She appeared to have a key in her hand, and signaled me to follow her. We tiptoed out of the chapel and she showed me into the building across the yard.

It was a graceful, harmonious space. Decoration was restrained but attractive. Above the altar, engraved stones remembered parsons past: the original John Evans and then his successor, who, remarkably, was called Evans too. I was beginning to feel quite at home.

"Will you be here tonight?" asked Miss Marple. "Our evening service will be held in the Welsh language. Twice a month it's held in Welsh, and twice a month in Spanish."

I admitted to her that, even if I could have spent the night in Gaiman (though goodness knows how I would have entertained myself there for an entire day), I wouldn't have been able to understand a single word of worship. My knowledge of Welsh was nonexistent. My branch of the Evans family, I'm sorry to say, falls into that shameful category of once-Welsh who spinelessly succumbed to the English oppressors.

I took a taxi back to Puerto Madryn. En route, we stopped to fill up with gas at a service station. The type of fuel this car used needed to be siphoned directly into the engine and by law, when a vehicle was being refilled in this way, the passengers had to stand outside the car. Duly, I climbed out as my driver requested, then slid back in when he went to pay. Across the forecourt, I noticed, a police car was refilling with the same type of fuel, but the policemen had stayed sitting in the car.

"Why are the police allowed to stay in the car when everyone else has to get out?" I asked the driver as we drove off.

"Did they stay in the car?" the driver asked. Then he became angry. "Yes, well, they would, wouldn't they? The law is that everyone has to get out, including them. But they think they're above it. That's the problem with this country—there's so much corruption! If the police see you driving with one of your indicator or brake lights out, they'll pull you over and they'll say, 'Well, either I can write you a ticket, or you could just give me such and such an amount.'"

"Do they all do that?" I asked.

"No, not all of them," the driver conceded. "I'd say about twenty-five percent of them are honest. But the rest are no good. I reckon three quarters of the police take bribes."

Back in Puerto Madryn, I walked along the beach. According to a towering thermometer, the temperature that day was seventy-three degrees. Sunday worship in this seaside town took a different form from that in Gaiman's chapel: This congregation had stripped down to bikinis and shorts and lay on towels on the sand, soaking up the sun. It seemed incredible to think that this was still Patagonia, the same region where yesterday I had been watching the snow drift down, and I felt suddenly overdressed in my T-shirt and jeans.

The tide was low. Long-legged wading birds stood and pecked in rock pools and shallow lagoons of seawater. The sand was wet and firm, imprinted with rutted little waves that echoed the undulations of the great Atlantic Ocean beyond. I strolled to the caves in which those original settlers had sheltered through that first, hauntingly dreadful winter. They were by no means cavernous chambers, but slight, shallow hollows in the fudge-colored rock. It was as though the cliff face were a giant slab of ice cream and the "caves" were the furrows made by the scoop. Those God-fearing pioneers had added wooden outer walls and roofs to their rocky abodes, but still, these can't have offered much protection from the treacherous sea that would have crept right up to their thresholds at high tide. On stormy nights in the depths of winter they must have been perilous, miserable shelters.

I hired a car and driver the following morning to take me to the wildlife reserve of the Península Valdés. We started out early: It would take two hours to drive to Caleta Valdés on the far east coast of the peninsula and I needed to be back in town by three o'clock to catch my bus for Buenos Aires. From Buenos Aires, I was returning home to London. This, then, would be the very last outing of my Argentine journey.

The driver picked me up from my *hostal* at seven o'clock and we drove through the seemingly endless, flat desert. The land was desperately dry, terrifyingly barren.

"It hardly rains at all here," my driver told me. He was a cheerful character, determined to act as guide as well as chauffeur. "This peninsula only gets about eight inches of rain each year."

Again, my thoughts went to those Welsh settlers—what on earth must they have thought when they first saw this place, so very different from their own verdant valleys? It was lucky that they had believed so fervently in their God.

The harsh conditions didn't seem to bother the guanacos. Many herds of those tall-necked creatures, some with calves, cantered across the wide expanses of sandy land as we drove through. They had an upright posture and their tight white bottoms seemed to bob as they ran, then vaulted effortlessly over the low wire sheep fences. *Choiques*—lesser rhea, or Darwin's rhea—strutted inelegantly on their gangly legs, while Patagonian hares lolloped through the sparse vegetation.

We arrived at Caleta Valdés and I walked down the boardwalks to the edge of the beach where scores of elephant seals lay inert like huge sleeping slugs. Their brown fur glistened in the sun. Occasionally, one of them would lift a flipper to shoot a scoop of warm pebbles over its back, or rouse itself sufficiently to *schlop-schlop-schlop* down to the water's edge. These creatures undulated as they moved, like big blubbery carpets being shaken out along the sand.

In the shallow water close to the shore a more enthusiastic couple courted. They faced each other and, pushing up with their flippers, balanced on their bellies like a pair of yogic cobras. Their noses stretched toward the heavens: The male was larger than the female so that she seemed to gaze up at him. Behind them, their tail fins just broke the surface of the water, turning upward in a smooth, flexible curve.

I walked around this stretch of the beach until the walkway ran out. Venturing onto the sand itself was strictly forbidden, for the seals can be aggressive and, at high tide, orcas feed here. They hurl themselves out of the water onto the beach at speeds of up to thirty-seven miles an hour, grab a seal in their mouths, and then use the rolling gravel to propel themselves back into the brine. But the tide was low now and the whales were far away. Emerald green seaweed lay in uneven stripes, interspersed by sandy channels where the water had recently flowed. A little way out, an anchor and chain lay embedded: this, according to an information board, had come from a Chilean ship that had been wrecked off this coast.

A short distance from the seals, a sandbank rose up from the ocean like a long, yellow island. Upon its grainy surface, a gaggle of Magellanic penguins stood in a circle. With their heads bowed gravely toward one another, they looked as though they were discussing matters of vital importance to the penguin world. Then, one by one, they turned and dived into the blue waters and swam away.

It was time for me, too, to leave. I returned to Puerto Madryn and, a few hours later, I climbed aboard that final Buenos Aires–bound bus. I really should have traveled overland more during my journey, I considered; these long-distance buses were supremely comfortable. After I'd been served dinner with wine later that evening, my spacious seat would recline to flat and I'd enjoy a good night's sleep as I trundled across the pampas. In the meantime it was wonderful just to sit and stare out at the world that filled my window.

Mile after mile, acre after acre of the same flat scrub passed by. Every now and then, a group of horses grazed on their poor, dry fare. Sometimes, the view opened out to wider, paler horizons. And then the scrub returned.

I was now cutting through exactly the same land across which so many explorers and pioneers had traveled on horseback before me. George Musters rode through this region in the company of the Tehuelche; Perito Moreno would have roamed these parts as he dreamed of a new, civilized Utopia. The landscape itself probably looked much the same now as it had done then. Those arid, sandy expanses wouldn't have altered much. But life had changed here beyond recognition. Moreno would have been delighted to see the place now, for the wilderness had been well and truly conquered. Tarmac roads weaved through the desert, towns had been built and were replete with shops, banks, and sunbathers. Argentina still had problems, that much was certain—but its transformation was nonetheless striking.

To my right lay the Atlantic Ocean, through whose waters so many mariners had sailed to reach the fabled

Patagonian coast: Ferdinand Magellan and his mutinous crews; Benjamin Franklin Bourne, who'd spent ninety-seven days held captive by the Tehuelche; Charles Darwin and his *Beagle*-bound companions. What would they make of twenty-first-century Patagonia? I wondered. No doubt they'd be astonished by it.

Night fell. The conductor pressed "play" and the video screen leaped to life with crazy Hollywood antics. I watched for a while, stupefied, then reclined my seat and let the motion of the bus lull me to sleep.

When I woke up, dawn was breaking. We were in the flat, open pampas now. I was traveling through those same plains across which Pedro Luro, the founder of Estancia Dos Talas, had cantered time and again as he'd traveled to the extremes of his burgeoning empire; where the naturalist W. H. Hudson had spent his dreamy childhood gazing awestruck at flowers and birds; where General Rosas had gathered his red-bedecked men around him and ridden out against the indigenous peoples. This was the land of the original gauchos, those free, nomadic horsemen whose spirit still gallops through these immense, magnificent plains.

I considered how these grasslands would have looked five hundred years ago, before any white man had spied them. There would have been no fences, no roads, and no trees except for the spongy ombú. The soft, misty dawn over this endless expanse of green would have been admired not by the passengers of a delightfully comfortable sleeper bus but by sparse tribes of natives. Little did those indigenous people know that, in just a few years' time, a small troupe of strange, four-legged creatures would appear on the pampas and change their world forever.

I thought of Ídolo and Gaucho, of Alenia, Larita, Picaflor, and Tony, and of all those other horses I'd ridden over the course of my journey, and wondered what they would make of their ancestors' momentous role in the creation of this fabulously hospitable, fantastically beautiful country—for without the horse, none of this change could have occurred. The horse not only secured victory for the conquistadors, it also allowed both Europeans and the native population to farm and to travel. Maybe, just maybe, I reflected, they'd have been quietly proud—and then they'd have given a snort and a whinny, and indulged in a nice long roll in the dust.

Acknowledgments

My adventures in Argentina were surprisingly comfortable, give or take odd incidents with the occasional ferocious dog or bolting horse. The fact that I only had to go to a hospital once and returned home with no life-altering injuries is in large part thanks to the following.

Without the help and hospitality of Robin and Teleri Begg at Estancia Los Potreros (www.ride-americas.com) I'd probably have tried to mount the horse backward, so huge thanks to them and to everyone at their wonderful *estancia* for a tremendous start to my stay in Argentina. It was difficult to leave.

Equally enormous thanks to Jane Williams, Yvonne Corbett, and everyone at Estancia Huechahue (www.hue chahue.com). They gave me terrific hospitality and unforgettable riding. And to Caroline van den Bos for her excellent company, as ever, and great stoicism in the face of chafed flesh.

304*Acknowledgments*

Thanks too to the folk at Movitrack (www.movitrack
.com.ar), whose jeep trip from Salta was quite simply one
of the best day trips I have ever been on. Jeremy Watson
(www.jeremywatson.com) and Margaret Schellerup very
kindly took me along on their wine tour in Mendoza. They
also introduced me to Harry and Lois Foster of Bodega
Enrique Foster (www.bodegafoster.com), who were boun-
teous with their fabulous wines (and several plates of empanadas to boot). Many thanks to them all.

A mention must also go to Tomás and Agustina, Luciana
and Marcelo, for their company in BA (and outstanding
beer and pizza at Marcelo's Buller Brewing Company in
Recoleta, www.bullerpub.com).

I am indebted to the Sheraton Hotel for putting me up
in Buenos Aires, to Howard Kirke at Aerolineas Argentinas,
and to Sarah Hill for her advice on all things Argentina. Sue
Ockwell at the Latin American Travel Association and Simon
Casson (www.outlawtrails.com) generously provided me
with contacts.

Massive thanks as always to Francesca Liversidge, Nicky
Jeanes, Sam Jones, and everyone at Transworld, and to
Jane Gregory, Emma Dunford, Claire Morris, Jemma
McDonagh, and everyone at Gregory and Company for
their wise counsel, clever ways with words, and warm
friendship.

Lastly, of course, thanks to all those long-suffering
horses—Ídolo, Gaucho, Flopi, Cheeseface, Pepino, Alenia,
Larita, Picaflor, Tony, and the others—who so tolerantly put
up with a hard-bottomed novice bouncing up and down on
their backs. I couldn't have done it without them.

Sources

Che Guevara: A Revolutionary Life, Jon Lee Anderson, Bantam Press

Over the Edge of the World: Magellan's Terrifying Circumnavigation of the Globe,
Laurence Bergreen, Harper Perennial

The Captive in Patagonia, Benjamin Franklin Bourne, Zagier & Urruty
Publications

Uttermost Part of the Earth, Lucas Bridges, Hodder & Stoughton

The Voyage of the Beagle, Charles Darwin, Wordsworth Editions

The Horses of the Conquest, Robert Cunninghame Graham, The Long
Riders' Guild Press

An Account, Much Abbreviated, of the Destruction of the Indies, Bartolemé de
las Casas, ed. Franklin W. Knight, translated by Andrew Hurley,
Hackett Publishing Company

Riding Across Patagonia, Lady Florence Dixie, The Long Riders' Guild
Press

Evita: The Real Lives of Eva Perón, Nicholas Fraser and Marysa Navarro,
André Deutsch

A State of Fear, Andrew Graham-Yooll, Eland

Far Away and Long Ago, W. H. Hudson, Eland

A Short History of the Argentinians, Félix Luna, Grupo Editorial Planeta

Argentine Caudillo: Juan Manuel de Rosas, John Lynch, Scholarly Resources Inc.

Perito Moreno's Travel Journal: A Personal Reminiscence, Eduardo V. Moreno, ed., El Elefante Blanco

At Home with the Patagonians, George Chaworth Musters, Nonsuch Publishing

The Argentina Reader, Gabriela Nouzeilles and Graciela Montaldo, ed., Duke University Press

Magellan's Voyage: A Narrative Account of the First Circumnavigation, Antonio Pigafetta, translated and edited by R. A. Skelton, Dover Publications

Argentina 1516–1982: From Spanish Colonization to the Falklands War, David Rock, I. B. Tauris

Life in the Argentine Republic in the Days of the Tyrants, Domingo Sarmiento, translated by Mrs. Horace Mann, Hafner Press

From Caledonia to the Pampas, Iain A. D. Stewart, ed., Tuckwell Press

Prisoner Without a Name, Cell Without a Number, Jacobo Timerman, translated by Toby Talbot, University of Wisconsin Press

The Tale of Two Horses, Aimé Tschiffely, The Long Riders' Guild Press

This Way Southward, Aimé Tschiffely, The Long Riders' Guild Press

Tschiffely's Ride, Aimé Tschiffely, Pallas Athene

El Presidio—The Prison: Ushuaia, Carlos Pedro Vairo, Zagier & Urruty Publications

Borges: A Life, Edwin Williamson, Viking

Permissions

Dixie, reprinted by permission of the Long Riders' Guild Press. Extracts from *The Voyage of the Beagle* by Charles Darwin, reprinted by permission of Wordsworth Editions. Extracts from *Prisoner Without a Name, Cell Without a Number* by Jacobo Timerman, translated by Toby Talbot, reprinted by permission of the University of Wisconsin Press. Extracts from *The Captive in Patagonia* by Benjamin Frank Bourne and *El Presidio— The Prison: Ushuaia* by Carlos Pedro Vairo, reprinted by permission of Zagier & Urruty Publications.

Every effort has been made to obtain the necessary permissions with reference to copyright material, and should there be any omissions in this respect we apologize and shall be pleased to make the appropriate acknowledgments in any future editions.